Community Structure Analysis from Social Networks

This book addresses social and complex network analysis challenges, exploring social network structures, dynamic networks, and hierarchical communities. Emphasizing network structure heterogeneity, including directionality and dynamics, it covers community structure concepts like distinctness, overlap, and hierarchy. The book aims to present challenges and innovative solutions in community structure detection, incorporating diversity into problem-solving. Furthermore, it explores the applications of identified community structures within network analysis, offering insights into social network dynamics.

- Investigates the practical applications and uses of community structures identified from network analysis across various domains of real-world networks.
- Highlights the challenges encountered in analyzing community structures and presents state-of-the-art approaches designed to address these challenges.
- Spans into various domains like business intelligence, marketing, and epidemics, examining influential node detection and crime within social networks.
- Explores methodologies for evaluating the quality and accuracy of community detection models.
- Examines a diverse range of challenges and offers innovative solutions in the field of detecting community structures from social networks.

The book is a ready reference for researchers and scholars of Computer Science and Computational Social Systems working in the area of Community Structure Analysis from Social Network Data.

Community Structure Analysis from Social Networks

Edited by
Sajid Yousuf Bhat, Fouzia Jan, and
Muhammad Abulaish

CRC Press
Taylor & Francis Group
Boca Raton London New York

CRC Press is an imprint of the
Taylor & Francis Group, an **informa** business
A CHAPMAN & HALL BOOK

Designed cover image: ConnectVector\shutterstock

First edition published 2026

by CRC Press
2385 NW Executive Center Drive, Suite 320, Boca Raton FL 33431

and by CRC Press
4 Park Square, Milton Park, Abingdon, Oxon, OX14 4RN

CRC Press is an imprint of Taylor & Francis Group, LLC

ISBN: 9781032847481 (hbk)
ISBN: 9781032849775 (pbk)
ISBN: 9781003515890 (ebk)

DOI: 10.1201/9781003515890

Typeset in Times New Roman
by Deanta Global Publishing Services, Chennai, India

Contents

Preface

The dynamic field of community structure analysis has become increasingly vital in comprehending the complexities of social and other real-world networks. This book explores the latest advancements and challenges in community detection and their applications across various domains, including biological systems, online social networks, and pandemic preparedness.

The book is organized into three sections. The first section focuses on the foundational elements of social network analysis, exploring dataset characteristics, challenges in data representation, and comparisons of open dataset repositories. It also highlights various strategies for analyzing and interpreting social networks, providing insights into their types, applications, and analytical challenges.

The second section focuses on methodologies and techniques for community detection. It delves into graph clustering, semi-supervised learning, and deep learning approaches, providing readers with an in-depth understanding of structure and dynamics. These chapters also offer a comparative perspective on classical and modern techniques, shedding light on their strengths and applications.

The final section emphasizes the practical applications of community detection. From identifying influential nodes and detecting implicit communities to managing pandemics and detecting plagiarism, the book underscores the versatility of community structure analysis in solving real-world challenges. It also explores the role of connected communities in pandemic preparedness and the use of overlapping community detection to identify spread blockers.

By presenting these topics in a structured and comprehensive manner, this book serves as a valuable resource for researchers, professionals, and students. It addresses critical aspects of social and complex networks, ranging from foundational theories to state-of-the-art applications, ensuring a detailed understanding of the field.

Editors

Sajid Yousuf Bhat holds a Bachelor's and Master's degree in Computer Science from the University of Kashmir and earned his PhD in Computer Science from Jamia Millia Islamia, New Delhi. He is currently serving as Senior Assistant Professor in the Department of Computer Science at the University of Kashmir, Hazratbal, Srinagar, Kashmir, India. He has over eight years of experience in academia and research. He has previously held faculty positions at the University of Delhi and the Central University of Kashmir. Dr Bhat has published research articles in prestigious international journals, including *IEEE Transactions*, as well as in books and conference proceedings. His research interests encompass complex networks, social network analytics, community analytics, machine learning, and computer vision.

Fouzia Jan has an MBA in Finance and Marketing from Bangalore University. She earned her PhD in Microfinance from Jamia Millia Islamia, New Delhi. She has published many research papers in renowned journals and presented various research papers in national as well as international journals. Besides, she was awarded the Maulana Azad National Fellowship by UGC, India, during her research. She qualified National Eligibility Test with JRF conducted by UGC, India, in June, 2012. At present, she is Assistant Professor in Management at the Department of Humanities and Social Sciences, National Institute of Technology, Srinagar, Kashmir. She has also worked as a management faculty at the University of Kashmir and Central University of Kashmir. Her areas of research interest include microfinance, service marketing, entrepreneurship, finance, and banking.

M. Abulaish, Professor of Computer Science at South Asian University (SAU), New Delhi, India, has over 26 years of academic and research experience. Since joining SAU in 2016, he has held key administrative roles, including Chairperson of the Computer Science Department, Director of Admissions and Examinations, and Acting Registrar. Previously, he served as Professor and Head of the Computer Science Department at Jamia Millia Islamia, New Delhi, and led a research group at King Saud University's Center of Excellence in Information Assurance. Dr Abulaish earned his PhD from IIT Delhi in 2007 and founded the Laboratory for Data Science and Analytics at SAU, focusing on data-intensive interdisciplinary research. His work spans data mining, AI, machine learning, and network analysis, with applications in text mining, social network analysis, rumor detection, sentiment analysis, health informatics, and cybersecurity. He has authored over 140 publications, including eight in IEEE/ACM Transactions.

Contributors

Shabnam Ahad
Islamic University of Science and Technology
Jammu and Kashmir, India

Arjumand Akbar
University of Kashmir
Jammu and Kashmir, India

Fayaz Ahmad Bhat
Department of Higher Education
Jammu and Kashmir, India

Sajid Yousuf Bhat
University of Kashmir
Jammu & Kashmir, India

Neda Binesh
Semnan University
Semnan, Iran

Fatemeh Daneshfar
University of Kurdistan
Kurdistan, Iran

Mona Dolati
University of Kurdistan
Kurdistan, Iran

Bazila Farooq
Lovely Professional University
Punjab, India

Aaquib Hussain Ganai
University of Kashmir
Jammu and Kashmir, India

Mehdi Ghatee
Amirkabir University of Technology
Tehran, Iran

Jayati Gulati
Rukmini Devi Institute of Advanced Studies
New Delhi, India

Rana Hashmy
University of Kashmir
Jammu and Kashmir, India

Bilal Ahmad Khan
Centre for Human Well-being Research Rehabilitation Foundation
Srinagar, India

Zarka Malik
Department of Higher Education
Jammu and Kashmir, India

Ankush Manocha
Lovely Professional University
Punjab, India

Irshad Ahmed Mir
Department of Higher Education
Jammu and Kashmir, India

Shabir Ahmad Najar
University of Kashmir
Jammu and Kashmir, India

Mudasir Ahmad Nazar
University of Kashmir
Jammu and Kashmir, India

Mohammad Saleem Sofi
G.M.C
Jammu and Kashmir, India

Sadegh Sulaimany
University of Kurdistan
Kurdistan, Iran

Tazeem Zainab
Department of Higher Education
Jammu and Kashmir, India

Wakar Amin Zargar
University of Kashmir
Jammu and Kashmir, India

Section I

Understanding and Analyzing Social Networks: Types, Dataset Analysis and Challenges

1 Deciphering Social Networks

Types, Applications, and Analytical Challenges

Bazila Farooq and Ankush Manocha

1.1 INTRODUCTION

Social networks refer to the interconnected structures made up of individuals or organizations, connected by various social relationships such as friendships, professional ties, or shared interests. These networks show how resources, influence, and information flow both within and across groups, making them crucial for understanding social dynamics [1]. One may learn more about how ideas spread, social norms are formed, and individual and group behavior by looking at these linkages. Social networks are crucial across various societal sectors, including business strategies, public health initiatives, and political campaigns, due to their capacity to reveal interaction and influence patterns that significantly affect outcomes [2]. Social network analysis (SNA), the study of these networks, has a long history that dates back to the early 1900s [3]. Pioneering sociologists such as Georg Simmel and Jacob Moreno laid the foundation for this field. Georg Simmel introduced the concept of studying the structure of social relationships systematically in the early 1900s [4]. His work emphasized the importance of social forms and the patterns of interaction that define social life. Simmel's insights into the dynamics of dyads (two-person groups) and triads (three-person groups) highlighted how the structure of a network influences individual behavior and social phenomena. Jacob Moreno further advanced the field in the 1930s by developing sociometry, a method for measuring social relationships [5]. Significant contributions from various disciplines, including anthropology, psychology, and mathematics, have further enriched SNA. For example, Claude Fischer's studies on personal networks in urban settings and Linton C. Freeman's exploration of the development of SNA as a scientific discipline have been instrumental in shaping contemporary understandings of social networks [6, 7]. The advent of powerful computing technologies and the internet in the late 20th century greatly accelerated the development of SNA. These advancements have enabled the analysis of large-scale networks with complex structures,

DOI: 10.1201/9781003515890-2

allowing researchers to explore intricate social dynamics and patterns of influence more effectively. Today, SNA employs advanced algorithms and sophisticated data analytics to delve into the complex web of social connections, providing insights that are crucial in our increasingly interconnected world [8]. In summary, the historical context of SNA is marked by foundational contributions from early sociologists and the integration of interdisciplinary research, culminating in a vibrant and dynamic field that continues to evolve with technological advancements. Social network analysis (SNA) has evolved significantly over time, with notable contributions from disciplines such as anthropology, psychology, and mathematics. The field experienced major advancements in the late 20th century due to the rise of the internet and advanced computer technology, enabling the analysis of complex, large-scale networks. SNA is a vibrant, multidisciplinary area that studies the complex web of social interactions using cutting-edge algorithms and sophisticated data analytics [9]. This exploration is crucial in our increasingly interconnected world, where understanding these networks can illuminate patterns of influence, information flow, and group dynamics. SNA's ability to map and analyze relationships has broad applications, from improving organizational efficiency to enhancing public health initiatives and informing policy decisions. Human connectivity has transformed dramatically in the digital age, with online social networks playing an increasingly vital role in our civic, professional, and personal lives. Social media sites like Facebook, X, and LinkedIn have developed into important forces shaping social relationships and institutions, going beyond just being platforms for communication. Trust is a complex yet important characteristic in these digital arenas that influences the emergence, growth, and longevity of online interactions. The concept of trust in digital environments is complex and encompasses judgments about the dependability, honesty, and skill of users as well as the platform itself. It is closely related to the ethical management of shared knowledge and expectations of reciprocal behavior. Even after a great deal of research on online communities, it is still unclear exactly how trust is established, preserved, and eroded in these settings, as illustrated in Figure 1.1. Interdisciplinary research has great potential and difficulty in filling this gap [10]. Through the integration of sophisticated machine-learning techniques with social science perspectives, researchers can begin to decipher these mechanisms. To develop tactics that promote stronger and more resilient digital communities, it is essential to understand how trust operates on the internet. This involves addressing problems that might undermine trust and jeopardize the integrity of digital interactions, such as privacy, disinformation, and online deceit. The insights gained from social network analysis and trust research will be crucial for creating environments that foster significant and trustworthy interactions as online platforms continue to develop [11].

1.2 LITERATURE REVIEW

Numerous academic fields have studied trust, emphasizing its importance in both private and public spheres. The significance of trust in digital economic activities has been highlighted by economists such as Arrow, who have highlighted its role

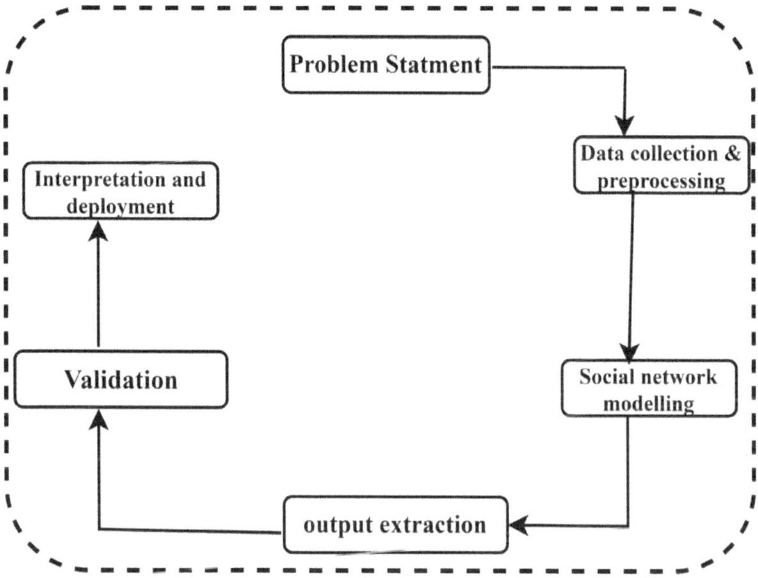

FIGURE 1.1 Process of social network analysis.

as a crucial enabler of economic transactions by lowering market friction. This idea applies equally to online transactions and interactions [12]. Rotter and other psychologists have studied how individual behavior and cognition shape views of trust, and their findings indicate that human relationships are greatly impacted by one's ability to be trusted. This dynamic is particularly significant in online environments since digital personas and interactions influence how these views are formed. Sociologists have integrated trust into the larger framework of societal institutions, highlighting its essential role in facilitating social cohesion and encouraging cooperative behavior [13]. A thorough basis for comprehending social trust is offered by Coleman's research [14]. Furthermore, theories like Burt's "structural holes" and Granovetter's "strength of weak ties" provide important insights into the complexities of trust in digital environments by implying that indirect relationships within network structures significantly impact on the development of trust and the exchange of information online [15, 16]. The emergence of social networks throughout the digital revolution has completely changed how people connect and brought about new dynamics in the building and maintenance of trust. Due to the expansion of social circles and the quickening of connection creation brought about by these platforms, building and sustaining trust in the absence of conventional face-to-face indicators present unique challenges. As Donath noted, the significance of online identities and reputation systems in trust dynamics has grown. These factors impact on how people portray themselves online and are seen by others, which in turn affects how much confidence is placed in them [17]. Existing research has major limitations, even though fundamental work across disciplines provides a sound framework for understanding trust. Economic models of trust frequently oversimplify the social and psychological nuances of interpersonal trust in digital interactions, concentrating primarily on transactional aspects [18]. Comparably, even though they are insightful, psychological and sociological research usually focuses on conventional face-to-face settings, which could not completely transfer to online settings where cues and interactions are very different [19].

1.3 TYPES OF SOCIAL NETWORKS

Social networks can be categorized based on the nature of connections they facilitate, such as personal relationships, professional ties, or digital interactions, and are depicted in Figure 1.2. These networks are essential for emotional support, career development, and modern communication [20]. Additionally, community networks foster social cohesion and collective action within specific groups or localities. Different types are mentioned one by one.

1. **Personal Networks**: Personal networks revolve around an individual and emphasize their relationships. These networks, which offer mental assistance, company, and a sense of belonging, are made up of family, friends, and intimate acquaintances. Personal networks are crucial for individual well-being, providing a basis for social interaction and emotional security [21]. They play a crucial role in shaping one's identity and social skills, as these relationships are often intimate and long-lasting [22]. The strength of personal networks lies in their depth and the quality of connections, which foster trust, loyalty, and mutual support.

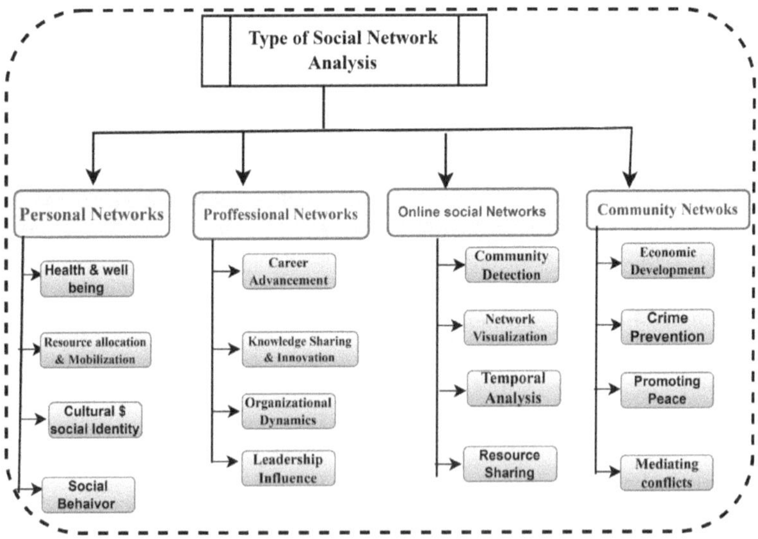

FIGURE 1.2 Types of social network analysis.

2. **Professional Networks**: Professional networks are centered around work-related connections and are critical for career development, job opportunities, and professional growth. These networks include colleagues, mentors, industry peers, and professional associations. By engaging in professional networks, individuals can access valuable resources, knowledge, and opportunities that can enhance their careers [23]. Networking events, conferences, and social media platforms like LinkedIn facilitate the building and maintaining of these connections. Professional networks often emphasize mutual benefits, where individuals share expertise, provide referrals, and collaborate on projects to advance their careers [24].
3. **Online Social Networks**: Online social networks are digital platforms that facilitate social interaction and communication over the internet. Platforms such as Facebook, X, LinkedIn, and Instagram have revolutionized modern communication by enabling users to connect with others globally. These networks allow for the rapid sharing of information, ideas, and media, and have become integral to personal and professional life. Online social networks can amplify the reach of one's personal and professional networks, provide platforms for self-expression, and foster virtual communities around shared interests [25]. However, they also pose challenges such as privacy concerns, misinformation, and the potential for superficial connections.
4. **Community Networks**: Community networks consist of social connections within specific communities, such as neighborhoods, interest groups, or social collectives. These networks are vital for fostering a sense of community, civic engagement, and collective action. Community networks can be geographically based, such as those in local neighborhoods, or interest-based, such as hobbyist groups, volunteer organizations, or cultural associations. They provide a platform for individuals to collaborate on common goals, support local initiatives, and enhance the overall quality of life within the community [26]. Community networks strengthen social cohesion, encourage civic responsibility, and create a supportive environment where members can rely on each other.

1.4 APPLICATIONS OF SOCIAL NETWORK ANALYSIS

Social network analysis (SNA) is used to explore and understand the intricate patterns of relationships and interactions within networks. By mapping and analyzing these connections, SNA helps identify key influencers, detect communities, and understand information flow. It leverages advanced algorithms and data analytics to provide insights into social structures, enhancing our comprehension of social dynamics, organizational behavior, and the spread of ideas [27]. Social network analysis (SNA) offers valuable insights across various fields by examining the patterns and structures of relationships within networks, as illustrated in Figure 1.3. These applications span from enhancing organizational efficiency to understanding social behaviors and improving public health.

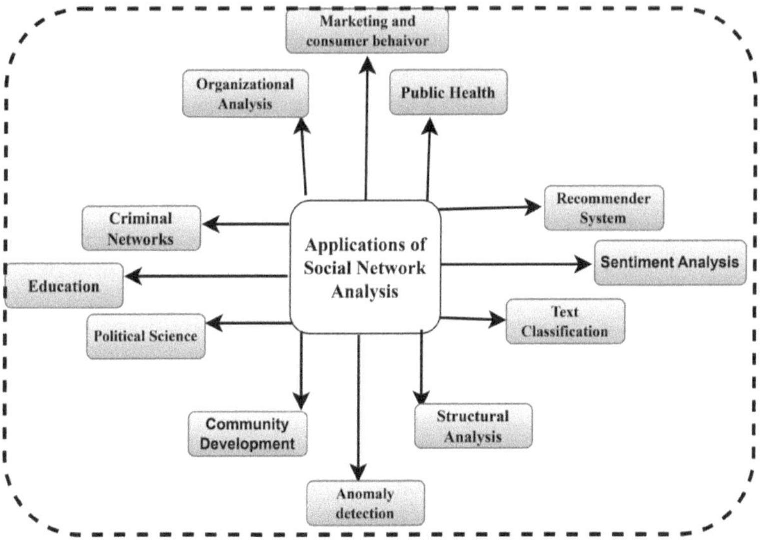

FIGURE 1.3 Illustration of social network analysis.

1. Organizational Analysis: SNA is used to understand communication and collaboration within organizations. By mapping employee interactions, it identifies key influencers, potential bottlenecks, and areas for improving information flow [28]. This helps in optimizing team structures, enhancing productivity, and fostering innovation.
2. Marketing and Consumer Behavior: In marketing, SNA helps in identifying influential customers who can impact others' purchasing decisions. By examining social media interactions and customer networks, businesses can customize marketing strategies, enhance customer targeting, and boost brand loyalty through word-of-mouth promotion [29].
3. Public Health: SNA is instrumental in public health for tracking the spread of diseases and understanding health behaviors. It helps identify how diseases propagate through social networks, enabling better-targeted interventions and more effective public health strategies [30]. It also aids in understanding the social determinants of health by analyzing how social connections influence health outcomes.
4. Criminal Networks: Law enforcement agencies use SNA to analyze criminal networks. By mapping out the connections between individuals involved in criminal activities, SNA helps in identifying key players, understanding the structure of criminal organizations, and disrupting illegal activities [31].
5. Education: In educational settings, SNA is applied to study student interactions and collaboration patterns. It helps in identifying students who are isolated or at risk, improving peer support networks, and enhancing overall educational outcomes through better-designed group activities and support systems [32].

6. Political Science: SNA is used to analyze political networks, including relationships between politicians, lobbying groups, and constituents. It helps in understanding power dynamics, coalition building, and the spread of political ideas and movements [33].
7. Community Development: SNA aids in community development by mapping out social ties within communities. It identifies key community leaders, assesses the effectiveness of community programs, and helps in building stronger, more cohesive communities by enhancing social capital and trust [34].

By leveraging SNA, researchers and practitioners can gain deeper insights into complex social structures, optimize strategies across various domains, and foster more effective and cohesive interactions within networks.

1.5 ANALYTICAL TECHNIQUES IN SOCIAL NETWORK ANALYSIS

Through social network analysis (SNA), analytical methods enable academics to explore and comprehend the dynamics and structure of social networks. These techniques measure interactions, identify important nodes, and understand the general topology of the network by employing a variety of metrics and techniques. Analysts can evaluate the degree of connectedness, identify subgroups within the network, and ascertain the importance of particular players by utilizing metrics like centrality, density, and clustering. To fully comprehend social interactions and their repercussions, complex network data must be interpreted with the use of statistical models and visualization tools [35]. SNA examines the dynamics and structure of social networks using a wide range of analytical tools, assisting in the discovery of connections and patterns that provide important insights into the actions and impacts of both people and organizations. In social network analysis (SNA), nodes (actors) represent entities such as individuals, organizations, or groups, while edges (ties or links) represent the relationships or interactions between these entities. Nodes can vary in type and may have attributes like demographic information, roles, activity levels, or influence. Edges can be directed (one-way) or undirected (mutual), and may be weighted to indicate the strength or frequency of interactions. They can also be temporal, reflecting dynamic changes over time, or multiplex, representing multiple types of relationships between the same nodes. Attributes of edges, such as the type of relationship, interaction frequency, duration, and strength of ties, provide deeper insights into the nature of connections within the network, helping to analyze influence, information flow, and network dynamics comprehensively.

1. Centrality Measures: Centrality metrics pinpoint the most significant or influential nodes within a network. Degree centrality quantifies the number of direct connections a node possesses, reflecting its level of activity. Betweenness centrality gauges the extent to which a node resides on the shortest paths between other nodes, underscoring its function as a bridge or gatekeeper. Closeness centrality measures a node's proximity to all other

nodes in the network, indicating its capacity for rapid interaction with others. Eigenvector centrality assesses a node's influence based on the importance of its neighbors' connections, highlighting its overall significance within the network [36].
2. Density: Density measures the proportion of possible connections in a network that are actual connections. A high-density network indicates a high level of interconnectedness, which can facilitate rapid information flow but may also lead to redundancy [37].
3. Clustering Coefficient: The clustering coefficient measures the degree to which nodes in a network tend to cluster together. It indicates the likelihood that a node's neighbors are also connected, reflecting the presence of tightly knit groups or communities within the network [38].
4. Community Detection: Community detection techniques identify subgroups or clusters within a network where nodes are more densely connected than to the rest of the network [39]. Methods such as modularity optimization and hierarchical clustering help in uncovering these communities, which can reveal important social structures and functional groupings.
5. Network Visualization: Visualization tools create graphical representations of networks, making it easier to identify patterns, clusters, and key nodes [40]. Tools like Gephi, Pajek, and Cytoscape offer various visualization options that can highlight different aspects of the network structure.
6. Path Analysis: Path analysis examines the paths between nodes, including the shortest path (geodesic distance) and other possible routes [41]. This analysis helps in understanding the efficiency of information flow and the role of specific nodes in facilitating communication within the network.
7. Structural Equivalence: Structural equivalence measures the similarity between nodes based on their connections to other nodes. Structurally equivalent nodes have similar patterns of ties and can often be substituted for one another in terms of their role in the network [42]. By applying these analytical techniques, SNA provides a comprehensive toolkit for exploring and understanding the intricate web of social connections, enabling researchers to uncover the underlying principles that govern social interactions and network dynamics.

1.6 CHALLENGES IN SOCIAL NETWORK ANALYSIS

Challenges in social network analysis (SNA) are multifaceted and rooted in the intricate nature of social networks. One significant hurdle is encountered during the data collection phase, where obtaining comprehensive and reliable data about social connections proves daunting [43]. The sheer volume of information, coupled with concerns about data quality and privacy, complicates this process. Additionally, representing real-world social interactions in a network format poses challenges [44]. Capturing the depth and context of relationships accurately, especially in dynamic or multi-layered networks, requires careful consideration and methodological rigor [45]. Furthermore, interpreting network structures and dynamics presents another layer of complexity[46]. Networks may exhibit varying patterns and meanings depending on the context and analytical approach employed. This necessitates a nuanced understanding and thoughtful interpretation of the data to draw accurate conclusions. Dealing with missing or incomplete data adds further complexity to the analysis, requiring researchers to employ techniques for data imputation or adjustment [47]. Addressing biases inherent in the data, such as sampling biases or response biases, is also crucial to ensure the validity and reliability of findings. Ethical concerns surrounding SNA, such as protecting the privacy and confidentiality of participants, further compound the challenges faced by researchers [48]. Navigating these ethical considerations requires careful adherence to ethical guidelines and principles, as well as transparent communication with participants about the purpose and potential implications of the study [49]. Despite these obstacles, overcoming them is essential for advancing our understanding of social networks and deriving meaningful insights that can inform various fields, including sociology, psychology, anthropology, and beyond [50]. By addressing these challenges with diligence and innovation, researchers can unlock the full potential of SNA to shed light on the complex dynamics of social interactions and networks.

1.7 CASE STUDIES AND EXAMPLES

Case studies demonstrate the diverse applications and significant impact of social network analysis (SNA) across various domains and are depicted in Table 1.1. In corporate settings, SNA is utilized to analyze email communication networks, identifying key influencers and communication bottlenecks within an organization. By mapping the flow of information and interactions among employees, SNA can reveal how information is disseminated, pinpoint areas where communication is stalled, and highlight influential employees who either facilitate or hinder the flow of information [51]. This insight helps organizations optimize communication strategies, enhance collaboration, and improve overall efficiency. For example, a case study of a large technology firm might reveal high internal communication within certain departments but poor inter-departmental links, leading to inefficiencies. Addressing these issues can foster better cross-departmental collaboration and innovation. In public health, SNA is pivotal for tracking the spread of infectious diseases within communities [52]. By examining social networks and patterns of contact between individuals or groups, researchers can identify high-risk clusters and develop targeted interventions to mitigate disease spread. During an outbreak like COVID-19, SNA helps public health officials understand how the disease spreads through different social groups and settings, allowing for targeted public health measures such as isolating specific clusters or enhancing contact tracing efforts, ultimately controlling the spread more effectively. In the realm of social media, SNA is employed to study the diffusion of information and the formation of online communities on platforms like X and Facebook. Researchers analyze the structure of these networks to understand trends, influence patterns, and the spread of misinformation [53]. SNA can identify influential users who act as hubs for information dissemination, helping amplify messages or spread misinformation. Understanding these dynamics is crucial for

TABLE 1.1
Summary of Case Studies and Examples

Objective	Background	Model	Outcome	References
Systematically review and synthesize existing social media research to identify key theories, constructs, and frameworks, and suggest future directions.	Motivated by the rapid growth and importance of social media and the need for a coherent synthesis of its theoretical underpinnings and frameworks.	Conducted a systematic literature review of articles from major academic journals, using qualitative content analysis to identify patterns and themes.	Outlined constructs including user engagement, trust, and social influence, are central to social media dynamics.	Kaplan et al. [59]
To empirically investigate the dynamics of an evolving social network, concentrating on how social networks develop, expand, and transform over time.	Social networks evolve through the creation and dissolution of social ties, but the mechanisms driving these dynamics were not well understood. The study aimed to provide empirical evidence on these underlying processes.	Utilized a large dataset of email communications from a university to construct a dynamic social network. Applied statistical and computational methods to analyze tie formation, dissolution, and overall network evolution.	Identified patterns such as triadic closure and preferential attachment in tie formation, observed high turnover of social ties, and provided support for existing network evolution theories while highlighting the need for new models.	Kossinets et al. [60]
To develop and test the use of social network sensors for the early detection of contagious outbreaks.	Motivated by the need for early detection of contagious outbreaks to prevent widespread transmission and minimize impact, the study explores innovative methods leveraging social networks.	Utilized social network analysis to identify central individuals in a network who could act as sensors for detecting the onset of contagious outbreaks. The model involved tracking these central individuals for early signs of infection.	Demonstrated that social network sensors could effectively provide early warning signals of contagious outbreaks, showing potential for improving public health surveillance systems.	Christakis et al. [61]

(Continued)

TABLE 1.1 (CONTINUED)
Summary of Case Studies and Examples

Objective	Background	Model	Outcome	References
Review the history, methods, and applications of network analysis in public health to highlight its utility and future potential in this field.	Motivated by increasing interest in using network analysis to address public health issues, aims to provide a comprehensive overview of its development and uses.	Conducted a historical and methodological review of network analysis in public health, examining key studies, methods, and applications across various contexts.	Demonstrated the broad applications of network analysis in public health, highlighted methodological advancements, and suggested future research directions to further integrate network analysis in public health practice.	Luke et al. [62]
To investigate the spread of true and false news online and analyze the factors influencing their propagation.	False information spreads rapidly on social media platforms, often reaching a larger audience than true information.	Analyzed a dataset of verified true and false news stories shared on X from 2006 to 2017. Examined the cascades of retweets to measure the spread of each story and identify characteristics associated with virality.	Found that false news spreads significantly faster, farther, deeper, and more broadly than true news. Falsehoods were 70% more likely to be retweeted than the truth, primarily driven by humans rather than bots. The diffusion of false news tends to target individuals with larger social networks, reinforcing the "fake news" effect.	Vosoughi et al. [63]

developing strategies to promote accurate information and combat fake news. For instance, a case study might involve analyzing how a viral tweet spreads across different communities and identifying key retweeters that significantly boost its reach [54]. In urban planning, SNA is applied to analyze transportation networks or social ties within neighborhoods. Researchers might use SNA to identify key transportation hubs critical for efficient urban mobility or understand patterns of social interaction influencing community cohesion and resilience [55]. Analyzing these networks helps urban planners design more efficient and resilient cities. For example, a study might reveal that certain neighborhoods have strong internal social ties but are poorly connected to other city parts, guiding investments in infrastructure to improve connectivity and support economic and social integration [56]. Interdisciplinary research opportunities further expand SNA's impact, such as in cybersecurity, where SNA helps identify network vulnerabilities and understand malicious entity behavior, enabling threat prediction and mitigation [57]. Technological advancements in artificial intelligence (AI) and machine learning are transforming SNA by automating data collection, network visualization, and pattern recognition, enhancing scalability and efficiency. However, as SNA delves deeper into personal data, ethical considerations regarding privacy and confidentiality become critical, requiring researchers to adhere to ethical guidelines, obtain informed consent, and communicate transparently with participants about the study's purpose and implications. Looking ahead, SNA will likely explore novel applications and adapt analytical techniques to keep pace with technological and societal changes. This includes developing methods to handle large-scale and complex network data, improving algorithms for more accurate analysis, and continuously updating ethical standards to protect privacy and data integrity [58]. By addressing these challenges and leveraging new technologies, SNA can unlock deeper insights into the complex web of social interactions, contributing to advancements across various fields and enhancing our understanding of social dynamics in an interconnected world. These examples illustrate how SNA can uncover hidden patterns and relationships within complex systems, informing decision-making and driving positive change across diverse fields.

1.8 FUTURE DIRECTIONS

Social network analysis (SNA) is shaped by technological advancements and emerging trends that influence the field's development and application.

1. **Technological Advancements**: The integration of artificial intelligence (AI) and machine learning techniques is poised to revolutionize SNA [64]. AI algorithms can enhance the scalability and efficiency of network analysis by automating tasks such as data collection, network visualization, and pattern recognition [65]. Real-time social interaction monitoring and predictive analytics are made possible by machine learning algorithms, which offer new insights into network dynamics [66]. Additionally, developments in natural language processing and data mining allow scholars to extract meaningful information from unstructured data sources, such as posts on

social media and online forums, expanding the scope of social network analysis (SNA) [67].

2. **Emerging Trends**: The field of social network analysis (SNA) is experiencing rapid growth, driven by technological advancements and the emergence of new applications. This evolution is marked by expanding areas of application and increased interdisciplinary research opportunities. With the proliferation of digital platforms, there is heightened interest in studying virtual communities and online collaboration networks. Researchers analyze how individuals interact, how information spreads, and how online communities form and evolve. Platforms such as X, Facebook, and LinkedIn provide valuable datasets that allow for the study of information diffusion, the creation of social ties, and the impact of network structures on behavior [68]. Additionally, the intersection of SNA with fields like public health, cybersecurity, and smart cities offers promising opportunities for cross-disciplinary research. For instance, in public health, SNA is utilized to monitor the spread of infectious diseases, identify high-risk populations, and design targeted interventions, offering crucial insights into disease transmission dynamics and the influence of social behaviors on health outcomes. In cybersecurity, SNA helps detect potential vulnerabilities in network structures and understand the behavior of malicious actors, enabling the prediction and mitigation of cyber threats [69]. In urban planning, SNA is applied to optimize transportation networks, boost community resilience, and enhance public services, thereby aiding city planners in making data-driven decisions that improve urban living conditions. Advancements in artificial intelligence (AI) and machine learning are significantly transforming SNA by streamlining data collection, network visualization, and pattern recognition, thus improving the scalability and efficiency of network analysis. Machine learning models offer predictive insights into network dynamics, facilitating real-time monitoring and forecasting of social interactions. Additionally, data mining and natural language processing technologies allow researchers to extract valuable insights from unstructured data sources, such as social media posts and online forums, thereby enhancing the analysis with new data dimensions [70]. However, as SNA explores deeper into personal and sensitive data, ethical considerations become increasingly paramount. Ensuring participant privacy and confidentiality poses a significant challenge, requiring strict adherence to ethical guidelines, obtaining informed consent, and maintaining clear communication with participants regarding the purpose and potential implications of the studies. Addressing these ethical concerns is essential to uphold trust and integrity in research practices. Looking ahead, the future of SNA is likely to involve exploring new applications and adapting analytical techniques to keep pace with technological and societal changes. This includes developing methods to handle large-scale and complex network data, improving algorithms for more accurate and meaningful analysis, and continuously updating ethical standards to protect participant privacy and data integrity.

By overcoming these challenges and leveraging new technologies, SNA can provide deeper insights into the intricate web of social interactions, thereby contributing to advancements in various fields and enhancing our understanding of social dynamics in an interconnected world [71].

1.9 CONCLUSION

In summary, the field of social network analysis (SNA) is on the cusp of significant progress propelled by technological advancements and evolving trends. The incorporation of artificial intelligence (AI) and machine learning into SNA methodologies offers a pathway to streamline analysis processes and extract deeper insights from the intricate fabric of social networks. With the continuous evolution of social networks fueled by the proliferation of online platforms and digital interactions, SNA is poised to explore new frontiers in understanding human behavior and interaction patterns. This includes delving into areas such as virtual communities, online collaboration dynamics, and the dissemination of information in digital spaces. However, alongside these opportunities, it is imperative to remain vigilant about ethical considerations surrounding data privacy, consent, and responsible data usage. By fostering interdisciplinary collaboration and harnessing the power of cutting-edge technologies, SNA is positioned not only to advance academic understanding but also to make meaningful contributions to addressing complex societal challenges. Through these efforts, SNA can play a pivotal role in deepening our comprehension of social dynamics and facilitating positive change in diverse domains, from healthcare to urban planning, paving the way for a more connected and informed society.

REFERENCES

1. Wasserman, S., & Faust, K. (1994). *Social Network Analysis: Methods and Applications*. Cambridge University Press.
2. Granovetter, M. S. (1973). The strength of weak ties. *American Journal of Sociology*, 78(6), 1360–1380.
3. Borgatti, S. P., & Halgin, D. S. (2011). On network theory. *Organization Science*, 22(5), 1168–1181.
4. Hollstein, B. (2021). Georg Simmel's contribution to social network research. In M. L. Small, B. L. Perry, B. Pescosolido, & E. B. Smith (Eds.), *Personal Networks: Classic Readings and New Directions in Egocentric Analysis* (pp. 44–59). Cambridge University Press.
5. Moreno, J. L. (1934). *Who Shall Survive?: Foundations of Sociometry, Group Psychotherapy, and Sociodrama*. Beacon House.
6. Barabási, A.-L. (2003). *Linked: How Everything Is Connected to Everything Else and What It Means*. Plume.
7. Freeman, L. C. (1979). Centrality in social networks conceptual clarification. *Social Networks*, 1(3), 215–239.
8. Scott, J. (2017). *Social Network Analysis*. Sage Publications.
9. Lazer, D., Pentland, A., Adamic, L., Aral, S., Barabási, A.-L., Brewer, D., & Van Alstyne, M. (2009). Computational social science. *Science*, 323(5915), 721–723.

10. Burt, R. S. (2005). *Brokerage and Closure: An Introduction to Social Capital.* Oxford University Press.
11. Golbeck, J. (2008). Computing and applying trust in web-based social networks. *AI Magazine*, 29(3), 43–52.
12. Arrow, K. J. (1974). *The Limits of Organization.* Norton.
13. Rotter, J. B. (1980). Interpersonal trust, trustworthiness, and gullibility. *American Psychologist*, 35(1), 1–7.
14. Coleman, J. S. (1990). *Foundations of Social Theory.* Harvard University Press.
15. Burt, R. S. (1992). *Structural holes: The social structure of competition.* Harvard University Press.
16. Granovetter, M. S. (1973). The strength of weak ties. *American Journal of Sociology, 78*(6), 1360–1380. https://doi.org/10.1086/225469
17. Donath, J. (2023). *The Social Machine: Designs for Living Online.* MIT Press.
18. Ivarsson, J., & Lindwall, O. (2023). *Suspicious Minds: The Problem of Trust and Conversational Agents.* Computer Supported Cooperative Work (CSCW).
19. Balogun, A. L., et al. (2023). Artificial intelligence and trust in online transactions. *Journal of Internet Commerce.* https://doi.org/10.1080/15332860802067706
20. Fischer, C. S. (2016). *Still Connected: Family and Friends in America Since 1970.* Russell Sage Foundation.
21. Agneessens, F., & Wittek, R. (2018). Social capital and employee well-being: Disentangling intricate dynamics of social networks at the workplace. *Social Networks*, 55, 69–79.
22. Seibert, S. E., Kraimer, M. L., & Liden, R. C. (2017). A social capital theory of career success. *Academy of Management Journal*, 60(2), 505–533.
23. Ellison, N. B., Vitak, J., Gray, R., & Lampe, C. (2014). Cultivating social resources on social network sites: Facebook relationship maintenance behaviors and their role in social capital processes. *Journal of Computer-Mediated Communication*, 19(4), 855–870.
24. Treem, J. W., & Leonardi, P. M. (2016). Social media use in organizations: Exploring The affordances of visibility, editability, persistence, and association. *Annals of the International Communication Association*, 40(1), 21–41.
25. Hampton, K. N., Lee, C. J., & Her, E. J. (2016). How new media affords network diversity: Direct and mediated access to social capital through participation in local social settings. *New Media & Society*, 18(9), 1806–1827.
26. Horgan, M. J., & Dimitrijevic, M. (2019). The role of community networks in strengthening social cohesion: Insights from a field study. *Community Development Journal*, 54(3), 499–516.
27. Barabási, A. L. (2016). *Network Science.* Cambridge University Press.
28. Freeman, L. C. (2004). *The Development of Social Network Analysis: A Study in the Sociology of Science.* Empirical Press.
29. Valente, T. W. (2010). *Social Networks and Health: Models, Methods, and Applications.* Oxford University Press.
30. Snijders, T. A. (2001). The statistical evaluation of social network dynamics. *Sociological Methodology*, 31(1), 361–395.
31. Marsden, P. V., & Lin, N. (1982). *Social Structure and Network Analysis.* Sage Publications.
32. Newman, M. E. (2010). *Networks: An Introduction.* Oxford University Press.
33. Hanneman, R. A., & Riddle, M. (2011). Concepts and measures for basic network analysis. In J. Scott & P. J. Carrington (Eds.), *The SAGE Handbook of Social Network Analysis* (pp. 340–369). Sage Publications.

34. Berkowitz, S. D. (2013). *An Introduction to Structural Analysis: The Network Approach to Social Research*. Elsevier.
35. Borgatti, S. P., Everett, M. G., & Johnson, J. C. (2013). *Analyzing Social Networks*. Sage Publications.
36. Freeman, L. C. (2004). *The Development of Social Network Analysis: A Study in the Sociology of Science*. Empirical Press.
37. Borgatti, S. P. (2005). Centrality and network flow. *Social Networks*, 27(1), 55–71.
38. Robins, G., Pattison, P., & Wasserman, S. (2009). Logit models and logistic regressions for social networks: I. *An introduction to Markov Graphs and Psychometrika*, 74(3), 491–525.
39. Carrington, P. J., Scott, J., & Wasserman, S. (Eds.). (2019). *Models and Methods in Social Network Analysis* (Vol. 27). Cambridge University Press.
40. Robins, G., Pattison, P., Kalish, Y., & Lusher, D. (2007). An introduction to exponential random graph (p) models for social networks. *Social Networks*, 29(2), 173–191.
41. Snijders, T. A. B., van de Bunt, G. G., & Steglich, C. E. G. (2010). Introduction to stochastic actor-based models for network dynamics. *Social Networks*, 32(1), 44–60.
42. Lospinoso, J. A., Schweinberger, M., Snijders, T. A., & Ripley, R. M. (2011). Assessing and accounting for time heterogeneity in stochastic actor-oriented models. *Advances in Data Analysis and Classification*, 5(2), 147–176.
43. Salter-Townshend, M., & Murphy, B. (2013). Review of statistical network analysis: Models, algorithms, and software. *Statistical Analysis and Data Mining: The ASA Data Science Journal*, 6(4), 260–264.
44. Marsden, P. V. (1990). Network data and measurement. *Annual Review of Sociology*, 16(1), 435–463.
45. Butts, C. T. (2003). Network inference, error, and informant (in) accuracy: A Bayesian approach. *Social Networks*, 25(2), 103–140.
46. Kadushin, C. (2012). *Understanding Social Networks: Theories, Concepts, and Findings*. OUP USA.
47. Prell, C. (2011). *Social Network Analysis: History, Theory, and Methodology*. SAGE Publication.
48. Edwards, G. (Ed.). (2010). *Social Capital and Social Network Analysis*. Edward Elgar Publishing.
49. Knoke, D., & Yang, S. (2019). *Social Network Analysis* (Vol. 154). SAGE Publications.
50. Hogan, B., Carrasco, J. A., & Wellman, B. (2009). Network analysis in the social sciences. *Science*, 323(5916), 892–895.
51. Ngai, E. W., Tao, S. S., & Moon, K. K. (2015). Social media research: Theories, constructs, and conceptual frameworks. *International Journal of Information Management*, 35(1), 33–44.
52. Kossinets, G., & Watts, D. J. (2006). Empirical analysis of an evolving social network. *Science*, 311(5757), 88–90.
53. Christakis, N. A., & Fowler, J. H. (2010). Social network sensors for early detection of contagious outbreaks. *PLoS One*, 5(9), e12948.
54. Luke, D. A., & Harris, J. K. (2007). Network analysis in public health: History, methods, and applications. *Annual Review of Public Health*, 28, 69–93.
55. Vosoughi, S., Roy, D., & Aral, S. (2018). The spread of true and false news online. *Science*, 359(6380), 1146–1151.
56. Gruzd, A., Wellman, B., & Takhteyev, Y. (2011). Imagining Twitter as an imagined community. *American Behavioral Scientist*, 55(10), 1294–1318.
57. Zhen, F., Cao, Y., & Wang, B. (2017). Understanding transportation modes from raw GPS data for urban areas. *IEEE Transactions on Intelligent Transportation Systems*, 18(11), 2993–3004.

58. Porta, S., Crucitti, P., & Latora, V. (2006). The network analysis of urban streets: A primal approach. *Environment and Planning B: Planning and Design*, 33(5), 705–725.
59. Kaplan, A. M., & Haenlein, M. (2010). Users of the world, unite! The challenges and opportunities of social media. *Business Horizons*, *53*(1), 59–68.
60. Kossinets, G., & Watts, D. J. (2006). Empirical analysis of an evolving social network. *Science*, 311(5757), 88–90.
61. Christakis, N. A., & Fowler, J. H. (2010). Social network sensors for early detection of contagious outbreaks. *PLoS One*, 5(9), e12948.
62. Luke, D. A., & Harris, J. K. (2007). Network analysis in public health: History, methods, and applications. *Annual Review of Public Health*, 28, 69–93.
63. Vosoughi, S., Roy, D., & Aral, S. (2018). The spread of true and false news online. *Science*, 359(6380), 1146–1151.
64. Lazer, D., Pentland, A. S., Adamic, L., Aral, S., Barabási, A. L., Brewer, D., & Van Alstyne, M. (2009). Computational social science. *Science*, 323(5915), 721–723.
65. Kivelä, M., Arenas, A., Barthelemy, M., Gleeson, J. P., Moreno, Y., & Porter, M. A. (2014). Multilayer networks. *Journal of Complex Networks*, 2(3), 203–271.
66. Wang, P., Gonzalez, M. C., & Hidalgo, C. A. (2014). Understanding the spreading patterns of mobile phone viruses. *Science*, 324(5930), 1071–1076.
67. De Domenico, M., Nicosia, V., Arenas, A., & Latora, V. (2015). Structural reducibility of multilayer networks. *Nature Communications*, 6(1), 1–8.
68. Golder, S. A., & Macy, M. W. (2011). Diurnal and seasonal moods vary with work, sleep, and day length across diverse cultures. *Science*, 333(6051), 1878–1881.
69. Yang, J., & Leskovec, J. (2015). Defining and evaluating network communities based on ground truth. *Knowledge and Information Systems*, 42(1), 181–213.
70. Mucha, P. J., Richardson, T., Macon, K., Porter, M. A., & Onnela, J. P. (2010). Community structure in time-dependent, multiscale, and multiplex networks. *Science*, 328(5980), 876–878.
71. Asur, S., & Huberman, B. A. (2010). Predicting the future with social media. In *2010 IEEE/WIC/ACM International Conference on Web Intelligence and Intelligent Agent Technology* (pp. 492–499). IEEE.

2 Social Network Analysis
Strategies and Challenges in Data Collection, Representation, and Analysis

Irshad A. Mir, Zarka Malik, and Tazeem Zainab

2.1 INTRODUCTION

A social network is a structured representation of the social actors (nodes) and their interconnections (ties) to form social groups that share common interests (Arif et al., 2012). These networks represent complex web relationships between individuals, groups, or organizations. The Digital 2024 Global Overview Report published in January 2024 reveals that there are more than 5 billion active social media user entities, with the global total touching 5.04 billion at the start of 2024. A social network connects these social media users by providing online platforms for content creation and interactions. Web 2.0 and social networks are intertwined concepts that represent a paradigm shift in how the Internet is used by people to communicate and interact (Arif et al., 2014).

Social network analysis (SNA) entails the study of the patterns and behavior of various social networks to gain insightful information. It helps in understanding the dependencies between social entities in the data, characterizing their behavior and their effect on the network as a whole and over time (Tabassum, Shazia et al., 2018). SNA relies on the use of mathematical and/or computational models that draw heavily on graphic imagery (Freeman, 2004). Very similar to social media analysis, social network analysis encompasses three main stages: capture, understand, and process, known as the CUP framework (Fan and Gordon, 2014). The first step involves the collection of historical and real-time data from various heterogeneous online sources. The understanding phase involves in-depth analytics of the captured data requiring high computational and storage facilities (Batrinca and Treleaven, 2015). Lastly, the process phase includes interpretation and visualization of the final data required for the specific purpose.

DOI: 10.1201/9781003515890-3

2.2 BACKGROUND OF SOCIAL NETWORKS

2.2.1 History

Social networking analysis (SNA) has a rich history spanning multiple domains, evolving from early sociological and psychological concepts to more advanced fields integrating mathematics, computer sciences, and social sciences.

Some renowned scholars provided the early frameworks for analyzing social relationships and structures that later helped in the development of the more formalized and advanced science of social networking analysis (SNA).

The leading among them was Émile Durkheim (1858–1917), a key figure in sociology who explored the structures of social relationships and these theories laid the foundational concepts for understanding social structures.

Another leading scholar during this era was Max Weber (1864–1920), whose work mainly focused on social action and the role of social structures in shaping individual behavior. His concepts of bureaucracy, authority, and rationalization provided insights into how social structures and relationships influence social organizations.

The third leading scholar in this area was George Simmel (1858–1918), who conducted extensive work on social circles and the impact of social relationships on individual identity, which proved to be very impactful in developing network theories (Zhang M, 2010).

2.2.2 Key Developments

1. **Jacob Moreno (1930s–1940s)**: A pioneer of social network analysis, aimed to both measure and illustrate social relations, referring to his work as "sociometry" and the drawings as "sociogram". He explored the structure and dynamics of social networks in groups (John Scott, 2012).
2. **Harrison White**: A breakthrough was made in the 1960s when Harrison and his colleagues Lorrain and White formalized network theory and structure analysis by applying mathematical and statistical methods to social networks. They developed algebraic and mathematical methods and took advantage of advances in computing to undertake matrix rearrangements for large-scale social networks.
3. **Mark Granovetter**: A prominent sociologist known for his paper published in 1973 titled "The strength of weak ties" that depicted that weak ties or less intimate connections are very important for accessing new information and opportunities. He conducted an in-depth study on how social networks affect economic behavior. By introducing the concept of embeddedness, Granovetter gave the idea that economic actions are deeply embedded in social relations (MS Granovetter, 1973).
4. **Linton Freeman**: The 1970s–1980s saw an era of methodological innovations, during which quantitative methods including measures of centrality such as degree centrality, betweenness centrality and closeness centrality were developed and refined by Freeman. This shift led to more precise and

scalable analysis allowing rigorous statistical methods to be employed in social network data.

5. **Steve Borgatti and Martin Everett**: During the 1990s UCINET, a comprehensive software package for social network analysis was developed by them. This and other computational tools like Pajek, Gephi, etc., revolutionized SNA by providing sophisticated algorithms for visualization and analysis of complex networks. These tools and many more have helped researchers to work on large data sets, analyzing their patterns and visualize the network structure in insightful ways.

2.2.3 Present Scenario

Since the 2000s, the fusion of social network analysis (SNA) with big data and social media has revolutionized the field, resulting in major advancements in the collection, analysis, and application of network data. The rise of social networking platforms like X, Facebook, Instagram, LinkedIn, etc., have become a source of rich data sets for researchers and analysts to access detailed information about user connections, interactions, and behaviors. The storage, processing, and analysis of this large-scale data using technologies like Hadoop and Spark provides a more comprehensive and detailed network analysis. This integration has yielded new insights across a range of fields, namely marketing, epidemiology, political science, economics, organizational behavior, social sciences, cyber security, and education. It is safe to say that currently, social network analysis (SNA) has advanced into a sophisticated discipline driven by technological advancements and the availability of large-scale data.

2.3 REPRESENTATION OF SOCIAL NETWORKS AND THEIR ANALYSIS

Representation of social network data is the key to visualize and analyze the social networks. A good representation method is vital for modeling the complex relationships of social structures and makes the job of analysis easy. Figure 2.1 depicts the various methods for the representation of social networks.

Among the methods presented below the graph-based and matrix-based methods are the most common methods used for the representation of social networks. The following sections present the basic understanding of each of representation methods.

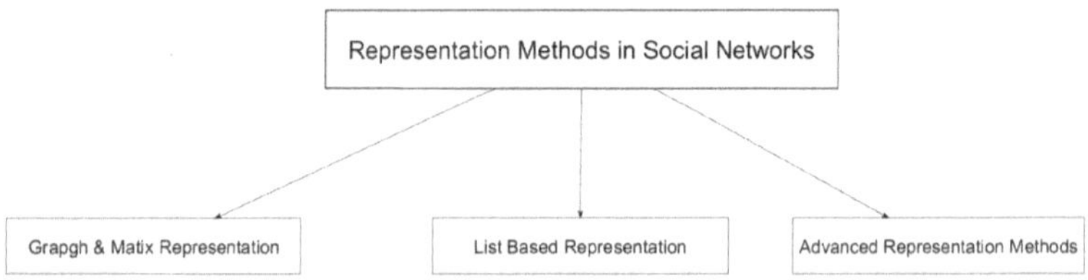

FIGURE 2.1 Types of representation methods.

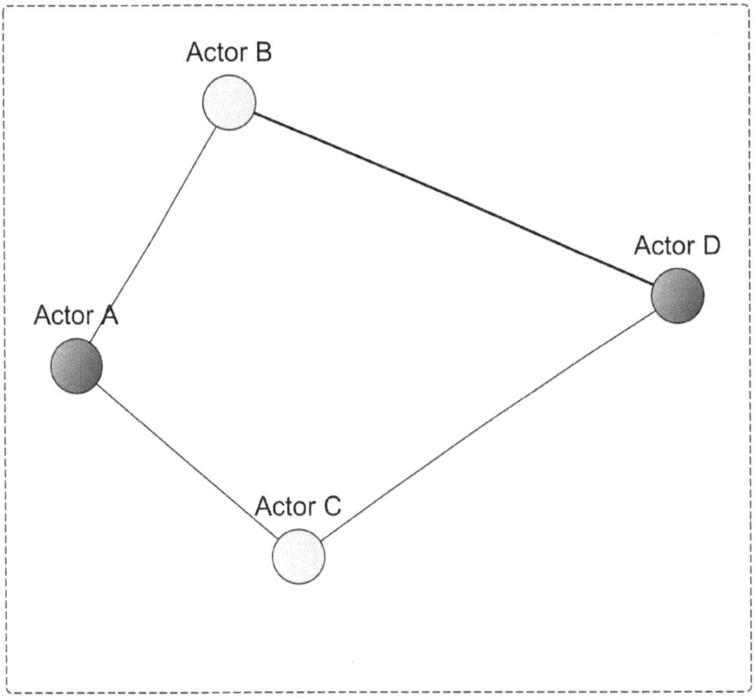

FIGURE 2.2 A simple network.

2.4 GRAPH-BASED REPRESENTATION

The graph and matrices-based representation method is the most common and widely used for the representation of social networks (Arif et al., 2012). The relationships among the social actors are represented using the edges of the graphs and can be easily transformed into matrices for mathematical modeling and analysis. In the graphical representation, the basic elements, that is, vertices and edges are used to represent the social actors and the relationship among them, respectively. As depicted in Figure 2.2, the graph formed of such actor and their relationships are referred to as sociograms in which labeled nodes represent the actors and an edge between these labeled nodes represents a social tie between the actors.

Before dwelling on further discussion, it is worth to introduce some basic terminologies and definitions related to the graph-based representation.

2.4.1 Definitions

2.4.1.1 Actor

In social network representation, a node or vertex is known as an actor that represents a user/individual as shown in Figure 2.3.

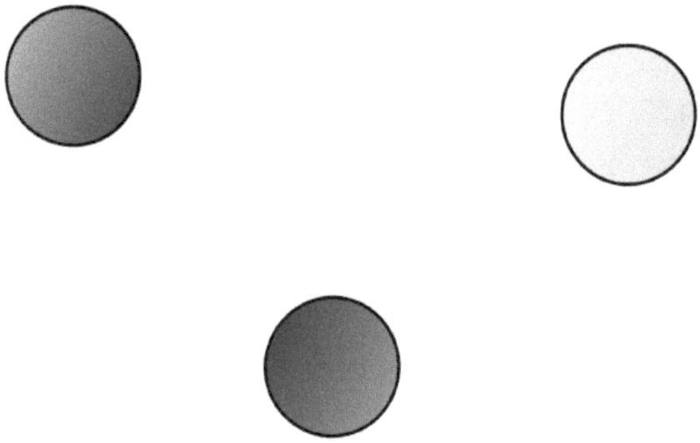

FIGURE 2.3 A node or actor.

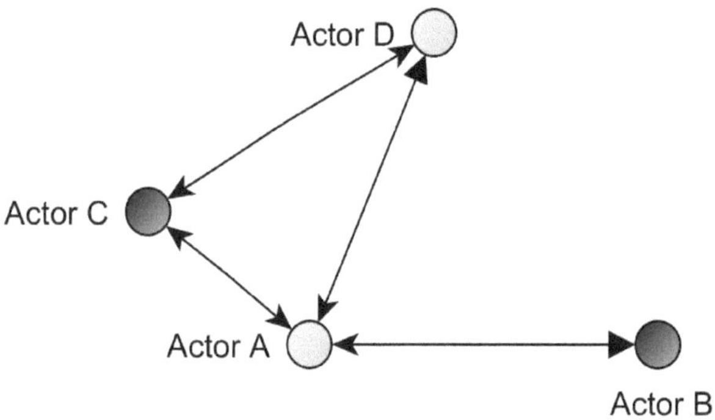

FIGURE 2.4 Ties and edges of a network.

Besides the label attached with a node, a node can be attributed with color coding (the number of colors to be used depending on the instance). As depicted in Figure 2.3, there are two colors attributed to the actors. The black color, for example, represents a male actor and the red one a female actor. In general, in social network representation, different colors, shapes, sizes, and shades can be used to attribute nodes or actors of a network.

2.4.1.2 Tie/Edge

The edges representing the tie between the actors can be either directed or undirected. An undirected edge simply represents the presence of a tie or relation between the actors, whereas a directed edge depicts which source actor intends to represent a relation with the destination actor. For example, Figure 2.4 shows a relation of actors on a social media platform in which a directed edge from actor A to D shows that D is in close group of A and a directed edge from D to B shows B to be in close group of A and so on.

The double-headed directed edges can also be used to represent the bidirectional tie between the actors, where both the actors intend to represent a tie or relation

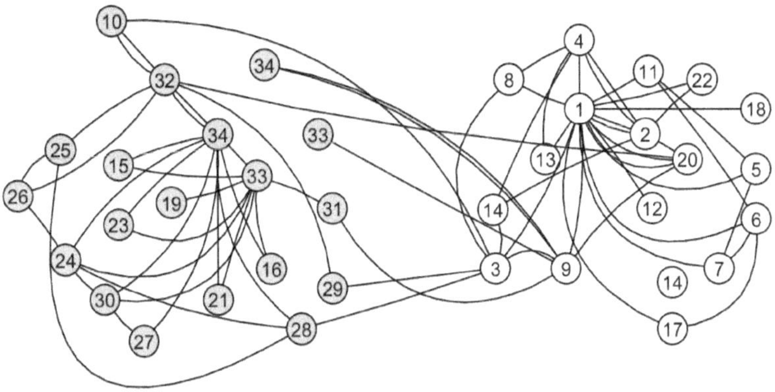

FIGURE 2.5 Network of friendship.

among them. Such bidirectional directed edges can minimize the complexity of the graph considerably. As in Figure 2.3, the relation between actor C to D, C to A, and A to B are bidirectional where the both actors with a directional edge among them intend to represent the same relation.

If there is relation or tie between the actors in which both are connected to each other than the connecting actor/nodes form a "clique". In Figure 2.3 , nodes A, C, and D form a clique (each node in the clique is connected to every other node in a bidirectional edge), whereas node B is connected to the network/group by only one edge and is called as pendent node.

In order to represent multiple relations in a graph, multiple edges with different color and shape of lines can be applied to represent the maximum data about the network.

2.4.1.3 Network

The collection of actors and the ties between them forming a graph is known as network, and Figure 2.5 depicts a network of friendship in an organization.

2.4.1.4 Weighted Ties

The relationship between the actors can be quantified and represented with the weighted edges between them. The weighted ties between the actors can be depicted either by the thickness of the edge or by the numeric weight that represents the measure of strength of the relationship. For instance, on a social network platform, there are many friends and the frequency of posts liked (showing the maximum association or best friends) by the friends can be depicted by using a weighted tie. Figure 2.6 depicts a scenario of weighted ties in a network.

2.4.1.5 Group

A subset of actors and their ties sharing some common attribute form a group. For instance, in a social network a group can be formed of all those actors having the same profession or same age group.

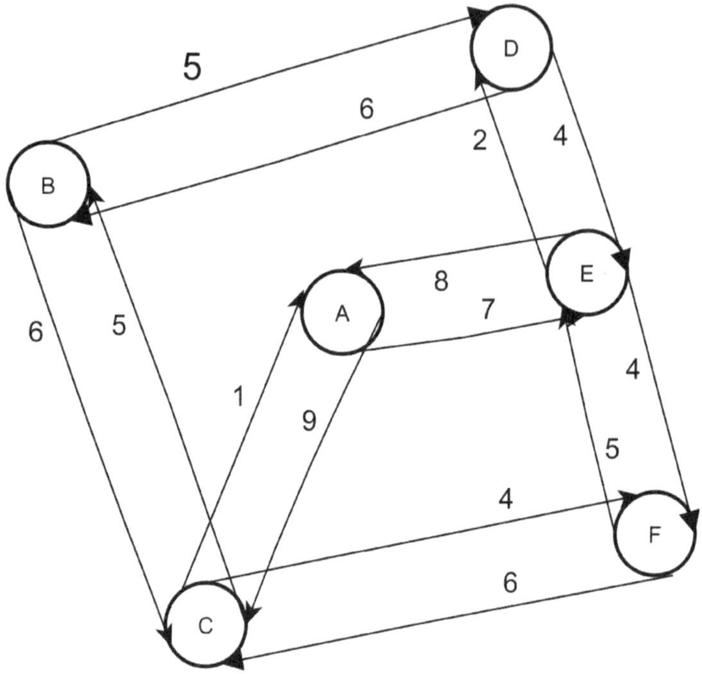

FIGURE 2.6 Weighted ties between actors.

2.4.1.6 Geodesic Distance

Geodesic distance can be defined as the minimum number of nodes/ties or the minimum total weight on the edges (if the weight on the edges representing the distance or cost of traversal) required to be traversed from a source node/actor to a destination node. For example, the geodesic distance between nodes A and D in Figure 2.7 is 3.

2.4.2 Properties of Relationships in a Network

2.4.2.1 Reciprocity

A relation/tie can be reciprocate, that is the relation from node A to node B can be treated as same from B to A. For instance, the relation between nodes A and B is reciprocated (Figure 2.8).

2.4.2.2 Transitive Relation

Transitive relations are binary relations defined on a set such that if the first element is related to the second element, and the second element is related to the third element of the set, then the first element must be related to the third element. For example, if for three elements a, b, c in set A, if a = b and b = c, then a = c. Here, equality "=" is a transitive relation. There are mainly three types of relations in discrete mathematics, namely, reflexive, symmetric, and transitive relations among many others.

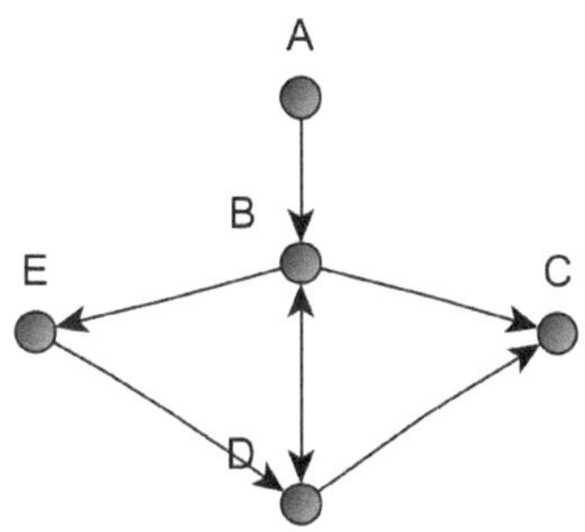

FIGURE 2.7 Geodesic distance between node A and D is 3.

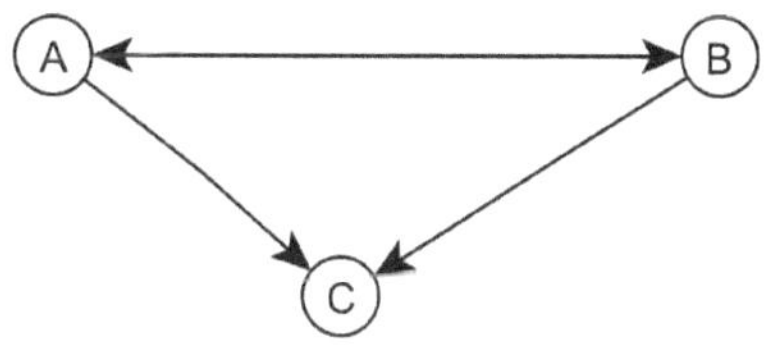

FIGURE 2.8 Reciprocated *relation.*

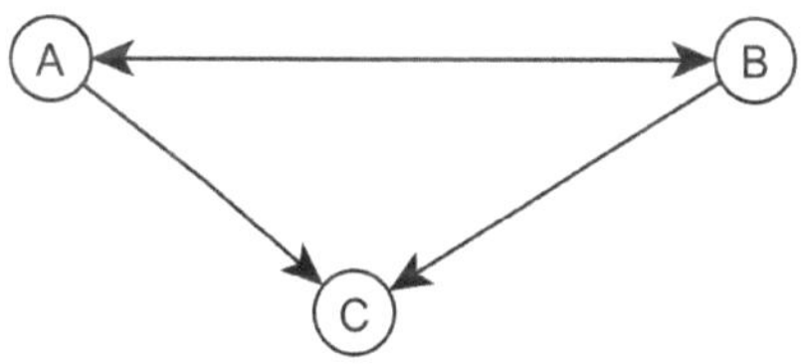

FIGURE 2.9 Transitive relation between nodes A and C.

Transitive relations between nodes **A** and **B** are those relations that are going through an intermediate node. Transitivity is important to assess the likelihood of future relations in a graph (Figure 2.9).

2.4.2.3 Popularity

It is the likelihood or prediction about the future relation gain of a node that is a focal point at present for majority of other nodes in the network. For example, node C is having high degree of popularity in the network (Figure 2.10).

2.4.3 Matrix-Based Representation

In order to represent a social network (the actors and their relationships) in a structured manner, the matrix mathematical representation is commonly adopted that enables the most effective and complex mathematical. This section presents the

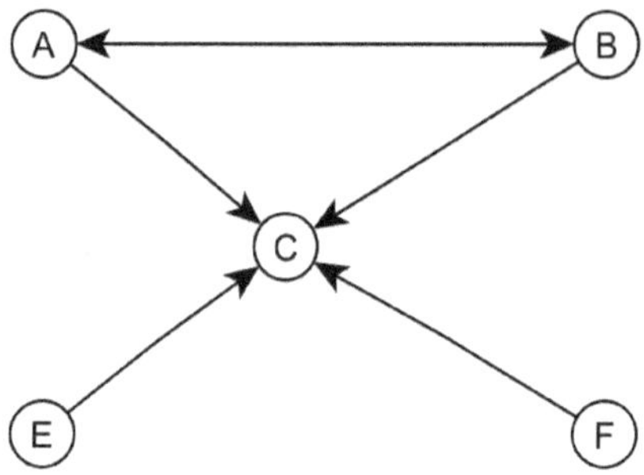

FIGURE 2.10 Popularity of node in a network.

0	2	1
3	0	7
1	-4	3
0	2	-5

FIGURE 2.11 A 4 * 3 matrix.

techniques used for the matrix based representation of social networks along with their advantages and limitation.

2.4.3.1 Sociomatrix/Adjacency Matrix

In its simplest form, a matrix is the arrangement of data in the form of rows and columns forming a rectangular array. The data in a matrix is called as elements or entities of the matrix, and each entity in the matrix is referred by its row and column index (i, j). A matrix having m rows and n columns the matrix is said to be an m by n or $(m*n)$ matrix. For example, the matrix in Figure 2.11 depicts a 3*4 matrix.

A matrix having only one row and n column is referred to be as row vector and a matrix with one column and n rows is known as column vector.

One of most commonly used matrix for the representation of social networks and the relationship is adjacency matrix, in which the total number of actors in the network forming the number of rows (m) and columns (n) of the matrix and the presence of a tie/relation is represented as an element with the numerical value 1 or 0 in the corresponding row *i and* column j for the presence or absence of a tie between actors, thus making it a binary matrix. In social network there are more complex ties than just the presence or absence of a tie, for instance, in a network of friendship R node A treats node B as close friend but node B may not treat the same way, hence making an asymmetric tie between them. In such cases, the corresponding element of row and column $R(i, j) \neq R(j, i)$ forming an asymmetric adjacency matrix R and the graph constructed to represent the asymmetric relations are directed graphs.

The elements of a matrix may not be always in binary form. In order to represent the complex ties between the actors other numerical indicators may be used to represent the complex relationships in a social network. The weighted graphs are constructed to represent the complex relationships with values showing the strength of the relationship.

There may be multiple ties between the actors of a network (represented by multiple edges with varying colors and weights of the edges in a sociogram). Such relations can be represented with multiple matrices of same dimension but with varying data elements. Figure 2.12 depicts the undirected, directed, and weighted networks and their corresponding adjacency matrices.

As depicted in Figure 2.12, in case of a directed graph, the corresponding adjacency matrix elements are absent if there is no directed edge from j to i. A network having simple unweighted and undirected edges can be represented by a binary matrix with elements either (presence or absence of a relation). In order to represent more complex relation, the network may have varying level of weight on the edges and the corresponding matrix elements also have the varying numerical values to represent those complex relations.

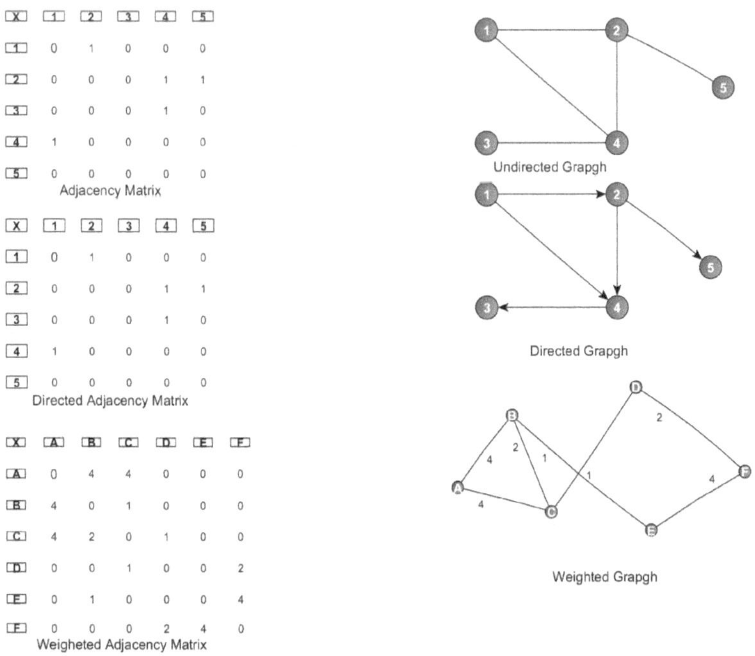

FIGURE 2.12 Undirected, directed, and weighted networks and their adjacency matrices.

2.4.4 Matrix Operations

Matrix-based representation is the most convenient easy method for the algebraic analysis of the network because of ease of using algebraic mathematical concepts. In this section we briefly present some of the basic operations that can be performed on a social network matrix required for basic analytical purposes.

2.4.4.1 Degree of Centrality of a Node

Degree of centrality of a node is defined as the number of direct ties a node is having in a network. Highest the degree of centrality for a node is an indicator for influence of the node in a network. In case of directed graph and directed adjacency matrix, there are two types of degrees of centrality, i.e, in-degree and out-degree. The former is a measure of the other nodes in a network or sub-network intends to represent a relation with the node, and later is the number of other nodes in a network that the node under study poses a direct relation. The degree of centrality can easily be determined by the matrix representation as follows:

Degree of centrality of a node for undirected adjacency matrix can be determined by counting the number of 1's in the corresponding row of the node. In an adjacency matrix, the degree of node indexed at row is calculated as follows:

$$k_i = \sum_j A_{j,i}$$

Degree of centrality of a node for directed adjacency matrix: As mentioned earlier in case of directed ties between the actors, there are two types of degrees, i.e., in-degree and out-degree. The in-degree of a node indexed at row can be calculated by summing up the number of 1's in the corresponding row in the corresponding column of the node. The out-degree of a node indexed at row can be calculated by summing up the number of 1's in the corresponding column in the corresponding row of the node. Mathematically:

$$K_i^{in} = \sum_j A_{j,i}$$

$$K_i^{out} = \sum_j A_{j,i}$$

2.4.5 Matrix Permutation, Blocks, and Images

In contrast to the graphs, the matrix representation can be used to rearrange the columns and rows to identify the different patterns. The shifting of rows also requires the shifting of columns to maintain the consistency in the data. The rearranging and shifting of rows and columns of matrix to identify the patterns is known has matrix permutation. For example is the matrix in Figure 2.9 where nodes are A, B, C, and D with subscripts of *m* and *f* to signify the sex of the actors.

*	A_m	B_f	C_m	D_f
A_m	–	1	1	0
B_f		–	1	0
C_m	1	1	–	1
D_f	0	0	1	–

If we permute the above matrix by rearranging the row and column is such a way that males and females become the adjacent in the matrix. Being the symmetric matrix, the rearranging requires changing the order of rows and their corresponding columns without changing the value of any element in the matrix, the resultant matrix is as follows:

*	A_m	C_m	B_f	D_f
A_m	–	1	1	0
C_m	1	–	1	1
B_f	0	1	–	0
D_f	0	1	0	–

It is also helpful, sometimes, to rearrange the rows and columns of a matrix so that we can see patterns more clearly. Shifting rows and columns (if you want to rearrange the rows, you must rearrange the columns in the same way, or the matrix won't make sense for most operations) is called "permutation" of the matrix. Some part of the matrix is highlighted with different colors and the elements having same color forming a block. Blocks in a matrix are divided by lines for example between male (*m*) and female (*f*) actors/nodes. Partitioning the matrix based on some parameter (sex in this case) forms the blocks. Such partitioning is required in analyzing the social network to gain an insight into the association among the different set of actors. For instance, in the matrix above, it is evident that male actor/node are forming a friendship and the female actors don't. Further the second and fourth blocks depict the male actors chose female actors as friend more than female actor choosing the male.

A block density matrix can be formed, if we chose only role in the above matrix (male and female) and select the proportion of the relations/ties in a block as follows:

Block Density Matrix

	Male (*m*)	**Female (*f*)**
Male (*m*)	1.0	0.75
Female (*f*)	0.50	0.0

An image matrix can be formed from the block density matrix if we further summarize the result by selecting some threshold level of density (0.60 in this case) and the density in the block density matrix satisfying the threshold level is recorded as 1 and below that as 0. The resulting image matrix is as follows:

Image Matrix		
	Male (*m*)	**Female (*f*)**
Male (*m*)	1	1
Female (*f*)	0	0

2.4.6 Other Mathematical Operations

2.4.6.1 Transposing a Matrix

The transpose of a matrix is the exchange of rows to columns and columns to rows. In the context of social network analysis, the transpose of a matrix of directed network results in identifying all the sources of relations directed at a particular actor/node. If we take the degree of an adjacency matrix and that of the transpose of that matrix, then we can find the symmetry of patterns between the actors. In other words, the comparison of a matrix and its transpose can identify the reciprocity of relations.

2.4.6.2 Inverse of a Matrix

The inverse of a matrix is denoted by such that it satisfies the property which is an identity matrix. In other words, the inverse of a matrix is just the opposite of the original matrix. The inverse operation can be used in the analysis of a social network to uncover the nonexistent facts.

2.4.6.3 Multiplication of a Matrix

In social network analysis, the network is represented as a matrix, and the multiplication operation is a useful tool. If we apply a multiplication operation on an an adjacency matrix, representing a network by itself, i.e., the squaring of an adjacency matrix, the resultant matrix provides us with the number of paths of length 2 between the nodes. Consider the undirected graph in Figure 2.13 and the corresponding adjacency matrix.

If we square the above adjacency matrix, i.e., multiply the matrix by itself, we get the following matrix.

	0	1	2	3
0	–	1	1	0
1	1	–	1	1
2	1	1	–	1
3	0	1	1	–

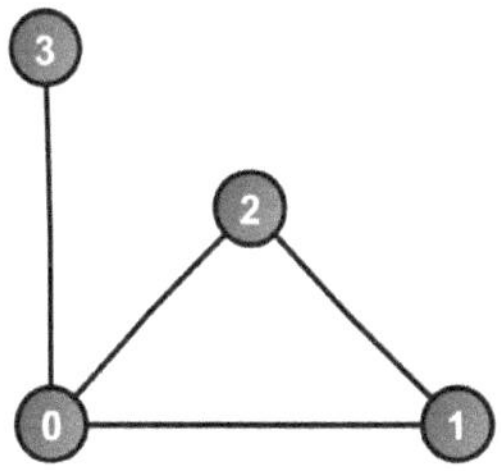

	0	1	2	3
0	0	1	1	1
1	1	0	1	0
2	1	1	0	0
3	1	0	0	0

FIGURE 2.13 Undirected graph and the adjacency matrix.

The elements of the squared adjacency matrix (1's) above show all the nodes connected to other nodes by a path of length 2. For instance, the node 3 is connected to nodes 1 and 2 by a path length of 2, and there is no path of length 2 from node 3 to node 0. Similarly, if we calculate the cube of the adjacency matrix, the resultant matrix will show all the paths between nodes of length 3 and so on. Hence, the basic multiplication operation on the matrix can reveal important aspect of a network that are quite handy for analysts. In analyzing a social network, it is very important to know the connectivity or strength of the association or relationships among the actors

In contrast to the normal product, if the Boolean product of the squared adjacency matrix is calculated, the resultant matrix will provide us with the answer as to whether there is any path of length 2 present between the nodes. A network having nodes interconnected to each other by a shorter path shows the strength of their relationship.

2.4.7 List-Based Network Representation

Yet another way to represent social network data is by using list-based representation techniques. The source graphs are still at the core for both list- and matrix-based representation techniques. There are two main techniques for list-based representation.

2.4.7.1 Edge List Method

An edge list is typically organized as a table where the first two columns list the IDs of pairs of nodes that have a connection. Additional columns can optionally provide details about the relationship between these nodes, such as the strength of the connection. Pairs of nodes without a connection are usually omitted from the edge list, which makes this format more efficient for storing network data compared to sociomatrices. Unobserved edges can be represented in the edge list by including "NA" in the value column.

2.4.7.2 Adjacency List

An adjacency list is a hybrid representation that combines elements of both an adjacency matrix and an edge list. It consists of an array of linked lists, where each list represents the neighbors of a specific vertex in a graph. This structure makes it easy to identify which vertices are adjacent to any given vertex. Each vertex can quickly access its neighboring vertices via the linked list, making the adjacency list a popular choice for graph representation. It is particularly useful for graph traversal problems, where knowing the neighbors of a node is often more critical than constructing the entire graph.

Adjacency lists are commonly used for sparse graphs, where the number of edges is generally proportional to the number of vertices, |V|.

In a standard adjacency list, there are two primary components: an array of vertices (ArrayV) and an array of edges (ArrayE). Each entry in the vertex array indicates the starting position of the edges in the edge array for the outgoing edges from that vertex. The edge array contains the destination vertices for these edges. To access the neighbors of a vertex v, you can read from Array[v] to Array[v + 1] in the edge array.

2.4.8 Properties and Terminologies of Nodes and Relationships

Now we have gained enough knowledge about the social networks and their representation; it is time to introduce some of the major terminologies and concepts required for the analysis of a network.

2.4.8.1 Degree of Centrality

As mentioned earlier in the matrix operation, the centrality degree is the most fundamental measure. It highlights the number of relationships incident upon a node/actor in a network. In case of an undirected network, it is just counting the number of total edges connected to a particular node/actor, whereas in directed networks, the in-degree (the number of edges incident upon a node) and out-degree (the number of nodes emanating from a node) are to be calculated. The degree of centrality is a measure to identify the importance and connectivity of a node in a network (Jennifer Golbeck, 2015).

2.4.8.2 Eigenvector

Once the degree of centrality is calculated and the most connected (prominent) nodes are identified, the eigenvector measures the interconnection of nodes having a high degree of centrality. In other words, it calculates which of the prominent nodes are connected to other prominent nodes (Denny, M., 2014; Costa and Putnik, 2014).

2.4.8.3 Betweenness Centrality

It is a measure to calculate the intermediateness of a node that acts as a link between the other nodes having the shortest path between them. In other words, it is the sum of shortest path lengths between every set of nodes where the path goes through the node under observation (Gómez et al., 2013).

2.4.8.4 Closeness Centrality

It is measure of the number of steps or ties required to be traversed for a particular node/actor to reach every other actor in the network (Denny, M., 2014). It is measured as 1 divided by the total geodesic distance from the current node to all other nodes in the network. If an actor is connected directly to every other actor in a network, the closeness of centrality will be maximum and it is minimum when it is not connected to any other actor in a network (Opsahl et al., 2010).

2.4.8.5 Brokerage

It is a measure which defines how important an actor is in the network that the interaction of other actors is dependent on it. It captures the sensitivity of a broker that serves as a mediator and thus can gain benefits from their position as an intermediary. There are five kinds of brokerage (Denny, M., 2014) relationships that are discussed briefly below:

- **Coordinator**: The node or actor belonging to same group that acts as an intermediate between other two actors in the group.
- **Itinerant**: Belongs to a separate group and connects two others sharing the group membership.
- **Gatekeeper**: Belonging to same group and acts as the only mean for other to connect to the group.
- **Representative**: Belonging to same group and the other actors in the group can only connect with other groups through it.
- **Liaison**: Is a member of a group that is distance from two actors that wish to connect but do not share group membership themselves. A delivery truck driver is a good example. Figure 2.14 depicts all the brokerage types discussed above.

2.4.9 Types of Networks

2.4.9.1 Single-Mode/Unipartite Network

This type of network consists of only one type of node. Here, all the nodes in the network belong to the same category and edges represent the relationship between these nodes. Example: Email communication network, wherein nodes represent individuals and edges represent email exchanges between them (Figure 2.15).

2.4.9.2 Two-Mode/Bipartite Network

This type of network consists of two distinct sets of nodes. Edges connect *only* nodes from one set to nodes with the other set, not within the same set. Example:

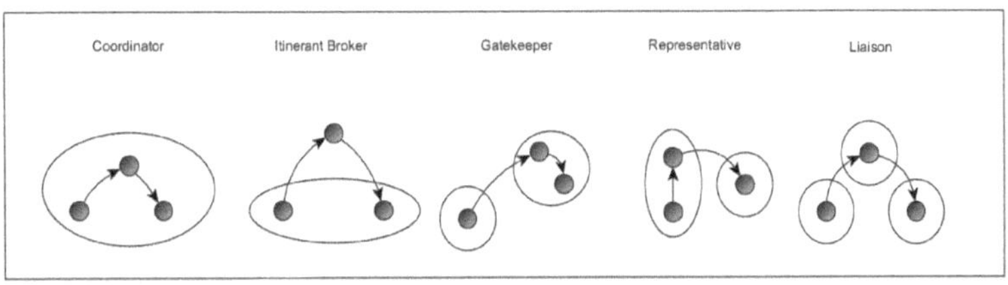

FIGURE 2.14 Brokerage relationship (Denny, M., 2014).

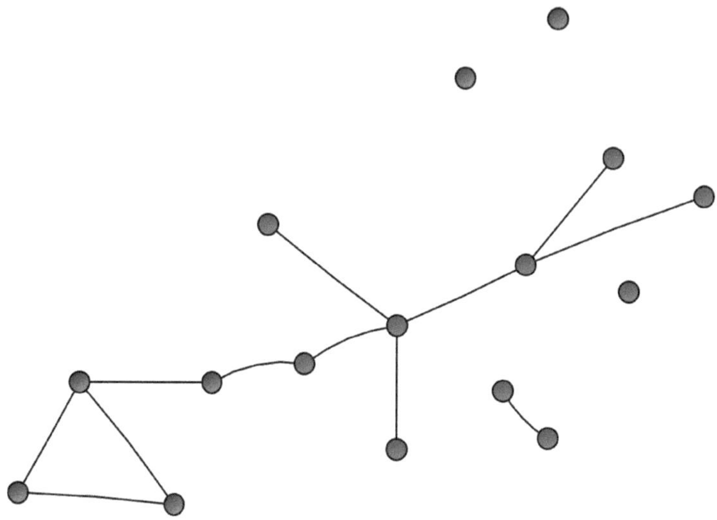

FIGURE 2.15 Single mode.

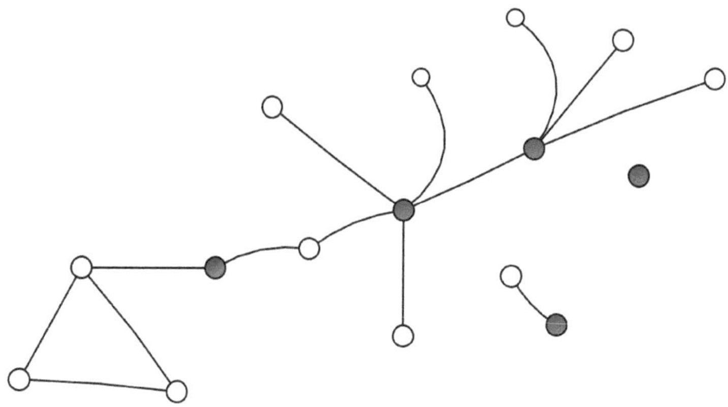

FIGURE 2.16 Bipartite network.

Customer–purchase network, wherein one set represents customers and the other set represents products and edges indicate the relationship of the customer with the product (Figure 2.16).

2.4.9.3 Multi-mode/Multipartite Network

It is also known as *k*-partite, where *k* represents any number. These networks consist of more than two distinct sets of nodes wherein edges always connect nodes of different sets never within the same set. Example: Project–employee–department network where edges connect projects to employees (that work on them) and employees to departments (they belong to) (Figure 2.17).

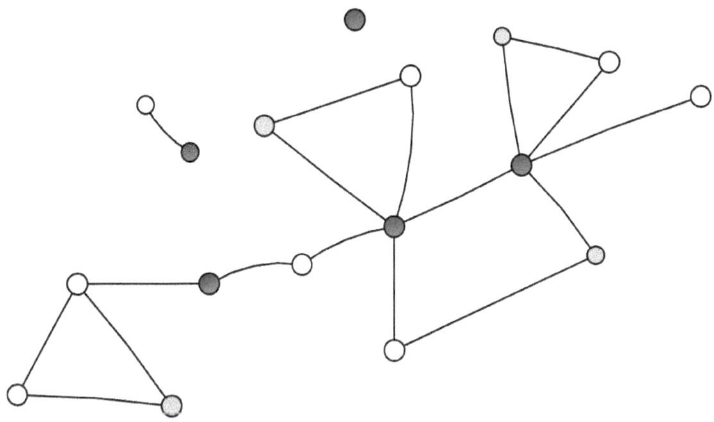

FIGURE 2.17 Multi-mode network.

2.4.10 Types of Social Network Data

In social network analysis (SNA), various types of data that provide insights into the structure, dynamics, and behavior of networks give a basis for understanding how the networks function and evolve (Aggarwal, C.C., 2011). Using data from multiple sources is imperative and is the future of analytics (Batrinca and Treleaven, 2015). Some of the major categories of data on social networks are as follows:

1. **Relational Data**: This data captures the interaction between the nodes (e.g., individuals, and organizations). The relationships can be binary, weighted, directed, or undirected. This type of data is mainly used to identify the overall network structure, impactful nodes, and types of interactions.

   Binary relationships depict the presence or absence of a connection. For example, friendships on social networks where each pair is either connected or not. Weighted relationships quantify the strength of the relationship. For example, number of messages exchanged on a social networking site. Directed relationships show the direction of connection between two nodes. For example, user A follows user B on a social networking site, so the relationship can be depicted as A › B. Conversely, undirected relationships depict mutual relationships where there is no specific direction. For example, a relation where user A is friends with user B, then user B is friends with user A.
2. **Attribute Data**: This data provides supplementary information about the nodes and edges beyond their connections. This type of data refines the understanding of the network dynamics in terms of the features of nodes and the relationship details. The attributes can be specific to the nodes called node attributes, e.g., information like age, designation, and gender or specific to the edges called edge attributes, e.g., type of interaction between nodes, such as collaboration and mentorship.

3. **Temporal Data**: This data tracks how network relationships and dynamics change over time. The data can be event-based, i.e., one which captures an action/event with time stamp, for e.g., dates when user A started following or unfollowing user B on a social networking site. The data can also be dynamic in nature and capture the transformation of networks over a period of time. For example, evolution of friendships or connections with time.
4. **Geographical Data**: This data provides spatial information about the nodes and their interactions. The data can be location-based, i.e., identifying the physical location of nodes, e.g., geographic location of users in a location-based social network. The data can also be distance-based, i.e., measures distance between impactful nodes, e.g., in a crisis management system distance can reveal the potential bottlenecks.
5. **Interaction Data**: This data details the nature and frequency of interactions, identifying active nodes and key relationships. The data can be communication data that records the interaction between nodes, e.g., e-mail logs, social media messages, etc. or it can be transaction data that records the exchanges and transactions, e.g., financial transactions between businesses.
6. **Behavioral Data**: This data is used to capture actions and engagement patterns of nodes in a network. The data can be activity data, i.e., capturing information about the activities performed by a node, e.g., social media posts, likes, and comments. The data can also be engagement data, i.e., measuring the level of interaction, e.g., number of people engaged in a reel posted on a social media platform.
7. **Content Data**: This data includes details about the content exchanged or shared on a network. This data can be textual, i.e., text of social media posts or emails, or multimedia data that includes photos, videos, or other formats of media shared on social networks.

Another way of classifying heterogeneous data, as presented in a review article on "A survey of privacy-preserving mechanisms for heterogeneous data types", by Mariana Cunha et al. (2021) can be illustrated in Figure 2.18.

2.4.11 Some Methods, Tools, and Techniques for Social Media Data Extraction

Extracting data from social media can be very beneficial for a variety of tasks including market research, trend forecasting, targeted advertising, sentiment analysis, expert findings for research guidance, and many more (Nasution et al., 2021) . Considering the humongous data that is available on the Web, extracting relevant information for specific tasks can be significantly challenging but at the same time, it can lead to transformative advancements across multiple fields (Jin et al., 2007).

This entire process consists of several interrelated steps. The first step is to **gather or capture the data** from various sources. This also involves data pre-processing, which involves data cleaning, transformation, integration, and extraction of relevant information. The next step is to **analyze or understand** the information captured.

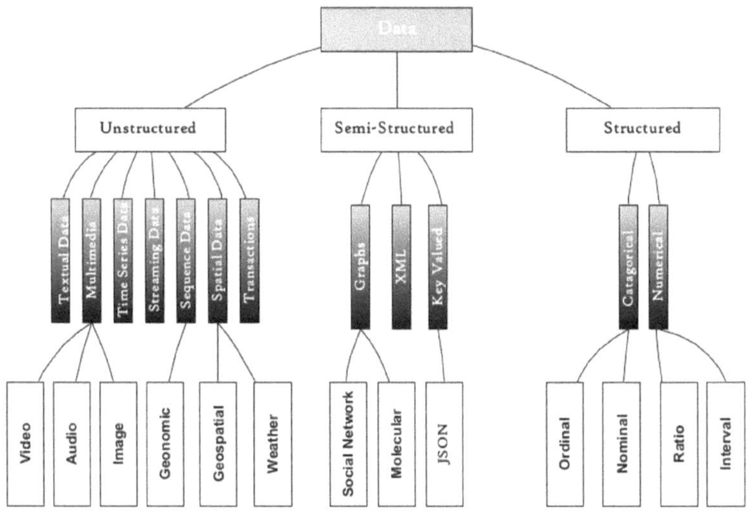

FIGURE 2.18 Heterogeneous data types.

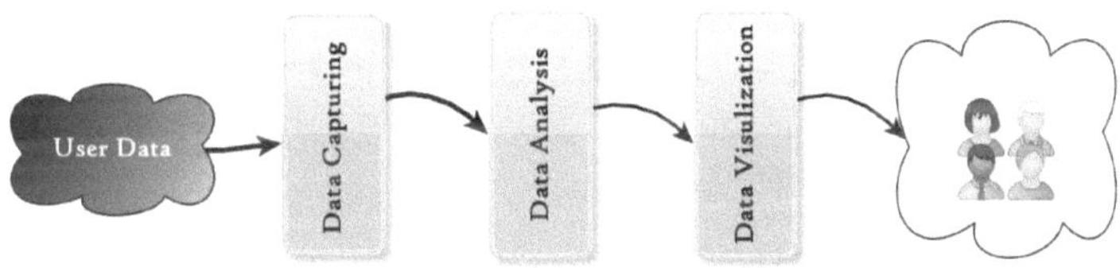

FIGURE 2.19 Stages involved in social media analytics.

This consists of the removal of noisy data (if any) and performing advanced analytics such as sentiment analysis and trend analysis. The last step is to **present or visualize** the findings of the second stage. This involves summarizing and evaluating the findings and the final presentation of the results (Arif et al., 2014) (Figure 2.19).

2.4.12 Methods Used in Data Extraction

2.4.12.1 Social Media Scraping

It is the process of systematically extracting data from social media platforms using automated web scraping solutions or scripts (Batrinca and Treleaven, 2015). This includes data from social media platforms such as profiles, hashtags, likes, and comments. There are several ways to scrape this data off the social media sites. Some of these are as follows:

1. **No-Code Web Scraping Tools**: These usually provide a pre-configured template for major social media platforms allowing users for a quick set-up of their scraping projects. Social media scrapers like Instagram scraper or TikTok scraper are used by leading brands to scrape through influencers' account to find the right ones for collaboration with their brand.
2. **Web Scraping APIs**: These allow users to retrieve and extract data from social media platforms using API calls/ requests (Devi et al., 2019). Some of the leading social media platforms like Facebook API or X (previously known as Twitter) API provide official APIs that allow developers to access the data programmatically. This provides a reliable way of integration with social media platforms but are bound by certain restrictions such as restrictions on the number of API requests per application or user, etc. However, code-based web scraping provides a level of customization to the users by allowing them to create scrapers based on their specific business requirements.
3. **Web Scraping Libraries:** A social media web scraper can be built using one or more web scraping libraries offered by various programming languages. For example, **Python** has libraries like *BeautifulSoup* that parses HTML and XML documents, allowing users to navigate, search, and modify the parse tree (Thivaharan *et al.*, 2020). **NodeJS** has libraries like *Cheerio* that parses and manipulates HTML, designed for server-side use and *Puppeteer* which provides a high-level API to control headless Chrome or Chromium. **Java** has *JSoup* that works with HTML, offering an API for extracting and manipulating data.

2.4.12.2 Challenges and Legality Issues Involved

Scraping the data which is publicly available is legal. However, private information and copyrighted content are protected by laws like GDPR (General Data Protection Regulation). Scraping data off **Facebook** is legal as of 2024. This includes information available publicly like username, profile URL, profile photo URL, followers and following information, etc. Another social media platform **X**, allows publicly accessible data to be scraped that can be utilized to track brand sentiment and gauge client responses (Yanchang Zhao, 2013). As long as the data is scraped in accordance with API requirements there's no issue; however, the API has some limits, e.g., it can only extract public information up to 100 tweets per profile as of January 2024. Another leading video-sharing website, **YouTube**, allows the scraping of data as long as it doesn't interfere with websites operation and doesn't collect PII (Personally Identifiable Information). The data that can be extracted includes video title and descriptions, video comments, and video likes and dislikes. This information proves to be extremely important for small and medium sized businesses (SMB) to reach new audience and enhance their customer base.

2.4.12.3 Top Outcomes of Scraped Social Media Data

1. **Consumer-Focused Approach**: Dynamic information is required to follow a customer-centric approach for consumer targeting and the same needs to

be updated regularly as and when new information is available. Customers use social media sites and/or online shopping sites to present their reviews, comments, and feedback about products. An efficient technique of data scraping can use this information which can be beneficial for businesses to make informed decisions regarding their products and strategies. For example, Spotify has a X account Spotify Cares which is specifically used to understand the concerns and expectations of its customers, develop relationships with potential customers, and improve their customer services.

2. **Keep Up with the Latest Trends**: To understand customers' expectations about the products and services extraction of current market data is a must. Social media sites, lifestyle blogs, and wikis are the source of such information. For example, a customer posting his feedback for a product on a shopping site extracted by a social media scraping bot will provide structured data that can be helpful for business owners to update their strategies and gain insight into the latest market trends.
3. **Conduct Sentiment Analysis**: Scraped data enables brands to identify positive or negative words describing the sentiment of the users regarding a product. For instance, you can collect specific tweets/comments with brand names or hashtags of a particular brand using a data collection or API tool. Based on this data, a positive, negative, or neutral public perspective about a product can be formed which is useful for business growth (Nemes and Kiss, 2020).
4. **API Integration**: Another very important tool used in data extraction in SNA is the API (Application Programming Interface) that is basically a set of rules and protocols that allows different software applications to communicate with each other. APIs are mainly of three types:

- **REST (Representational State Transfer) API:** It utilizes HTTP methods (like GET, POST, PUT, DELETE) to perform operations on resources. Data is received mainly in JSON and XML formats (Batrinca and Treleaven, 2015).
- **SOAP (Simple Object Access Protocol) API:** With a high level of complexity and security this technique employs XML-based messaging protocol for structured communication between systems.
- **GraphQL (Query language) API:** This technique entails a flexible query language that can be used by clients to give precise data requests for fetching only the required data from the heterogeneous collection of social media APIs (C. Wang et al., 2019) (Figure 2.20).

Some of the most used social media APIs include X API, which allows access to tweets, user profile, and trends; Facebook Graph API, which allows access to Facebook data including posts, user profile, and pages; and the Instagram Graph API, which is used to access Business Account data, including media, insights, and user interaction.

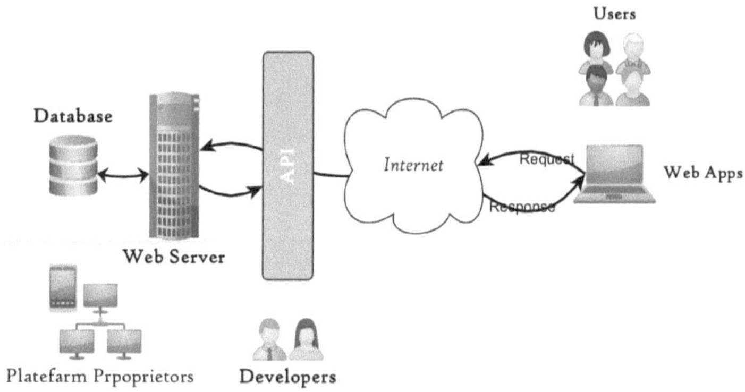

FIGURE 2.20 A basic API diagram (adapted from Eising, 2017). Source: Perrotta (2021).

2.4.12.4 Challenges and Considerations

1. **Data Privacy**: When accessing and using personal data, ensuring compliance with data privacy regulations (e.g., GDPR) is very essential.
2. **Rate Limiting and Quotas**: APIs often impose restrictions on the number of requests that can be made within a certain timeframe which can impact data collection efforts.
3. **Changes and Deprecations**: APIs may evolve or become obsolete over time, requiring updates to integrations or the adoption of alternative methods for accessing data.
4. **Data Mining and Text Analysis**: This involves extracting useful information from text-based data using algorithms and machine learning. The various techniques involved in this method are NLP (Natural Language Processing), Topic modeling, etc. This method is used to process large volumes of unstructured text data. Data mining primarily involves discovering patterns, correlations, and insights from large data sets using statistical and computational methods. There are a large number of techniques that are used in this method like classification, clustering, association rule learning, regression analysis, etc. Data mining encompasses a vast array of applications including customer segmentation, fraud detection, market basket analysis, risk management, and others (Bhanuse et al., 2016).

Text analysis also known as text mining involves extracting meaningful information from unstructured text data encompassing various techniques to analyze and process this data. Key techniques involved in text analysis include Tokenization, speech tagging, sentiment analysis, text summarization, text classification, etc. The major applications of text analysis include social media monitoring, customer feedback

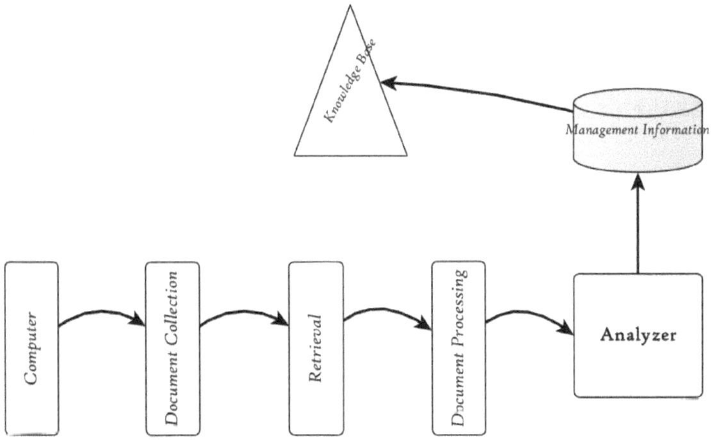

FIGURE 2.21 Flow diagram of text-mining.

analysis, document classification, information retrieval, and research (Figure 2.21) (Bartal et al., 2007).

2.4.12.4.1 Challenges Involved

1. **Data Quality and Cleaning**: The data extracted by these techniques might be inaccurate, inconsistent, or incomplete including duplicates, incorrect fields, and missing values (Singh and Dwivedi, 2020) usually requiring a lot of pre-processing and normalization. Similarly, the integration of data from multiple sources is also a challenge due to differences in format, structure, and quality.
2. **Scalability**: Processing and analyzing large volumes of data can be resource intensive as well as require significant computational power and storage. An array of efficient optimization algorithms is required as and when the size of data grows.
3. **Privacy and Security**: As with other data extraction techniques, this technique also requires adherence to data privacy rules and regulations (GDPR, CCPA) to protect sensitive user information (Velásquez, 2013). The use of powerful processing tools may threaten users' privacy. Prevention of unauthorized access and breaches during data storage and processing is a prerequisite of this technique.
4. **Feature Extraction:** Text data is usually considered high dimensional data involving numerous features. Identifying and managing such data and selecting relevant features can be quite cumbersome impacting the performance of various models.

Other than these above mentioned methods there are a few other methods that are used in data extraction, like Network Surveys, Database Queries, Web crawling,

Sensor data collection, etc. Each of these techniques has its share of advantages and challenges involved.

5. **Data Pre-processing**

After the data has been extracted from one or more of the already mentioned data extraction methods, the next step essential for preparing the raw data for interpretation is data pre-processing. This step ensures the data is clean, complete, structured, and ready for modeling and analysis. Properly pre-processed data allows researchers to accurately detect and report defects, thereby improving the suitability of datasets for training models. This ensures that models can learn independently from unbiased data and generate reliable results (Felix and Lee, 2019).

This process comprises a sequence of steps like data cleaning, data reduction, data transformation, and data integration (Roy et al., 2018). Some additional steps may also be involved when the extracted data in question is to be used in SNA. These may be steps like node and edge definition, attribute encoding, handling self-loops, and multiple edges, filtering and subsetting, etc. In this section, we will briefly discuss each of the stages involved in data pre-processing.

2.4.12.4.2 Data Cleaning

This is one of the most crucial data pre-processing steps in SNA which deals with situations leading to inconsistent and incomplete input. The first issue deals with eliminating **duplicate values**, to ensure the data is unique. This can be accomplished by **node deduplication** involving the identification and merging of duplicate nodes and **edge deduplication** involving the merging of multiple edges that represent the same relationship.

The second scenario deals with handling the **missing values**, which can occur in both node and edge attributes. This can be accomplished by **imputation,** i.e., replacing missing values with estimates such as mean, median, or mode of particular attribute, or simple **removal,** i.e., removing the nodes and edges with missing data but only if the data is small enough that its removal doesn't distort the analysis. The third deals with fixing errors like typos, or incorrect data entries to maintain data quality (Singh and Dwivedi, 2020). Data cleaning also involves the detection and handling of outlier nodes and edges representing extreme cases. This can be handled with **manual inspection** and **pruning,** i.e., removal of nodes/edges or capping their values to avoid biased analysis.

2.4.12.4.3 Node and Edge Definition

This is one of the crucial steps in data cleaning that ensures that the structure of the network represents the relationships and interactions within the data. The key consideration in node definition is **identifying the nodes** (entities) and ensuring each node is properly labeled ensuring there are no duplicates, ambiguous identities, or misrepresented actors. Another important consideration is **attribute consistency** which involves ensuring that attributes of nodes are consistently and accurately linked to each node. Edges, also called as links or connections, represent the relationships between various nodes. Well-defined edges have the following key considerations: **relationship type**, i.e., the nature of interaction needs to be captured whether it is collaboration, communication, friendship, or influence. While defining edges it is very important to identify its **direction**, whether it is a directed edge or an undirected edge. This property can further influence the various metrics involved in the network. Edges also have weights, representing the relationship's strength, frequency, or importance. Ensuring that the edge weights are consistent and meaningful is an essential data pre-processing technique.

2.4.12.4.4 Data Transformation

This technique involves converting raw data networks into a structured format that can be analyzed. It may involve steps like smoothing, aggregation, generalization, normalization, etc. (Alasadi et al., 2017). Some of the data transformation techniques are as follows:

- **Binarization**:

It involves the conversion of network data into a binary format, where edges are represented as zero or one, i.e., present or absent. This, in turn, determines the presence or absence of connections in a network.

- **Aggregation**:

This involves combining multiple interactions or relationships between nodes into one single edge for network simplification and reduction in redundancy.

- **Normalization**:

This technique is very effective in networks where data comes from multiple sources. It ensures that the network features are on a consistent scale, making them comparable across the network.

- **Attribute Encoding:**

This involves converting categorical variables into numerical representations and adjusting numerical values to a common scale if required. It has various types:

a. **Label Encoding:**

To maintain an ordinal relationship between categories, this technique assigns a unique numerical value to each category of a given attribute.

b. **One-Hot Encoding:**

In the case of nominal data where there is no inherent order in categories, this encoding converts categorical variables into binary vectors where each category is represented by a separate column.

c. **Frequency Encoding**:

To provide a compact representation of categorical data, this technique replaces categories with their frequency of occurrence in data.

d. **Embedding Encoding**:

In complex networks, this type of encoding converts high-dimensional categorical data into low-dimensional vectors using machine learning models.

2.4.12.4.5 Handling Self-Loop and Multiple Edges

This step includes the elimination of edges where nodes connect to themselves and tackling multiple connections between the same nodes (e.g., summing or averaging the edge weights). **Self-loop** typically occurs when an edge of a node in a network points back to itself. This can be handled by removing self-loops, counting self-loops separately, and weighing self-loops. Multiple edges occur when there is more than one edge between the same pair of nodes causing redundancy, misleading metrics, algorithm limitations, etc. This can be handled by various techniques, namely edge aggregation, edge differentiation, thresholding, etc.

2.4.12.4.6 Sub-setting and Filtering

This step involves the removal of nodes or edges that seem irrelevant to the analysis and focusing on a particular section of the network that is specifically required for analysis thereby narrowing the scope. Some of the common sub-setting approaches are **attribute-based sub-setting** which involves extracting a subset of nodes and edges based on their attributes. Another approach is **time-based sub-setting** also known as temporal slicing which involves creating a subset of the network that focuses on specific time intervals.

Filtering helps to clean the network by removing irrelevant or noisy data. Some of the common filtering techniques are **degree-based filtering,** wherein the filtering of the nodes is done based on their degree or number of connections they have. Another approach is **edge-weight filtering,** wherein filtering of edges is done based on their weights retaining only those with a certain threshold of strength. In contrast, **attribute-based filtering** involves removing of nodes or edges based on their attributes or interaction types.

2.4.12.4.7 Validation and Quality Assurance

This step involves verifying the data integrity by checking that the pre-processed data aligns with the expected quality and standards and accurately represents the network and addressing discrepancies, if any. There are several key checks that data has to undergo to be validated like **consistency checks**, **data integrity**, **range validation, data duplication**, **data completion check**, etc. Similarly, the data needs to undergo several quality assurance checks to ensure that it reflects the social network being studied accurately and without bias. This includes **anomaly detection**, **cross-validation checks**, **sensitivity analysis**, **data documentation and provenance checks, bias detection and correction checks**, etc.

2.4.12.4.8 Prepare Data for Analysis

This is a cross-over step that leads to analysis and involves saving the data in formats that are compatible with SNA analysis tools (CSV etc.). It also involves setting up visualization parameters to facilitate effective analysis.

2.4.12.4.9 Metadata and Documentation

This step involves recording the details of the transformations applied in the pre-processing phases for record ability and reproducibility purposes. Metadata is also created in this step which describes the data attributes, sources, and any changes made to the data. The following details are captured in the metadata: Data source information, node and edge description, attribute definition and formats, data transformation and cleaning steps, limitations and assumptions, file formats, provenance of data, and versioning and updates. This ensures the quality and reliability of social network analysis along with the creation of more useful stores of information (López-Acosta, Araceli, et al., 2020).

2.4.12.4.10 Export/Import Data

This is the final step in data pre-processing wherein the cleaned and processed data is stored in the desired formats and imported to the SNA tools for analysis and exploration (Camacho et al., 2020). While importing data that is loading cleaned network data into an SNA tool for analysis, many steps are performed like **data format compatibility** (common import formats: GraphML, GML, Pajek, JSON, CSV, etc.), **mapping nodes and edges**, **software-specific import requirements**, **and handling node and edge attributes**. Similarly, while exporting the data that is saving processed network data for external use or sharing again a series of steps needs to be followed, like **choosing the right export format** (common export formats: CSV, GraphML, GEXF, JSON, Pajek.net), **preserving attributes and structures**, **software specific export features**, **file size and data complexity handling**, **metadata handling**, etc.

2.5 CONCLUSION

Social network analysis is a multifaceted field that requires the knowledge of other related field of science, sociology and mathematics to understand and analyze the complex social structure. This chapter covers the most basic aspect of visualisation and representation of social structure into different forms that allows the mathematical and analytical operations to be applied to mine or uncover the patterns in a social structure. To get the ball rolling the chapter began with the history and the present scenario in the field of SNA. It further examines the type of networks and the social network data. In order to gain an insight into the analysis the chapter presents the various data extraction techniques and their representation methods along with the basic analytical operations to be performed.

REFERENCES

Aggarwal, Charu C. *An introduction to social network data analytics.* Springer US, 2011.

Alasadi, Suad A., and Wesam S. Bhaya. "Review of data preprocessing techniques in data mining." *Journal of Engineering and Applied Sciences* 12, no. 16 (2017): 4102–4107.

Arif, Tasleem, Rashid Ali, and M. Asger. "Scientific co-authorship social networks: A case study of computer science scenario in India." *International Journal of Computer Applications* 52, no. 12 (2012): 38–45.

Arif, Tasleem, Rashid Ali, and M. Asger. "Social network extraction: A review of automatic techniques." *International Journal of Computer Applications* 95, no. 1 (2014): 16–23.

Bartal, Alon, Elan Sasson, and Gilad Ravid. "Predicting links in social networks using text mining and SNA." In *2009 International conference on advances in social network analysis and mining*, pp. 131–136. IEEE, 2009.

Batrinca, Bogdan, and Philip C. Treleaven. "Social media analytics: A survey of techniques, tools and platforms." *Ai & Society* 30 (2015): 89–116.

Bhanuse, Shraddha S., Shailesh D. Kamble, and Sandeep M. Kakde. "Text mining using metadata for generation of side information." *Procedia Computer Science* 78 (2016): 807–814.

Camacho, David, Angel Panizo-LLedot, Gema Bello-Orgaz, Antonio Gonzalez-Pardo, and Erik Cambria. "The four dimensions of social network analysis: An overview of research methods, applications, and software tools." *Information Fusion* 63 (2020): 88–120.

Costa, Eric, and Goran Putnik. "An introduction to the state-of-the-art review of social network-based manufacturing system: social network analysis definitions, terminology and application areas." In *4th International Conference on Business Sustainability–Management, Technology and Learning for Individuals, Organisations and Society in Turbulent Environments*. 2014.

Cunha, Mariana, Ricardo Mendes, and João P. Vilela. "A survey of privacy-preserving mechanisms for heterogeneous data types." *Computer science review* 41 (2021): 100403.

Denny, Matthew. "The importance of generative models for assessing network structure." Available at SSRN *2798493* (2014).

Dewi, Lusiana Citra, and Alvin Chandra. "Social media web scraping using social media developers API and regex." *Procedia Computer Science* 157 (2019): 444–449.

Eising P. What exactly is an API?, 2017. Available at: https://medium.com/@perrysetgo/what-exactly-is-an-api-69f36968a41f.

Fan, Weiguo, and Michael D. Gordon. "The power of social media analytics." *Communications of the ACM* 57, no. 6 (2014): 74–81.

Felix, Ebubeogu Amarachukwu, and Sai Peck Lee. "Systematic literature review of preprocessing techniques for imbalanced data." *Let Software* 13, no. 6 (2019): 479–496.

Freeman, Linton. "The development of social network analysis." *A Study in the Sociology of Science* 1, no. 687 (2004): 159–167.

Golbeck, Jennifer. *Introduction to social media investigation: A hands-on approach.* Syngress, 2015.

Gómez, Daniel, José Rui Figueira, and Augusto Eusébio. "Modeling centrality measures in social network analysis using bi-criteria network flow optimization problems." *European Journal of Operational Research* 226, no. 2 (2013): 354–365.

Granovetter, Mark S. "The strength of weak ties." *American Journal of Sociology* 78, no. 6 (1973): 1360–1380.

Jin, YingZi, Yutaka Matsuo, and Mitsuru Ishizuka. "Extracting social networks among various entities on the web." In *The Semantic Web: Research and Applications: 4th European Semantic Web Conference, ESWC 2007, Innsbruck, Austria, June 3–7, 2007. Proceedings 4*, pp. 251–266. Springer Berlin Heidelberg, 2007.

López-Acosta, Araceli, Alejandra García-Hernández, Sodel Vázquez-Reyes, and Alejandro Mauricio-González. "A Metadata Application Profile to Structure a Scientific Database for Social Network Analysis (SNA)." In *2020 8th International Conference in Software Engineering Research and Innovation (CONISOFT)*, pp. 208–215. IEEE, 2020.

Nasution, Mahyuddin KM, and Shahrul Azman Noah. "Social network extraction based on Web: A Review about Supervised Methods." In *Journal of Physics: Conference Series*, vol. 1898, no. 1, p. 012046. IOP Publishing, 2021.

Nemes, László, and Attila Kiss. "Social media sentiment analysis based on COVID-19." *Journal of Information and Telecommunication* 5, no. 1 (2021): 1–15.

Opsahl, Tore, Filip Agneessens, and John Skvoretz. "Node centrality in weighted networks: Generalizing degree and shortest paths." *Social networks* 32, no. 3 (2010): 245–251.

Perrotta, Carlo. "Programming the platform university: Learning analytics and predictive infrastructures in higher education." *Research in Education* 109, no. 1 (2021): 53–71.

Roy, Swarup, Pooja Sharma, Keshab Nath, Dhruba K. Bhattacharyya, and Jugal K. Kalita. "Pre-processing: A data preparation step." *Encyclop Bioinform Comput Biol ABC Bioinform* 463 (2018): 1–5.

Scott, John. *What is social network analysis?*. Bloomsbury Academic, 2012.

Singh, Santosh Kumar, and Dr Rajiv Kumar Dwivedi. "Data mining: dirty data and data cleaning." *Available at SSRN 3610772* (2020).

Tabassum, Shazia, Fabíola SF Pereira, Sofia Fernandes, and João Gama. "Social network analysis: An overview." *Wiley Interdisciplinary Reviews: Data Mining and Knowledge Discovery* 8, no. 5 (2018): e1256.

Thivaharan, S., G. Srivatsun, and S. Sarathambekai. "A survey on python libraries used for social media content scraping." In *2020 International Conference on Smart Electronics and Communication (ICOSEC)*, pp. 361–366. IEEE, 2020.

Velásquez, Juan D. "Web mining and privacy concerns: Some important legal issues to be consider before applying any data and information extraction technique in web-based environments." *Expert Systems with Applications* 40, no. 13 (2013): 5228–5239.

Wang, Chen, Luigi Marini, Chieh-Li Chin, Nickolas Vance, Curtis Donelson, Pascal Meunier, and Joseph T. Yun. "Social media intelligence and learning environment: An open source framework for social media data collection, analysis and curation." In *2019 15th International Conference on eScience (eScience)*, pp. 252–261. IEEE, 2019.

Zhang, Mingxin. "Social network analysis: History, concepts, and research." *Handbook of Social Network Technologies and Applications* (2010): 3–21.

Zhao, Yanchang. "Analysing Twitter data with text mining and social network analysis." In *Proceedings of the 11th Australasian data mining and analytics conference (AusDM 2013)*, p. 23. 2013.

3 Comparative Study of Open Dataset Repositories for Community Detection and Information Diffusion in Online Social Networks

Aaquib Hussain Ganai and Rana Hashmy

3.1 INTRODUCTION

People and their interactions are involved in virtual social media platforms [1]. Social network analysis (SNA) is the term for the analysis conducted on these virtual social networks [2]. Girvan and Newman's research on these online social networks began in 2002 [3], marking the onset of SNA's study of these networks. The meaning of community in virtual social media is taken as per the nature of study under investigation [4]; loosely, a subset of nodes that are intra-densely and inter-sparsely connected is known as the community. [5]. The technique of exploring this community structure within a given virtual network is called community detection in that network [6].

There are two types of techniques for community detection in online social networks: nonoverlapping community detection [7] and overlapping community detection.

These two types of techniques can be best understood as described in the Table 3.1.

3.1.1 Nonoverlapping Community Detection (Disjoint Community Detection)

In this type of community detection, a node belongs to a single community within the community structure of the given online social network [7]. In the virtual social networks, a node inherently belongs to multiple communities, so this disjoint

 DOI: 10.1201/9781003515890-4

TABLE 3.1
Types of Community Exploration Techniques in Online Social Networks

Type of Community Detection	Node Membership	Whether Representing a Real Online Social Network or Not
Nonoverlapping community detection	Node belongs to a single community	Not representing the real online social networks
Overlapping community detection	Node belongs to multiple communities	Representing the real structure of online social networks

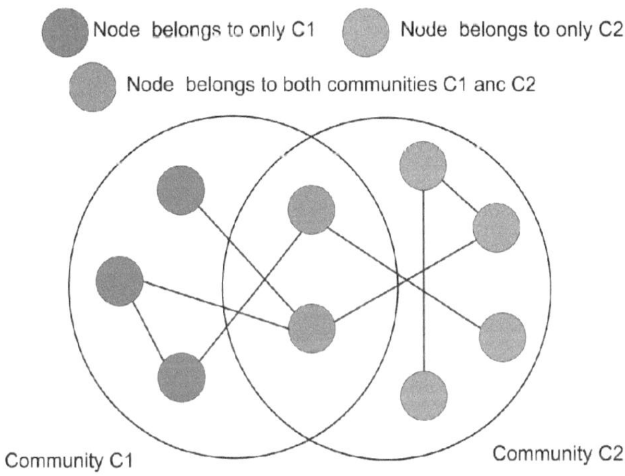

FIGURE 3.1 Nonoverlapping community structure.

community detection is not a natural way of detecting community structure in virtual social media platforms. This disjoint community detection method only provides a way for preliminary investigation into community detection in online social networks.

The nonoverlapping community detection can be best understood by Figure 3.1, in which the community structure has two communities, C1 and C2, and none of their members belong to more than one community.

Some of the recent methodologies for detecting disjoint communities are described in the following section.

3.1.1.1 Interest Group Identification Method (IGI)

This method detects disjoint community structure in a given online social network. It uses the DFS algorithm to detect community structure in the given social network by applying the concept of strongly connected components. This method performs best on real online social networks [8].

3.1.1.2 MDP Cluster Method

It is an efficient modularity-based community detection method and is successful in detecting disjoint communities. It detects the communities in large-scale social networks. This method uses the Louvain method to address the high dimensionality. It uses MPdd, so direct parsing swarm optimization is used to detect communities from this super network model. The model works well on real and artificial datasets in terms of community detection and run time [9].

3.1.1.3 CoMRCA Method

This method detects multirelational communities from multirelational networks. It is successful in detecting disjoint communities. This method has two steps:

1. In this step, the given social network has to be modeled on the relational analysis concept.
2. During this step, the extraction of multidimensional communities takes place [10].

The comparative analysis of these well-known methodologies for the detection of disjoint communities is shown in Table 3.2.

3.1.2 Overlapping Community Detection

This type of community detection is instrumental in identifying a community structure from the given online social network in which a node belongs to multiple

TABLE 3.2
Nonoverlapping Community Detection Techniques

Method	Based on	Advantages	Disadvantages
IGI [8]	DFS for getting strongly connected components	Having very less runtime	Model doesn't study the relationship between interest groups/communities
MDP Cluster [9]	Uses Louvain method to address high dimensionality and uses the direct swarm optimization method to find communities from the network	Gives best results on real and artificial networks that have high dimensions in nature. This model shows the best results in terms of community structure detection and run time	Datasets for the application of this model need a good amount of preprocessing and preparation
CoMRCA [10]	First models the social networks on the relational analysis concept and then extracts the multidimensional communities	Detects multidimensional community structures from multirelational social networks	Limited applications to different types of datasets

communities. Thus, a node can belong to more than one community in the given detected community cover. This type of community detection is naturally a realistic approach for uncovering true community structure in online social networks. This overlapping community detection can best be understood by Figure 3.2, in which some nodes have shared memberships in more than one community.

Some of the recent studies that have been conducted for handling overlapping community detection are as follows.

3.1.2.1 ILPA (Improved Label Propagation Algorithm)

This method detects overlapping community structure. This algorithm has two stages:

Stage 1: This stage performs label propagation.

Stage 2: During this stage, overlapping community structure is detected. This algorithm works best on real and synthetic datasets [11].

3.1.2.2 SL3PA Method

This method is based on a speaker–listener propagation approach. It has three stages:

1. Graph splitting
2. Label propagation
3. Community detection

It is a parallel algorithm but takes the given social network as undirected [12].

3.1.2.3 INOVIN

This approach detects overlapping communities in social networks. Fuzzy clustering is used to detect community structure in online social networks. This method uses two concepts:

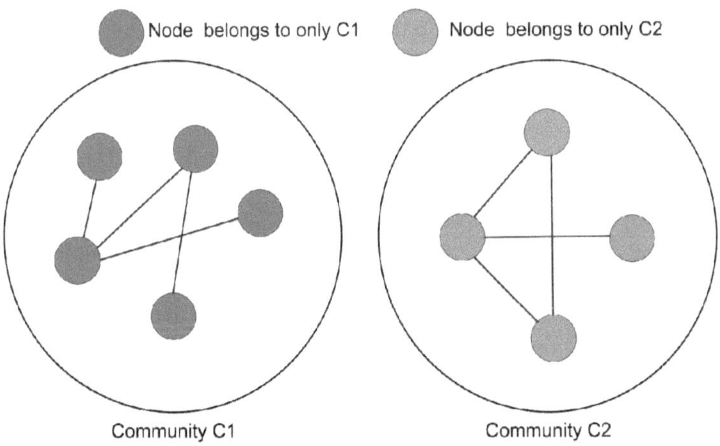

FIGURE 3.2 Overlapping community structure

First, a fuzzy membership for measuring the dynamic membership of a node toward a community, and second, a density variation detection technique is used to detect embedded communities [13].

3.1.2.4 Local Random Walk Method

This method detects overlapping community structure in online social networks. This method uses a limited random walk approach to generate attribute vectors for nodes and then uses them in the identification of community structure by grouping nodes with similar feature sets. This model works best on real and synthetic datasets. This method has been tested for the detection of sparse and dense community structure [14].

3.1.2.5 Density-Based Local Community Detection Method

This method finds overlapping community structures in complex networks.

This method is implemented via the map reduce framework. This method is divided into two stages:

1. The first stage identifies a mutual-core connected subgraph of underlying network.
2. During this second stage, an existing connected components detection method is used to identify components in the mutual-core connected subgraph generated in the first stage [15].

The comparative analysis of these recent studies that have been made in the field is given in Table 3.3.

To work on uncovering community cover, researchers face the major challenge of selecting the best-fit datasets for their research. The open dataset repositories provide a way to researchers to choose the respective datasets for their work on community detection. To provide researchers a systematic way of choosing the datasets for their research study, we aim to fill the gap in this chapter by making a concrete comparative study of major dataset repositories for working on community uncovering and information dispersion.

The spread of information is currently a significant component of SNA. The process of disseminating data or knowledge in these virtual networks is known as information dissemination [16, 17]. Sources for obtaining datasets of these online social networks, which vary in size from small to large, are the primary obstacle facing researchers studying the dissemination of information in these virtual networks. The dissemination of information can be examined with the help of these publicly available datasets. These online social network datasets can be weighted or unweighted based on whether the communications have any tangible magnitudes [18–20]. They can also be directed or undirected based on whether the user communications are symmetric or asymmetric between users in the specific network. All the kinds of datasets should be employed in the research of information dissemination in virtual social networks since the datasets of online social networks can range in size from small to large. A social network can be mathematically represented by a graph G (V,

TABLE 3.3
Overlapping Community Detection Techniques

Method	Based on	Advantages	Disadvantages
ILPA [11]	Label propagation	Gives best results on real and synthesized datasets	The model's scalability to the large real datasets is unknown
SL3PA [12]	Speaker-listener propagation model	Gives advantage of parallel computing	Memory requirement for running the algorithm is a challenging aspect
INOVIN [13]	Fuzzy clustering	Shows best results for detection of overlapping community structure	Model attributes for the datasets are synthesized, so dataset preparation is hard
Local random walk method [14]	Limited random walk method	Approach is efficient for detecting sparse and dense community structures	Model can't be applied to dynamic networks in the current form
Density-based local [15] community detection method	Connected components	Implemented through map reduce	The model can't be applied to dynamic and evolving networks in the current form

E), where V is the set of nodes that represent the network's users, and E is the set of edges that reflect the users' communications with one another [21, 22].

The online social network graph can be represented in two different ways: either as adjacency lists or as square matrices with dimensions V * V. The former method is the most commonly used format for online social graph representations.

The majority of the datasets in the public dataset repositories are in the .paj, .csv, .xlsx, .txt, .json, .md, .jpeg, .png, .mtx, .tsv, .edgelist, and .net file formats.

To better understand the process of community detection and information spread across online social networks, we will compare the main public dataset repositories in this chapter.

The chapter comprises four sections, this introduction section is followed by Section 3.2 on related work, Section 3.3 on social network dataset repositories and their comparative study, and Section 3.4 on conclusions and future work.

3.2 RELATED WORK

In the discipline of social media analysis, the comparative analysis of various dataset repositories has been investigated previously. Several notable attempts that are relevant to our study are as follows: Weber et al. studied the two datasets that have been generated/collected using developed software tools [23]; Masoumzadeh et al. studied the geo-social network datasets [24]; Shu et al. conducted a comparative study of many datasets for detecting fake news in virtual social networks [25];

Cecajet al. examined the online social network analysis using the crawler generated datasets and existing datasets [26]. The expanded Stanford Network Analysis Platform (SNAP) dataset repository and associated graphing library were described by Lescovec et al. [27], while Nadeem examined social network tools and their comparative analysis [28].

The following well-known attempts are relevant to our study: utilizing the strongly connected component concept to cluster online social networks into several interest groups and identify the most influential and final members [29]. Silva et al. proposed the profile rank approach [30] for locating prominent users and relevant information. Bakshy investigates how users affect one another [31]. A mathematical formula for simulating the dissemination of information is proposed by Wang et al. [32]. A multiplex influence maximization (MIM) method is suggested by Kunle et al. [33] for identifying influential users. In order to uncover overlapping communities, Kahef suggests a hierarchical algorithm [34]. To address information dissemination, Gatti et al. offer a multi-agent social network simulation [35]. An enriched attribute network serves as the foundation for Lin et al.'s proposed overlapping community discovery technique [36]. In the vast field of linked online social network analytics, these are just a few attempts.

3.3 SOCIAL NETWORK DATASET REPOSITORIES AND THEIR COMPARATIVE STUDY

We can use a variety of publicly accessible dataset repositories to investigate knowledge dissemination and community detection in online social networks. The best-known and most-used dataset repositories for studying community detection and information diffusion in online social networks are as follows.

3.3.1 Stanford Network Analysis Platform (SNAP) Dataset Repository

An enormous number of online social network datasets are available in this repository. This repository's networks range in size from medium to large. This repository contains at least 50 datasets that can be used to disseminate information. The dataset file and the metadata file for each dataset are contained in the relevant dataset [37].

3.3.2 Pajek Dataset Repository

The most popular SNA dataset repository is called Pajek. Small datasets are included in the repository; these datasets are benchmarks for research on community detection and the spread of information in virtual social networks. The datasets in the repository are most useful for studies that aim to explain the diffusion of knowledge [38].

3.3.3 Arizona State University (ASU) Dataset Repository

The University of Arizona built the repository. Datasets of online social networks are available in the ASU collection, which can be utilized to study community detection and to investigate the spread of information within these networks. The majority of extensive datasets for online social networks are available in the repository [39].

3.3.4 UCI Network Dataset Repository

Datasets from both small and large online social networks are available in the repository; these datasets can be used for the study of community detection and in the research of how information spreads across these networks. The University of California is the creator of this library of datasets. The datasets are available for free download by users, who may then utilize them for analysis.

3.3.5 KONNECT Dataset Repository

It is a German University of Lolenz-Landau's Koblenz's network collection. The collection includes 1326 network datasets ranging in size from small to large, which can be used to research how information spreads through online social networks [40].

3.3.6 Kaggle Dataset Repository

The library of open-source datasets can be utilized to investigate community detection and the spread of information inside virtual social networks. Datasets from the repository can be utilized to investigate mostly the information dissemination using machine learning models [41].

The two main research areas of social network analysis (SNA) are community detection and information dissemination, which may be studied using all these dataset repositories. The factors required for the particular research project may influence the final selection of these dataset repositories. The comparative study of the above-mentioned dataset repositories based on various parameters is given in Table 3.4.

This comparative study of open dataset repositories can be used by researchers who are eager to study community detection and information dissemination.

TABLE 3.4
Comparative Study of Various Open Dataset Repositories

	Direction		Magnitude		Scale	
Dataset Repository	**Undirected**	**Directed**	**Unweighted**	**Weighted**	**Small**	**Large**
SNAP	Yes	Yes	Yes	Yes	No	Yes
Pajek	Yes	Yes	Yes	Yes	Yes	No
ASU	Yes	Yes	Yes	Yes	No	Yes
UCI Network	Yes	Yes	Yes	Yes	Yes	Yes
KONNECT	Yes	Yes	Yes	Yes	Yes	Yes
Kaggle	Yes	Yes	Yes	Yes	Yes	Yes

3.4 CONCLUSIONS AND FUTURE WORK

We have presented a comparative analysis of the main public dataset repositories available for use in researching community detection and the spread of information. Based on the structural characteristics of these networks, like direction, magnitude, and scale, we have conducted a comparative analysis of the various dataset repositories that were utilized in the aforementioned studies. Researchers can select various datasets from these public dataset repositories to investigate community detection and the dissemination of information. In the future, our research study will make use of datasets from the Pajek and SNAP dataset repositories.

REFERENCES

1. R. Han, "More Talk , More Support? The effects of social network interaction and social network evaluation on social support via social media," *Psychology Research and Behavior Management*, vol. 16, pp. 3857–3866, 2023. [Online]. https://doi.org/10.2147/PRBM.S424443.
2. C. Haythornth Waite, "Social network analysis: An approach and technique for the study of information exchange," *Library & Information Science Research*, vol. 18, no. 4, pp. 323–342, 1996. [Online]. https://doi.org/10.1016/S0740-8188(96)90003-1.
3. M. Girvanand, and M. E. J. Newman, "Community structure in social and biological networks," *Proceedings of the National Academy of Sciences of the United States of America*, vol. 99, pp. 7821–7826, 2002. [Online]. https://doi.org/10.1073/pnas.122653799.
4. M. M. Daliri Khomami, A. Rezvanian, A. M. Saghiri, and M. R. Meybodi, "Overlapping Community Detection in Social Networks Using Cellular Learning Automata," in 2020 28th Iranian Conference on Electrical Engineering (ICEE), Tabriz, Iran, 2020, pp. 1–6. https://doi.org/10.1109/ICEE50131.2020.9260792.
5. M. Wang, C. Wang, J. X. Yu, and J. Zhang, "Community detection in social networks: An in-depth benchmarking study with aprocedure-oriented framework," *Proc. VLDBEndow.*, vol. 8, no. 10, pp. 998–1009, June 2015. [Online]. https://doi.org/10.147.
6. P. Bedi, and C. Sharma, "Community detection in social networks," *Wiley Interdisciplinary Reviews: Data Mining and Knowledge Discovery*, vol. 6, pp. 1–25, 2016. [Online]. https://doi.org/10.1002/widm.1178.
7. Y. Xu, H. Xu, and D. Zhang," A novel disjoint community detection algorithm for social networks based on backbone degree and expansion," *Expert Systems with Applications*, vol. 42, pp. 10–21, 2015. [Online]. https://doi.org/10.1016/j.eswa.2015.06.042.
8. Abd Al-Azim, Nouran Ayman R., Tarek F. Gharib, Yasmine Afify, and Mohamed Hamdy. "Influence propagation: Interest groups and node ranking models." *Physica A: Statistical Mechanics and its Applications*, p. 124247, 2020.
9. M. Fozuni Shirjini, S. Farzi, and A. Nikanjam, "MDPCluster: A swarm-based community detection algorithm in large-scale graphs," *Computing,* vol. 102, pp. 893–922, 2020. https://doi.org/10.1007/s00607-019-00787-4.
10. S. Guesmi, C. Trabelsi, and C. Latiri, "Multidimensional community discovering in heterogeneous social networks," *Concurrency Computat Pract Exper*, vol. 33, p. e5809, 2021. https://doi.org/10.1002/cpe.5809
11. S. Dong, "Improved label propagation algorithm for overlapping community detection,' *Computing*, vol. 102, pp. 2185–2198, 2020. https://doi.org/10.1007/s00607-020-00836-3.

12. Keshab Nath, Swarup Roy, and Sukumar Nandi, "InOvIn: A fuzzy-rough approach for detecting overlapping communities with intrinsic structures in evolving networks," Applied Soft Computing, vol. 89, C, April 2020. https://doi.org/10.1016/j.asoc.2020.106096.
13. S. Bahadori, P. Moradi, and H. Zare, "An improved limited random walk approach for identification of overlapping communities in complex networks," *ApplIntell*, 2020. https://doi.org/10.1007/s10489-020-01999-4
14. Muhammad Abulaish, Ishfaq Majid Bhat, and Sajid Yousuf Bhat. "Scaling density-based community detection to large-scale social networks via map reduce framework," 1 Jan. 2020 : 1663 – 1674
15. R. Chelehchaleh, M. Salehi, R. Farahbakhsh, et al., "BRaG: Ahybrid multi-feature-framework for fake news detection on social media," *Social Network Analysis and Mining*, vol. 14, p. 35, 2024. [Online]. https://doi.org/10.1007/s13278-023-01185-7.
16. G. Gallo, M. Goglia, and V. DeSimone, "Network and social media: The digital surgeon," in Towards the Future of Surgery. New Paradigms in Healthcare, J. Martellucci and F. Dal Mas, Eds. Springer, Cham, 2023. [Online]. https://doi.org/10.1007/978-3-031-47623-5_4.
17. S. Catanese, P. D. Meo, E. Ferrara, G. Fiumara, and A. Provetti," Extraction and Analysis of Facebook Friendship Relations," 2011. [Online]. https://doi.org/10.1007/978-1-4471-4054-2_12.
18. E. Sadikov and M. M. Martinez," Information Propagation on Twitter," Stanford University, 2021. [Online]. https://snap.stanford.edu/class/cs224w-2010/proj2009/TwitterWriteup_Sadikov.pdf.
19. S. Das, Ö. Eğecioğlu, and A. E. Abbadi," Anonymizing weighted social network graphs," in 2010 IEEE 26th International Conference on Data Engineering, 2010, pp. 237–242. https://doi.org/10.1109/PerComW.2014.6815210. [Online]. Available:https://sites.cs.ucsb.edu/~omer/DOWNLOADABLE/graph_anonymization_ICDE10.pdf.
20. P. Dey, S. Bhattacharya, and S. Roy, "A survey on the role of centrality as seed nodes for information propagation in large scale network," *ACM/IMS Transactions on Data Science*, vol. 2, pp. 1–25, 2021. [Online]. https://doi.org/10.1145/3465374.
21. H. B. Khalfallah, M. Jelassi, N. B. B. Saoud, and J. Demongeot, "Social and community networks and obesity," in Metabolic Syndrome, R. S. Ahima, Ed. Springer, Cham, 2023, pp. 1–19. https://doi.org/10.1007/978-3-031-40116-9_19.
22. D. Weber, M. Nasim, L. Mitchell, and L. Falzon, "A method to evaluate the reliability of social media data for social network analysis," 2020. [Online]. https://doi.org/10.48550/arXiv.2010.08717.
23. A. Masoumzadeh, and J. Joshi, "Anonymizing geo-social network datasets," in Proceedings of the 4th ACM SIGSPATIAL International Workshop on Security and Privacy in GIS and LBS (SPRINGL '11), New York, NY, USA, 2011, pp. 25–32. https://doi.org/10.1145/2071880.2071886. [Online]. https://doi.org/10.1145/2071880.2071886.
24. K. Shu, D. Mahudeswaran, S. Wang, D. Lee, and H. Liu, "Fake news net: A data repository with news content, social context, and spatiotemporal information for studying fake news on social media," *Big Data*, vol. 8, no. 3, pp. 171–188, June 2020. https://doi.org/10.1089/big.2020.0062.
25. A. Cecaj, M. Mamei, and N. Bicocchi, "Re-identification of anonymized CDR datasets using social network data," in 2014 IEEE International Conference on Pervasive Computing and Communication Workshops (PERCOM WORKSHOPS), Budapest, Hungary, 2014, pp. 237–242. https://doi.org/10.1109/PerComW.2014.6815210.
26. J. Leskovec and R. Sosic," SNAP: A general-purpose network analysis and graph mining library," *ACM Transactions on Intelligent Systems and Technology*, vol. 8, pp. 1–1, 2016. https://doi.org/10.1145/2898361.

27. N. Akhtar," Social network analysis tools," in 2014 Fourth International Conference on Communication Systems and Network Technologies, Bhopal, India, 2014, pp. 388–392. https://doi.org/10.1109/CSNT.2014.83.
28. A. Al-Azim, T. Gharib, Y. Afify, and M. Hamday, "Influence propagation: Interest groups and node ranking models," *Physica A: Statistical Mechanics and Applications*, vol. 553, 2020. [Online]. https://doi.org/10.1016/j.physa.2020.124630.
29. A. Silva, S. Guimaraes, W. Merira, and M. Zaki, "Profile rank: Finding relevant content and influential users based on information diffusion," in Proceedings of the 7th Workshop on Social Network Mining and Analysis (SNAKDD '13), New York, USA, Article 2, pp. 1–9, 2013. [Online]. https://doi.org/10.1145/2501025.2501033.
30. E. Bakshy," Information Diffusion and Social Influence in Online Networks," PhD Thesis, University of Michigan, 2011. [Online]. http://hdl.handle.net/2027.42/89838.
31. H. Wang, F. Wang, and K. Xu, "Modelling information diffusion in online social networks with partial differential equations," arXiv: 1310.0505v1 [cs.SI], Oct. 2013. [Online]. https://arxiv.org/abs/1310.0505v1.
32. A. Kuhnle, M. Alim, X. Liu, H. Zhang, and M. Thai, "Multiple influence maximization in online social networks with heterogeneous diffusion models," *IEEE Transactions on Computational Social Systems*, vol. 5, no. 2, pp. 418–429, 2018. https://doi.org/10.1109/TCSS.2018.2810259.
33. R. Kashef, "Detecting overlapping communities in social networks using a modified segmentation by weighted aggregation approach," in International Conference on Data Science, E-Learning and Information Systems (DATA '21), Association for Computing, 2021.
34. M. Gatti, A. Appel, C. Santos, C. Pinhanez, P. Cavalin, and S. Neto," A simulation based approach to analyze the information diffusion in online social networks," in Winter Simulations Conference (WSC), Washington, DC, 2013, pp. 1685–1696. https://doi.org/10.1109/WSC.2013.6721550.
35. H. Lin, Y. Zhan, Z. Zhao, Y. Chen, and C. Dong," Overlapping community detection basedon attribute augmented graph," *Entropy*, vol. 23, p. 680, 2021. [Online]. https://doi.org/10.3390/e23060680.
36. https://snap.stanford.edu/data/#socnets.
37. http://vlado.fmf.uni-lj.si/pub/networks/data/.
38. https://lib.asu.edu/data/datasets.
39. https://networkdata.ics.uci.edu/http://konect.cc/.
40. http://konect.cc.
41. https://www.kaggle.com/datasets.

Section II

Exploration of Community Detection in Social Networks

4 Community Detection
Exploring Structure and Dynamics

Jayati Gulati

4.1 INTRODUCTION

A social network can be used to express any real-world network. It can be described as a structure represented by a number of nodes and the connections between them, which are typically referred to as ties. The term social actor refers to a node in a social network that can represent a person, group, document, organization, or nation. A connection between a pair of nodes can reflect associations such as common interest areas, dislikes, friendships, exchange of information, hyperlinks, or common citations. Social network analysis (SNA) (Wasserman and Faust 1994) studies the relation between entities including social structures, social position, role analysis, etc., and analyzes it for finding useful patterns or flow of information.

With the advent of Web 2.0, there has been tremendous growth in the study of different networks like Internet (for marketing or other business ventures), social networks or other links between individuals (e.g., X), protein networks, food webs, distribution networks such as blood vessels (Newman 2003). SNA considers large-scale networks, revealing patterns not visible in small networks, therefore, their analysis becomes very important (Tang and Liu 2010). The links between the elements that make up these networks offer deep understanding of their numerous dynamic interactions and may be useful in a number of contexts. Graphs are employed as data structures in the analysis and research of these networks. A graph is a non-linear data structure that consists of a set of nodes joined by links or edges which can be labeled/unlabeled or directed/undirected or signed/unsigned (Cook and Holder 2006). A network can be easily visualized and interpreted with greater ease when it is presented in the form of a graph (Cook and Holder 2006).

A social graph is defined as a data structure used to model social networks with densely populated nodes based on certain similarities. Large social graphs tend to show properties like scale-free distribution, small-world effect, and strong community structure as mentioned by Tang and Liu (2010). In general, it can be seen from statistics that many data samples have a particular scale. But the nodes in a social graph do not follow this rule and are bound to show a behavior called

DOI: 10.1201/9781003515890-6

as the scale-free distribution. A scale-free distribution also known as power law distribution is a skewed distribution, where a tail depicts that the majority of nodes in a social graph have a low degree as compared to those having dense connections. Another feature shown by a social graph is the small-world effect. According to Milgram (1967), social networks can be categorized as small worlds since the average path length in a well-defined population for two individuals to meet is six hops. This finding gave rise to the well-known expression "six degrees of separation." Also, it is seen by the researchers that two entities in a network are not too far away considering the number of hops between them, in general they are shown to have six degrees of separation (Leskovec and Horvitz 2008). Different measures like diameter, eccentricity, and path length are used to depict the same.

A social graph exhibits the presence of a robust community structure. This indicates that groups of entities interact with one another more frequently than the rest of the network. Communities in social networks frequently correspond to significant functional or interest groups of the underlying nodes, and it might be challenging to develop methodologies and strategies to pinpoint these groups. Social networks display community structures, which are groupings of nodes that are more similar or closely connected, due to the crucial attribute of network transitivity. Clustering coefficient is used to capture transitivity, which plays a crucial role in identifying the community structure. There are two categories of clustering coefficients—local clustering coefficient and global clustering coefficient (Watts and Strogatz 1998). Local clustering coefficient identifies the cliques formed among a node's immediate neighbors. A clique represents a complete graph. While global clustering coefficient identifies the number of triangles in a given network which helps in identifying high-density regions in a graph. These two measures help in detecting communities.

Information is extracted from a dataset that can be characterized as a graph through the process of graph mining. Traditional graph mining includes frequent subgraph mining, graph matching, graph classification, graph clustering, etc. (Atastina, Sitohang, Saptawati, and Moertini 2017). Also, frequent graph mining extracts the frequently occurring subgraphs in a network, i.e., the subgraphs having a count above a certain threshold value (Jiang, Coenen, and Zito 2013). These subgraphs depict some repeating patterns or can be beneficial for finding isomorphic graphs (Corneil and Gotlieb 1970). Classification and clustering handle the data by dividing it into smaller groups or labels based on supervised or unsupervised learning approaches, respectively. One of the important applications of graph mining is community detection, which studies the cohesive groups in a graph. These groups are tightly coupled and have high association among themselves and a smaller number of associations outside the group (Lancichinetti and Fortunato 2009). In contrast to nodes located outside a community, nodes within a community might have similar features, which provide input to several applications like target marketing (Pool, Bonchi, and Leeuwen 2014), studying common interest groups (Lim and Datta 2012), recommendations and user interface adaptations (Planti´e and Crampes 2013).

4.2 LITERATURE REVIEW OF COMMUNITY DETECTION ALGORITHMS

Community in a given network is defined as a close-knit group of objects that interact more frequently with each other as compared to the other parts of the network as shown in Figure 4.1. Also, according to Lin and Kernighan (1973), "Communities are those parts of graph that have less ties with rest of the graph." Therefore, detection of communities extracts the group of nodes that have a high number of interactions among themselves than with the rest of the network.

Networks are frequently investigated at various granularities, from the macroscopic descriptions of statistical aspects (degree distribution, total clustering coefficient, etc.) to the microscopic features (degree, centrality, etc.) of nodes. A "mesoscopic" explanation attempts to describe the community organization in networks between these two levels. Sets of nodes in a network that are more densely connected to one another than to the rest of the network are referred to as communities. Community structures, such as social groups interacting in a society (Girvan and Newman 2002; Arenas, Danon, Dz-Guilera, Gleiser, and Guimer 2004), topic-related webpages (Flake, Lawrence, Giles, and Coetzee 2002), and sections within food webs (Krause, Frank, Mason, Ulanowicz, and Taylor 2003), are significant because they are frequently closely linked to the functional units of a system.

A fundamental job in social network analysis, community detection has attracted a lot of attention recently and the subject is still developing quickly Fortunato and Castellano 2012). In the field of community detection, some of the most widely used work is the one developed by Girvan and Newman (2002). The algorithm develops a divisive strategy by deleting the edge with the largest betweenness value modularity. It aims to eliminate edges progressively using the concept of edge betweenness. After removal of this edge, the betweenness is calculated for the affected nodes and edges. Another popular work by Newman (2006) is where the quality function for modularity is introduced. Modularity is expressed as eigenvectors that use a spectral algorithm for community detection and return densely packed communities with shorter run time. Spectral clustering in (Auffarth 2007) is based on the problem of graph partition where the input data matrix is in the form of eigenvectors. This data is represented as coordinates in multi-dimensional space and k-means clustering is applied, which results in communities. The community detection problem is formalized as an optimization problem in Genetic Algorithm

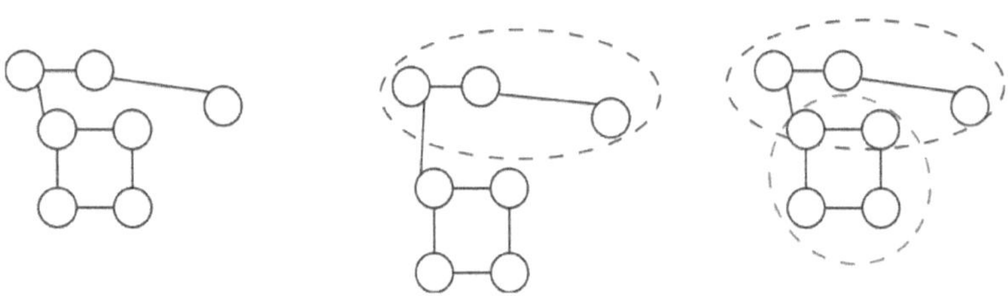

FIGURE 4.1 (a) Social graph, (b) disjoint communities from social graph, and (c) overlapping communities from social graph

(GA) (Bui and Moon 1996). GAs are used to optimize modularity (Lehnerer 2018) and community score (Hafez, Ghali, Hassanien, and Fahmy 2012) to detect community structure in a graph. Community detection has many real-world applications (Bhat and Abulaish 2015; Bhat and Abulaish 2013; Asur, Parthasarathy, and Ucar 2009; Fu, Song, and Xing 2009; Backstrom, Huttenlocher, Kleinberg, and Lan 2006; Dunlavy, Kolda, and Acar 2011).

A few algorithms in community detection are random walk-based, spin models, synchronization, etc. In random walk, nodes are traversed over randomly and merged into groups using different strategies (Zeitouni 2006; Zhou 2003). Spin models are used in statistical mechanics. A network graph is transformed into the Potts model and each node with a community is associated with spin variables (Reichardt and Bornholdt 2004). The algorithm defines a modified Potts Hamiltonian, combining a ferromagnetic variable that encourages intra-community connections with an antiferromagnetic variable that promotes diversity among spin configurations. Another work in Reichardt and Bornholdt (2006) assumes nodes to be in a spin state and introduces the spin glass technique. A method for community detection is introduced by mapping the problem onto finding the ground state of an infinite-ranged Potts spin glass model. The energy of the spin system corresponds to a quality function for clustering, where the spin states represent group indices. This method bridges hierarchical and partitional clustering by adjusting a parameter that influences the weights of missing and existing links, providing insights into community overlap and hierarchy.

A few works based on snowball sampling-inspired community detection have been mentioned in Gulati and Abulaish (2019), Gulati and Abulaish (2023), Gulati, Abulaish, and Bhat (2022). They introduce a new set of algorithms that are based on snowball sampling techniques for undirected (both disjoint and overlapping communities) social graphs. The algorithms start with identifying the seed nodes, i.e., the nodes with high connectivity in their neighborhood. It progresses by merging seed nodes with their best neighbors, forming snowball chains called communities.

Table 4.1 shows a few popular state-of-the-art techniques in the field of community.

TABLE 4.1
A Summarized Literature Review

State-of-the-Art Approach	Category/Type of Network	Advantages	Disadvantages
DBSCAN (Ester, Kriegel, Sander, and Xu 1996)	Traditional approach/ Undirected social graph	It allows arbitrary-shaped communities.	It uses two parameters that decide upon the structure of the community.
k-Means clustering (MacQueen 1967)	Traditional approach Undirected social graph	It can determine communities of various shapes and size.	The algorithm depends on the value of k. It clusters outliers by forcing the centroids to expand or can lead to formation of a community consisting of only outliers.

(*Continued*)

TABLE 4.1 (CONTINUED)
A Summarized Literature Review

State-of-the-Art Approach	Category/Type of Network	Advantages	Disadvantages
Hierarchical clustering (Newman and Girvan 2004)	Traditional approach/ Undirected social graph	It forms a tree of communities that can be cut at any given level as per a given metric value.	A node with low degree value is unable to join the bigger communities. Also, once a node joins a wrong community it can never re-enter another community.
Spectral clustering (Auffarth 2007)	Traditional approach/ Undirected social graph	It is a generic class of algorithms that is easy to implement. It is robust to noise and outliers in the data.	Its efficiency reduces when the size of dataset increases as it requires a large storage space and a lot of time to process the eigenvectors. It also requires number of clusters at the beginning of the algorithm.
LPA (Raghavan, Albert, and Kumara 2007)	Undirected social graph	Its linear time complexity for sparse graphs and quadratic for other graphs	The resulting community structure may vary in every execution of LPA. It has another issue that it can result in formation of a monster community.
Stepping LPA-S (Li, Huang, Wang, and Chen 2017)	Undirected social graph	This method considers both similarity among nodes as well as the topology of the network unlike LPA and hence, form meaningful partitions.	The time complexity is no more linear than LPA, it is quadratic for this algorithm.
SLPA (Xie, Szymanski, and Liu 2011)	Overlapping community detection approach	It has a linear time complexity for sparse networks.	It is an extension of LPA that makes use of a hyper-parameter. It restricts the label updation to only the border nodes to save time.
DEMON (Coscia, Rossetti, Giannotti, and Pedreschi 2012)	Overlapping community detection approach	It is a deterministic method and has limited time complexity.	It uses hyperparameters for setting the threshold value and minimum community size.
ANGEL (Rossetti 2019)	Overlapping community detection approach	It provides low time-complexity with high-quality overlapping partitions.	The evolving nature of a community remains an unanswered question and can have several interpretations, which need attention.

(Continued)

TABLE 4.1 (CONTINUED)
A Summarized Literature Review

State-of-the-Art Approach	Category/Type of Network	Advantages	Disadvantages
Infomap (Rosvall and Bergstrom 2008)	Disjoint/Overlapping Community detection approach	It is a scalable algorithm that can organize communities as per hierarchy.	This algorithm does not seem to work well for random networks.
Louvain (Blondel, Guillaume, Lambiotte, and Lefebvre 2008)	Disjoint community detection approach	It performs well on large networks.	This technique is unable to separate outliers.
BigClam (Yang and Leskovec 2013)	Overlapping community detection approach	It scales up to large networks containing millions of nodes and edges.	This algorithm does not consider the content of the node and the edge weights and focuses on the relationship among edges.
Multicomm (Hollocou, Bonald, and Lelarge 2018)	Overlapping community detection approach	This technique helps in identifying communities from multilayered networks that have a wide range of connections among themselves.	It requires number of communities as an input parameter. The use of conductance diminishes the quality of the identified seed nodes Liu, Shao, and Su (2020).
CONGA (Gregory 2007)	Overlapping community detection approach	It uses edge as well as vertex betweenness to determine quality partitions.	It has high computational complexity.
COPRA (Gregory 2010)	Overlapping community detection approach	It works for directed and weighted graphs.	It produces a number of small size communities for networks.
CFinder (Adamcsek, Palla, Farkas, Der´enyi, and Vicsek 2006)	Overlapping community detection approach	It uses a local, density-based approach which identifies cliques rather than k-cliques.	This approach requires locating all maximal cliques rather than the individual k-cliques, which is an NP-hard problem. It also fails to terminate in many large social networks.

4.3 APPLICATIONS

Community detection seeks to uncover or draw attention to information that is less widely recognized or that would remain overlooked without prudent data analysis. Community detection is used in a variety of applications by diverse network types, including biological, social media, academic, etc., to gather insightful information. The current subsection discusses a few of the real-world applications in several fields.

Online Social Network: X being a popular social network utilizes community detection techniques for understanding the features of a network, analyzing public emotions, visualizing association among users, and analyzing a group of users with a specific interest (Diakopoulos and Shamma 2010; Choudhury, Lin, Sundaram, Candan, Xie, and Kelliher 2010; Ozer, Kim, and Davulcu 2016). In Ferrara (2012), large-scale community structures are studied using more than 500 million Facebook users, identifying a high degree of similarity. Community identification methods can also be applied to detect threats like attacks by terrorist groups in social networks (Waskiewicz 2012). Another social media Flickr uses community detection to organize content for users' ease. In the work by Papadopoulos, Zigkolis, Tolias, Kalantidis, Mylonas, Kompatsiaris, and Vakali (2010), a group of related images is extracted for users to navigate through them easily. Another similar work in Mo¨ellic, Haugeard, and Pitel (2008) uses the nearest neighbor approach to identify similar photos. Event tracking is another application of community detection in social media (Sayyadi, Hurst, and Maykov 2009). It is characterized based on similar keywords, i.e., documents describing a common event will be associated with a common set of keywords.

Recommender Systems: In order to target customers with marketing techniques, offer recommendations, and improve the online purchasing experience, e-commerce uses data mining technologies (Javed, Younis, Latif, Qadir, and Baig 2018). According to Ricci, Rokach, and Shapira (2011) and Reddy, Kitsuregawa, Sreekanth, and Rao (2002), customers are given product recommendations based on their prior purchases.

By integrating elements like links between users, social connections, and geographic location, community detection improves this process. Another application in this field mentioned in Beigi, Jalili, Alvari, and Sukthankar (2014) is based on the prediction and propagation of trust among users in social media. By considering the similarity between a customer's trust values and the trust relations in a network, like-minded consumers in a community are found. Also, in order to identify authors working in the same field of study or to locate relevant research from citation networks and co-operation networks, one useful tool is community detection (Wang, Li, Zhang, and Lu 2016). Similar to this, Xin, E, Song, Song, and Tong (2014) discuss book recommendations based on a user's social conduct. For statisticians, another comparable work in Ji and Jin (2016) organizes the co-authorship and citation data. A work in Gasparetti, Sansonetti, and Micarelli (2021) highlights a graph created with X users and their tweets as vertices. The edges represent the follow-followee relationship and user-tweet interactions. By using a community detection algorithm, the partitions C = C1, C2, ..., CN are identified based on similar characteristics.

The technique can also be viable for future link prediction, which is the essence of a recommender system. It sets a utility function that needs to be maximized. This function finds the likelihood of existence of a link between two nodes given communities C.

Healthcare: Due to the great number of interactions between entities, biological networks such as protein-protein interaction, metabolic networks, etc., also have applications in this area, like Spirin and Mirny (2003), Dunn, Dudbridge, and Sanderson (2005), which identify functional modules in a protein network. A principle component analysis (PCA)-based method was created to disclose the community structure for the sake of illness diagnosis and prevention. Using k-means and fuzzy C means to cluster IR (infrared) spectra from tissues, community detection also assisted in finding malignant cells in lung tissues given by Bechtel, Kelley, Coons, Klein, Slagel, and Petty (2005) and an early-stage breast cancer given by Wang and Garibaldi (2005).

Fraud Detection and Link Prediction: Community detection is another technique used in fraud detection to locate network peaks. In Pinheiro (2012), the communities are first identified from a telecommunication network, and then the outliers are found using graph topological properties such as degree and betweenness. Similar to this, two strategies are developed in Gangopadhyay and Chen (2016) for a healthcare network to discover exclusive partnerships utilizing suspicious groups. In many aspects of life, including recommending new products to users on e-commerce sites, friend recommendations on social networking sites (Jalili, Orouskhani, Asgari, Alipourfard, and Perc 2017), and determining the connection between two proteins (Lei and Ruan 2013), link prediction uses community detection. It forms the basis of hyperlink prediction on the World Wide Web by Liben-Nowell and Kleinberg (2003) and recommender systems by Cao, Liu, and Yang (2010).

4.4 COMMUNITY DETECTION USING PYTHON

Python is a popular programming language for community detection because of its wide variety of libraries, simple syntax, and ease of integration with other computer languages. CDlib ((C)ommunity (D)iscovery Library) is a Python library used for identifying and extracting communities from networks. The library helps in community discovery analysis. CDlib is a Python package built upon the network facilities offered by networkx and igraph. The library provides a standardized input/output for several Community Detection algorithms as mentioned by Rossetti, Milli, and Cazabet (2019). A few popular sub-libraries have been discussed below.

4.5 ALGORITHMS

Some of the popular community detection algorithms are coded in this library. In 2008, the Louvain community detection algorithm (Que, Checconi, Petrini, and Gunnels 2015) was introduced as a fast method to unfold communities in huge networks. This method is based on modularity and it maximizes the gap between the actual number of edges within a community and the expected number of edges within a community as mentioned in Figure 4.2.

```
from cdlib import algorithms
import networkx as nx
G = nx.karate_club_graph()
coms = algorithms.louvain(G, weight='weight', resolution=1., randomize=False)
```

FIGURE 4.2 Louvain algorithm for identifying communities.

```
from cdlib import algorithms
import networkx as nx
G = nx.karate_club_graph()
coms = algorithms.leiden(G)
```

FIGURE 4.3 Leiden algorithm for identifying communities.

```
from cdlib import algorithms
import networkx as nx
G = nx.karate_club_graph()
coms = algorithms.walktrap(G)
```

FIGURE 4.4 Random walk for identifying communities.

Subsequent studies revealed that Louvain community detection frequently finds internally unconnected communities (poor internal connections). Moving a node that has served as a bridge between two components in a community to a new community could cause the old community to become disconnected in the Louvain algorithm. In order to maximize a modularity score for each community, the algorithm divides nodes into disjoint communities. The Leiden method in Figure 4.3 is a hierarchical clustering algorithm that works recursively by combining communities into single nodes through greedy modularity optimization. It makes adjustments to the Louvain method to mitigate some of its flaws, such as the situation where some of the communities Louvain finds are not highly connected. This is accomplished by dividing communities into smaller, more interconnected groups at random intervals (Traag, Waltman, and van Eck 2019).

Another method for identifying communities based on random walks is called Walktrap (Pons and Latapy 2005) shown in Figure 4.4. In this method, the network's random walks are used to calculate the distance between each vertex.

4.6 EVALUATION

Evaluation can be done in two ways: internally and externally. The internal evaluation is calculated based on fitness scores like modularity, average internal degree, conductance, etc. Whereas the external evaluation is done based on comparison of partitions like the ground truth and the identified partition. It can be calculated using Normalized Mutual Information, Omega score, Rand Index, etc.

The Python code in Figure 4.5 calculates the average distance which is defined average path length across all possible pairs of nodes containing it.

```
from cdlib.algorithms import louvain
from cdlib import evaluation
g = nx.karate_club_graph()
communities = louvain(g)
scd = evaluation.avg_distance(g, communities)
```

FIGURE 4.5 Average path length calculation.

```
from cdlib.algorithms import louvain
from cdlib import evaluation
g = nx.karate_club_graph()
communities = louvain(g)
scd = evaluation.avg_transitivity(g, communities)
```

FIGURE 4.6 Transitivity calculation.

```
from cdlib import evaluation, algorithms
import networkx as nx
g = nx.karate_club_graph()
louvain_communities = algorithms.louvain(g)
leiden_communities = algorithms.leiden(g)
evaluation.normalized_mutual_information(louvain_communities, leiden_communities)
```

FIGURE 4.7 Normalized mutual information calculation.

```
from cdlib import algorithms, viz
import networkx as nx
g = nx.karate_club_graph()
coms = algorithms.louvain(g)
position = nx.spring_layout(g)
viz.plot_network_clusters(g, coms, position)
```

FIGURE 4.8 Graph visualization.

The code in Figure 4.6 calculates the average transitivity of a community defined as the average clustering coefficient of its nodes w.r.t. their connection within the community itself.

The external evaluation is done by the code in Figure 4.7 that implements the normalized mutual information (NMI). It is a normalization of the mutual information (MI) score to scale the results between 0 (no mutual information) and 1 (perfect correlation).

4.6.1 Viz

This library as the name suggests is used for visualization of the social graph and the identified communities. It can be color coded and polygons can be drawn from the communities using this library. The code for the same is mentioned in Figure 4.8.

Using a color-coded system based on community assignments, this function creates a graph with nodes. Every node is part of an individual community, which is visualized by this function by assigning each community and its nodes a different color.

4.7 ADVANTAGES

Networks like OSNs, biological networks, etc. offer enormous amounts of data about users and their preferences (via profiles), and allow them to publish and share stuff about themselves, their lifestyles, etc., with other network users. The ability for users to communicate with other users who they may connect with is one of the most significant and noteworthy advantages offered by these OSNs. With the help of these user-centered features, a user can establish and maintain social connections, locate and connect with other users who share their interests and preferences, and share, discover, and support user-contributed information and knowledge (Mislove, Marcon, Gummadi, Druschel, and Bhattacharjee 2007). There is an exceptional potential to research, comprehend, and utilize the qualities of OSNs given their extreme popularity, massive membership, and enormous volume of social network data generated. A thorough examination of OSN growth and structure can not only help in designing and assessing existing systems but also improve the design of future OSN-based systems and provide a better understanding of how online social networks affect society. Social network analytics is experiencing an information explosion as a result of the massive amount of data that social networks are producing on a daily basis. This makes it necessary to employ computational methods for effectively analyzing the nature and structure of these intricate networks. In addition to collaborating with sociologists to develop social network analysis techniques for identifying social network features, computer scientists are developing and utilizing data mining technologies to uncover hidden patterns in social network data. As a result, social graphs are utilized to model OSNs because they enable easier analysis utilizing a wide range of topological properties and better visualization.

A social network can be transitioned into a social graph, but it is difficult to analyze and assess patterns with the naked eye. Therefore, powerful algorithms are required for its analysis. Community detection being one of them focuses on identifying strongly connected or highly interacting entities. It helps in evaluation of large and complex networks and provides useful insights.

Social media algorithms can identify and maintain strong connections with people who share interests by utilizing community detection techniques. In machine learning, community detection can be used to identify groups with shared characteristics and extract groupings for a variety of purposes. This method can be applied, for instance, to identify manipulative organizations inside a stock market or social network.

4.8 CHALLENGES

Many other social network analysis tasks are based on the identification of groups, clusters, or communities in a social graph. The goal of community detection is to identify groupings (communities) by analyzing network topologies and structures. It becomes difficult to identify community structures because it depends on a number of variables, such as whether the structure is based on global or local structural properties, whether a node can simultaneously belong to more than one community, whether link weights are taken into account or not, and, last but not least, how the seed nodes are chosen. The following are a few challenges that keep coming up when analyzing communities in social graphs:

Computational Cost: The complicated nature and scope of social graphs make it increasingly challenging to handle the enormous volumes of data. The enormous amount of data on social media sites like X, pertaining to tweets, hashtags, etc. places a heavy computational overhead on community detection algorithms. Considering the time parameter, the social network is dynamic and ever-evolving. To capture this essence is important for a community detection algorithm. The number of resources required to handle large complex computation of algorithms on huge networks is another facet of this challenge.

Community Validation Measures: There are no means for validating the discovered community to determine whether it is accurate or not. When ground-truth data is available, normalized mutual information (NMI) can be used to assess how closely the communities identified by a specific algorithm and the ground-truth data align. Although there are a very few datasets providing such information, the availability of ground-truth data also becomes a problem. Additionally, a lot of quality measures have been researched and developed over the years, but none of them can be used consistently to ratify all community detection methods. It is observed that various algorithms use various measures depending on the situation (Hafez, Hassanien, and Fahmy 2014). As an illustration, assessing disparate groups makes use of NMI, and assessing overlapping communities makes use of overlapping NMI (ONMI). Finding the appropriate assessment metric for a given algorithm is therefore a difficult task.

Interpretation of Results: The detected communities can only be interpreted with the domain knowledge about the network under consideration, which might not be always available. It is not always possible to assess the quality of the identified communities because of the different use cases, i.e., different network distribution might produce different type of communities. The identification of appropriate metrics also becomes troublesome in such cases. In the case of social media, overlapping communities might prove to be beneficial but the presence of high overlaps might lead to unclear results.

Overlapping/Hierarchical Nature of Communities: In real-world networks, interacting with multiple groups is extremely common, therefore many nodes in social graphs typically show affinity for numerous communities. In a social network, a person could belong to multiple interest groups, hence it may be crucial to identify all of these overlaps. Additionally, research on the development of hierarchical communities is useful in projecting the potential growth of the network. The majority of community identification methods employed in literature, however, frequently reveal mutually exclusive community structures. Therefore, it is especially desirable to develop techniques for finding overlapping and hierarchical community structures.

Handling of Multimodal Data: Managing the multiple attributes of an actor in an OSN (e.g., name, hashtags, user ID, etc.) or their relationships (represented by friendship, number of common interest groups, etc.) require multimodal data handling. The network structure and other text or image attributes need to be stored and processed for finding similarity or establishing connections between users. For managing such type of data, a more complex structure is required that can be accomplished using numerous layers in an algorithm or using complex models.

Seed Node Identification: The selection of the starting or seed node for the detection process is still an unresolved question. This is significant since the quality of the community to be identified depends on the identification of the seed node. For instance, the detection process may become trapped in the local maxima if the seed node is not chosen wisely. The process also might become tedious for dynamic networks as the temporal variability affects the quality of the detected communities.

4.9 CONCLUSION

Effective tools are required to provide social analysts with simple exploratory insights or large-scale, significant social patterns and trends for major organizations since social network analysis is a diverse topic. The integration of all community research techniques into a single framework is a difficult but highly desirable task. Because most network analysis tasks in the literature have only been handled in isolation, there is currently a lot of space for improvement when it comes to the collective analysis of social network data. The term "community" which is typically defined in terms of the environment being researched is one of many keywords used in the subject of SNA that lacks a common meaning. Similar to this, the notions of influential nodes (or seed nodes) and information flow are handled differently in various circumstances.

One of the major issues with various social network analysis tasks is determining the suitable assessment parameters for the examination of a given technique. The lack of significant, annotated real-world social networks with knowledge about communities with ground truth is primarily accountable for this. For particular SNA tasks, a variety of ways have been proposed, and it has been shown that the majority of them work well. As a result, selecting the optimal approach for social network analysis can be difficult for a user. For instance, there are numerous methods for community detection, but none have been proven to be more efficient than the others. Since community detection methods behave differently on distinct contexts in a social network, it is necessary to contextually evaluate different approaches on real-world social network datasets. The majority of methods are also rarely put to use; for instance, most scholars in the area of community analysis do not address ways to use communities that have been identified through community detection methods. Another issue in the community detection field is managing massive networks. They require powerful processors and good data structures for quick data traversal. Good hardware can therefore speed up the delivery of reliable data and help in the development of a community detecting technique. Community detection also has challenges including determining the seed nodes. Finding core/seed nodes is an essential component of community detection as this can form the basis for detection of high-quality communities. This is a crucial stage that demands meticulous attention. Overall, the discipline of community detection is extremely expansive and multifaceted. Therefore, it must be examined from different perspectives based on the current context.

REFERENCES

A. Arenas, L. Danon, A. Dz-Guilera, P.M. Gleiser, and R. Guimer. Community analysis in social networks. *The European Physical Journal B*, 38:373–380, March 2004.

A. E. Krause, K. A. Frank, D. M. Mason, R. E. Ulanowicz, and W. W. Taylor. Compartments revealed in food-web structure. *Nature*, 282–285, November 2003.

A. Mislove, M. Marcon, K. P. Gummadi, P. Druschel, and B. Bhattacharjee. Measurement and analysis of online social networks. In *Proceedings of the 7th ACM SIGCOMM Conference on Internet Measurement*, 29–42, October 2007.

Ahmed Ibrahem Hafez, Aboul Ella Hassanien, and Aly A. Fahmy. Testing community detection algorithms: A closer look at datasets. *Social Networking: Mining, Visualization, and Security* (2014): 85–99.

Ahmed Ibrahem Hafez, Neveen I Ghali, Aboul Ella Hassanien, and Aly A Fahmy. Genetic algorithms for community detection in social networks. In *Proceedings of 12th International Conference on Intelligent Systems Design and Applications (ISDA)*, 460–465. IEEE, 2012.

Alexandre Hollocou, Thomas Bonald, and Marc Lelarge. Multiple local community detection. *ACM SIGMETRICS Performance Evaluation Review*, 45:76–83, March 2018.

Andrea Lancichinetti and Santo Fortunato. Community detection algorithms: A comparative analysis. *Physical Review E*, 80(5):056117-1–056117-11, November 2009.

Aryya Gangopadhyay and Song Chen. Health care fraud detection with community detection algorithms. In *IEEE International Conference on Smart Computing (SMARTCOMP)*, 1–5, May 2016.

Bal´azs Adamcsek, Gergely Palla, Ill´es J. Farkas, Imre Der´enyi, and Tam´as Vicsek. CFinder: Locating cliques and overlapping modules in biological networks. *Bioinformatics*, 22(8):1021–1023, April 2006. ISSN 1367-4803.

Benjamin Auffarth. Spectral graph clustering. *Universitat de Barcelona, course report for Technicas Avanzadas de Aprendizaj, at Universitat Politecnica de Catalunya*, 1–12, 2007.

Bin Cao, Nathan Nan Liu, and Qiang Yang. Transfer learning for collective link prediction in multiple heterogenous domains. In *Proceedings of the 27th International Conference on International Conference on Machine Learning, Haifa, Israel*, 159–166, November 2010. ISBN 9781605589077.

Carlos Andr´e Reis Pinheiro. Community detection to identify fraud events in telecommunications networks. *SAS SUGI Proceedings: Customer Intelligence*, 2012.

Chengwei Lei and Jianhua Ruan. A novel link prediction algorithm for reconstructing protein– protein interaction networks by topological similarity. *Bioinformatics*, 29(3):355–364, 2013.

Chuntao Jiang, Frans Coenen, and Michele Zito. A survey of frequent subgraph mining algorithms. *The Knowledge Engineering Review*, 28(1):75–105, 2013.

Daniel M. Dunlavy, Tamara G. Kolda, and Evrim Acar. Temporal link prediction using matrix and tensor factorizations. *ACM Transactions on Knowledge and Discovery of Data*, 5(2):1–27, February 2011. ISSN 1556-4681.

David Liben-Nowell and Jon Kleinberg. The link prediction problem for social networks. In Proceedings of the 12th International Conference on Information and Knowledge Management, New Orleans, LA, USA, 556–559, November 2003.

Derek G. Corneil and Calvin C. Gotlieb. An efficient algorithm for graph isomorphism. *Journal of the ACM*, 17(1):51–64, 1970.

Diane J. Cook and Lawrence B. Holder. *Mining Graph Data*. John Wiley and Sons, 2006.

Duncan J. Watts and Steven H. Strogatz. Collective dynamics of 'small-world' networks. *Nature*, 393(6684):440–442, July 1998.

Emilio Ferrara. Community structure discovery in facebook. *International Journal of Social Network Mining*, 1:67–90, January 2012.

Fabio Gasparetti, Giuseppe Sansonetti, and Alessandro Micarelli. Community detection in social recommender systems: A survey. *Applied Intelligence*, 51(6):3975–3995, 2021.

Francesco Ricci, Lior Rokach, and Bracha Shapira. Introduction to recommender systems handbook. In *Recommender Systems Handbook*, 1–35. Springer, 2011.

G. W. Flake, S. Lawrence, C. L. Giles, and F. M. Coetzee. Self-organization and identification of web communities. *Computer*, 35(3):66–71, March 2002.

Ghazaleh Beigi, Mahdi Jalili, Hamidreza Alvari, and Gita Sukthankar. Leveraging community detection for accurate trust prediction. In *Proceedings of ASE Big-data/socialcom/cybersecurity Conference, Stanford University*, 1–8, June 2014.

Giulio Rossetti, Letizia Milli, and Remy Cazabet. Cdlib: a python library to extract, compare and evaluate communities from complex networks. *Applied Network Science*, 4, July 2019. Xinyu Que, Fabio Checconi, Fabrizio Petrini, and John A. Gunnels. Scalable community detection with the louvain algorithm. In *2015 IEEE International Parallel and Distributed Processing Symposium*, pages 28–37, 2015.

Giulio Rossetti. Exorcising the demon: Angel, efficient node-centric community discovery. In *Proceedings of International Conference on Complex Networks and Their Applications VIII, Lisbon, Portugal*, 152–163, November 2019.

Haijun Zhou. Distance, dissimilarity index, and network community structure. *Physical Review E*, 67(6):061901–1–061901–8, 2003.

Hassan Sayyadi, Matthew Hurst, and Alexey Maykov. Event detection and tracking in social streams. In *Proceedings of the International AAAI Conference on Web and Social Media*, 3:311–314, January 2009.

Imelda Atastina, Benhard Sitohang, G.A. Putri Saptawati, and Veronica S. Moertini. A review of big graph mining research. In *Proceedings of IOP Conference Series: Materials Science and Engineering*, 180:012065–1–012065–9, 2017.

J MacQueen. Classification and analysis of multivariate observations. In *Proceedings of the 5th Berkeley Symposium on Mathematical Statistics and Probability*, 281–297, January 1967.

J¨org Reichardt and Stefan Bornholdt. Detecting fuzzy community structures in complex networks with a potts model. *Physical Review Letters*, 93(21):218701–1–218701–4, 2004.

J¨org Reichardt and Stefan Bornholdt. Statistical mechanics of community detection. *Physical Review E*, 74(1):016110–1–016110–14, 2006.

Jaewon Yang and Jure Leskovec. Overlapping community detection at scale: A nonnegative matrix factorization approach. In *Proceedings of the 6th ACM International Conference on Web Search and Data Mining (WSDM), Rome, Italy*, 587–596, February 2013. ISBN 9781450318693.

Jayati Gulati and Muhammad Abulaish. A novel snowball-chain approach for detecting community structures in social graphs. In *2019 IEEE Symposium Series on Computational Intelligence (SSCI)*, 2462–2469. IEEE, 2019.

Jayati Gulati and Muhammad Abulaish. SbChain+: An enhanced snowball-chain approach for detecting communities in social graphs. *International Journal of Advanced Computer Science and Applications*, 14(6), 2023.

Jayati Gulati, Muhammad Abulaish, and Sajid Yousuf Bhat. OvSbChain: An enhanced snow- ball chain approach for detecting overlapping communities in social graphs. *International Journal of Advanced Computer Science and Applications*, 13(5), 2022.

Jiaxu Liu and Yingxia Shao, and Sen Su. "Multiple local community detection via high-quality seed identification." In *Web and Big Data: 4th International Joint Conference, APWeb-WAIM 2020, Tianjin, China, September 18–20, 2020, Proceedings, Part I 4*, 37–52. Springer International Publishing, 2020.

Jierui Xie, Boleslaw K. Szymanski, and Xiaoming Liu. SLPA: Uncovering overlapping communities in social networks via a speaker-listener interaction dynamic process. In *Proceedings of the 11th IEEE International Conference on Data Mining (ICDM) Workshops, Vancouver, Canada*, pages 344–349, September 2011.

Joel J Bechtel, William A Kelley, Teresa A Coons, M Gerry Klein, Daniel D Slagel, and Thomas L Petty. Lung cancer detection in patients with airflow obstruction identified in a primary care outpatient practice. *Chest*, 127(4):1140–1145, 2005.

Jure Leskovec and Eric Horvitz. Planetary-scale views on a large instant-messaging network. In *Proceedings of the 17th International Conference on World Wide Web, Beijing, China*, pages 915–924, 2008. ISBN 9781605580852.

Kwan Hui Lim and Amitava Datta. Finding Twitter communities with common interests using following links of celebrities. In *Proceedings of the 3rd International Workshop on Modeling Social Media*, 25–32, 2012.

Lars Backstrom, Dan Huttenlocher, Jon Kleinberg, and Xiangyang Lan. Group formation in large social networks: Membership, growth, and evolution. In *Proceedings of the ACM SIGKDD International Conference on Knowledge Discovery and Data Mining, Philadelphia, PA, USA*, 44–54, August 2006.

Lei Tang and Huan Liu. *Graph Mining Applications to Social Network Analysis*, 487–513. Springer, 2010.

Liu Xin, Haihong E, Junde Song, Meina Song, and Junjie Tong. Book recommendation based on community detection. In *Joint International Conference on Pervasive Computing and the Networked World, Vina del Mar, Chile*, 364–373, 2014.

M. E. J. Newman. Modularity and community structure in networks. *Proceedings of the National Academy of Sciences (PNAS)*, 103(23):8577–8582, April 2006.

M. Girvan and M. E. J. Newman. Community structure in social and biological networks. *Proceedings of the National Academy of Sciences (PNAS)*, 99(12):7821–7826, January 2002.

Mahdi Jalili, Yasin Orouskhani, Milad Asgari, Nazanin Alipourfard, and Matjaˇz Perc. Link prediction in multiplex online social networks. *Royal Society Open Science*, 4(2):160863–1–160863–11, 2017.

Mark E. J. Newman. The structure and function of complex networks. *Society for Industrial and Applied Mathematics (SIAM) Review*, 45(2):167–256, March 2003.

Mark EJ Newman and Michelle Girvan. Finding and evaluating community structure in networks. *Physical Review E*, 69(2):026113–1–026113–15, March 2004.

Martin Ester, Hans-Peter Kriegel, J¨org Sander, and Xiaowei Xu. A density-based algorithm for discovering clusters in large spatial databases with noise. In *Proceedings of the Second International Conference on Knowledge Discovery and Data Mining, Portland, Oregon*, 226–231, August 1996.

Martin Rosvall and Carl T. Bergstrom. Maps of random walks on complex networks reveal community structure. *Proceedings of the National Academy of Sciences (PNAS)*, 105(4):1118–1123, February 2008.

Mert Ozer, Nyunsu Kim, and Hasan Davulcu. Community detection in political Twitter networks using nonnegative matrix factorization methods. In *Proceedings of IEEE/ACM International Conference on Advances in Social Networks Analysis and Mining (ASONAM)*, 81–88, 2016.

Michel Planti´e and Michel Crampes. *Survey on Social Community Detection*, 65–85, Springer, 2013.

Michele Coscia, Giulio Rossetti, Fosca Giannotti, and Dino Pedreschi. DEMON: A local-first discovery method for overlapping communities. In *Proceedings of the 18th ACM SIGKDD International Conference on Knowledge Discovery and Data Mining, Beijing, China*, 615–623, August 2012. ISBN 9781450314626.

Muhammad Aqib Javed, Muhammad Shahzad Younis, Siddique Latif, Junaid Qadir, and Adeel Baig. Community detection in networks: A multidisciplinary review. *Journal of Network and Computer Applications*, 108:87–111, 2018.

Munmun Choudhury, Yu-Ru Lin, Hari Sundaram, K. Selcuk Candan, Lexing Xie, and Aisling Kelliher. How does the data sampling strategy impact the discovery of information diffusion in social media? In *Proceedings of the 4th International AAAI Conference on Weblogs and Social Media (ICWSM)*, 4:34–41, January 2010.

Nicholas A. Diakopoulos and David A. Shamma. Characterizing debate performance via ag- gregated Twitter sentiment. In *Proceedings of the SIGCHI Conference on Human Factors in Computing Systems, Atlanta, Georgia, USA*, 1195–1198. ACM, April 2010.

Ofer Zeitouni. Random walks in random environments. *Journal of Physics A: Mathematical and General*, 39(40):R433–R464, 2006.

P. Krishna Reddy, Masaru Kitsuregawa, P. Sreekanth, and S. Srinivasa Rao. A graph based approach to extract a neighborhood customer community for collaborative filtering. In *Proceedings of Databases in Networked Information Systems*, 188–200, 2002.

Pascal Pons and Matthieu Latapy. Computing communities in large networks using random walks. In *Computer and Information Sciences - ISCIS 2005*, 284–293, Berlin, Heidelberg, 2005. Springer Berlin Heidelberg.

Pengsheng Ji and Jiashun Jin. Coauthorship and citation networks for statisticians. *The Annals of Applied Statistics*, 10(4):1779–1812, 2016.

Pierre-Alain Mo¨ellic, Jean-Emmanuel Haugeard, and Guillaume Pitel. Image clustering based on a shared nearest neighbors approach for tagged collections. In *Proceedings of the Inter-national Conference on Content-Based Image and Video Retrieval, Niagara Falls, Canada*, 269–278, 2008.

Qisen Wang, Wenzhong Li, Xiao Zhang, and Sanglu Lu. Academic paper recommendation based on community detection in citation-collaboration networks. In *Proceeding of 18th Asia Pacific Web Conference, Web Technologies and Applications, Suzhou, China*, 124–136, 2016.

Ruth Dunn, Frank Dudbridge, and Christopher Sanderson. The use of edge-betweenness clustering to investigate biological function in protein interaction networks. *BMC Bioinformatics*, 6:39–1–39–14, February 2005.

S. Milgram. The small world problem. *Psychology Today*, 2(1):60–67, 1967.

Sajid Yousuf Bhat and Muhammad Abulaish. Community-based features for identifying spammers in online social networks. In *Proceedings of International Conference on Advances in Social Networks Analysis and Mining (ASONAM), Niagara Falls, ON, Canada*, 100–107, August 2013.

Sajid Yousuf Bhat and Muhammad Abulaish. HOCTracker: Tracking the evolution of hierarchical and overlapping communities in dynamic social networks. *IEEE Transactions on Knowledge and Data Engineering*, 27(4):1019–1031, April 2015.

Santo Fortunato and Claudio Castellano. *Community Structure in Graphs*, 490–512.

Shen Lin and Brian W. Kernighan. An effective heuristic algorithm for the traveling-salesman problem. *Operations Research*, 21(2):498–516, 1973.

Simon Lehnerer. Community detection in complex networks using genetic algorithms. *SKILL- Studierendenkonferenz Informatik*, 35–46, 2018.

Simon Pool, Francesco Bonchi, and Matthijs Van Leeuwen. Description-driven community detection. *ACM Transactions on Intelligent Systems and Technology (TIST)*, 5(2):1–28, 2014.

Sitaram Asur, Srinivasan Parthasarathy, and Duygu Ucar. An event-based framework for characterizing the evolutionary behavior of interaction graphs. *ACM Transactions on Knowledge Discovery from Data (TKDD)*, 3(4):1–36, December 2009. Springer New York, 2012.

Stanley Wasserman and Katherine Faust. *Social Network Analysis: Methods and Applications. Structural Analysis in the Social Sciences.* Cambridge University Press, 1994.

Steve Gregory. An algorithm to find overlapping community structure in networks. In *Proceedings of Knowledge Discovery in Databases (PKDD), Berlin, Heidelberg*, 91–102, September 2007.

Steve Gregory. Finding overlapping communities in networks by label propagation. *New Journal of Physics*, 12(10):103018–103043, October 2010.

Symeon Papadopoulos, Christos Zigkolis, Giorgos Tolias, Yannis Kalantidis, Phivos Mylonas, Yiannis Kompatsiaris, and Athena Vakali. Image clustering through community detection on hybrid image similarity graphs. In *Proceedings of IEEE International Conference on Image Processing, Hong Kong, China*, 2353–2356, 2010.

Thang Nguyen Bui and Byung Ro Moon. Genetic algorithm and graph partitioning. *IEEE Transactions on Computers*, 45(7):841–855, 1996.

Todd V. Waskiewicz. Friend of a friend influence in terrorist social networks. In *Proceedings on the International Conference on Artificial Intelligence (ICAI)*, 1–5, 2012.

Traag V., Waltman L., and Nees Jan van Eck. From louvain to leiden: guaranteeing well- connected communities. *Scientific Reports*, 9:5233, 2019.

Usha Nandini Raghavan, R´eka Albert, and Soundar Kumara. Near linear time algorithm to detect community structures in large-scale networks. *Physical Review E*, 76(3):036106–(1–11), October 2007. ISSN 1550-2376.

Victor Spirin and Leonid A. Mirny. Protein complexes and functional modules in molecular networks. *Proceedings of the National Academy of Sciences*, 100(21):12123–12128, September 2003.

Vincent D. Blondel, Jean Loup Guillaume, Renaud Lambiotte, and Etienne Lefebvre. Fast unfolding of communities in large networks. *Journal of Statistical Mechanics: Theory and Experiment*, 2008(10):P10008–1–P10008–12, January 2008.

Wei Li, Ce Huang, Miao Wang, and Xi Chen. Stepping community detection algorithm based on label propagation and similarity. *Physica A: Statistical Mechanics and its Applications*, 472:145–155, April 2017.

Wenjie Fu, Le Song, and Eric P Xing. Dynamic mixed membership blockmodel for evolving networks. In *Proceedings of the 26th Annual International Conference on Machine Learning*, 329–336, June 2009.

Xiao-Ying Wang and Jon M Garibaldi. A comparison of fuzzy and non-fuzzy clustering techniques in cancer diagnosis. In *Proceedings of the 2nd International Conference in Computational Intelligence in Medicine and Healthcare, BIOPATTERN Conference, Costa da Caparica, Lisbon, Portugal*, 28, 2005.

5 Graph Clustering Techniques for Community Detection in Social Networks

Fatemeh Daneshfar, Mona Dolati, and Sadegh Sulaimany

5.1 INTRODUCTION

Social networks [1] are not merely collections of isolated users; they represent intricate ecosystems where individuals interact, collaborate, and share information. These interactions can be depicted as a graph, where users are depicted as nodes and their relationships are depicted as edges. Analyzing the structure of this graph allows us to understand the underlying dynamics of the network. One crucial aspect of this analysis is uncovering communities [2]—groups of users who exhibit a significantly higher density of connections within their group compared to connections with users outside.

The concept of community detection is central to many applications and disciplines. Communities within social networks often correspond to real-world groups such as circles of friends, professional clusters, or groups with shared interests. These communities are more than just random groupings; they can reflect shared interests, professional affiliations, or even ideological stances. Understanding the composition and structure of these communities offers a wealth of benefits. For instance, it can help us predict user behavior. By identifying communities with similar interests, we can gain insights into how users might interact with information or products. This knowledge can be leveraged by social media platforms to personalize user feeds and recommendations [3].

Additionally, communities can act as natural target audiences for specific advertising campaigns. Businesses can tailor their messaging and product offerings to resonate with the interests and needs of specific communities, thus enhancing the effectiveness of their marketing strategies. Furthermore, community detection can aid in detecting anomalies within the network. Identifying sudden shifts in community structure or activity can help detect potential issues such as the spread of misinformation or the emergence of malicious actors [4]. By monitoring community

DOI: 10.1201/9781003515890-7

dynamics, network administrators can proactively address such anomalies, safeguarding the integrity and security of the network.

Given the vast potential of social network community detection [5], this chapter investigates the key techniques used to uncover these hidden structures. We focus on both traditional graph clustering methods and the recent advancements in graph embedding techniques. Traditional graph clustering methods, such as hierarchical clustering, partitioning methods, and spectral clustering, have been widely used to detect communities by grouping nodes based on graph topology. These methods rely on the structural properties of the graph and often require predefined parameters or criteria to function effectively.

On the other hand, graph embedding techniques represent a modern approach that transforms high-dimensional graph data into low-dimensional vectors while preserving the graph's structural properties. Techniques such as DeepWalk, node2vec, and graph neural networks (GNNs) enable the learning of continuous node representations that can capture complex patterns and community memberships. These embeddings can then be used with clustering algorithms to identify communities more efficiently [6]. However, both traditional clustering methods and modern embedding techniques have their own strengths and limitations. Traditional methods are often straightforward and interpretable but may struggle with scalability and the detection of overlapping communities. Embedding techniques, while powerful and scalable, can be complex and require substantial computational resources.

In this chapter, we introduce a unified framework that integrates the advantages of both traditional clustering and embedding techniques. By integrating these approaches, we aim to provide a more comprehensive and robust solution for detecting communities within social networks. This unified perspective not only enhances the accuracy and efficiency of community detection but also offers deeper insights into the underlying structures of social networks. By exploring and combining these methodologies, we seek to advance the domain of social network research and provide valuable tools for researchers and practitioners. The subsequent sections of this chapter will delve into the detailed review of traditional and embedding techniques, the development of the unified framework, and the evaluation of its performance on various social network datasets.

5.2 LITERATURE REVIEW

Over the past decades, the field of community detection on social networks has been dynamic and continuously progressing, with a variety of methodologies and techniques being devised. This section offers a summary of the key developments and contributions in the field, particularly emphasizing conventional graph clustering approaches and contemporary graph embedding strategies.

5.2.1 Traditional Graph Clustering Methods

Traditional graph clustering methods have been instrumental in the analysis and understanding of complex networks. These methods leverage the structural properties of graphs to identify clusters or communities within the network. Fundamental techniques encompass graph partitioning, hierarchical clustering, spectral clustering, and methods based on modularity. Each of these methods offers distinct advantages and has been extensively studied and applied in various domains, from social network analysis to bioinformatics.

5.2.1.1 Graph Partitioning

The goal of graph partitioning techniques is to separate a graph into non-overlapping subsets, minimizing the interconnecting edges between these subsets. One traditional method is the Kernighan-Lin algorithm, which reduces cut size by repeatedly exchanging nodes between different partitions [7]. Another prominent method is the multilevel graph partitioning scheme, which involves coarsening the graph, partitioning it, and then refining the partition [8]. These methods are particularly useful for load balancing in parallel computing and have been applied in VLSI design and data mining.

5.2.1.2 Hierarchical Clustering

Hierarchical clustering techniques construct a cluster hierarchy using either agglomerative (bottom-up) or divisive (top-down) strategies. In the agglomerative approach, clusters are formed by initially treating each node as a separate cluster and then successively merging the most similar clusters [9]. Conversely, the divisive approach starts with the entire graph as a single cluster and recursively splits it. The Girvan-Newman algorithm is a notable example that uses edge betweenness to iteratively remove edges and detect community structures [10]. Hierarchical clustering is advantageous for its ability to reveal multi-level community structures.

5.2.1.3 Spectral Clustering

Spectral clustering leverages the eigenvalues and eigenvectors of the graph's Laplacian matrix for dimensionality reduction before applying clustering algorithms. This method is based on the intuition that the eigenvectors of the Laplacian provide a good embedding of the nodes into a lower-dimensional space where clustering is easier [11]. One of the pioneering works in this domain is by Shi and Malik, who introduced the normalized cut criterion for graph partitioning, which balances the cut size and the volume of the partitions [12]. Spectral clustering is known for its robustness and ability to handle complex structures in data.

5.2.1.4 Modularity-Based Methods

Modularity-based techniques enhance the modularity measure, which assesses how well a network is divided into modules (or communities) [13, 14]. The modularity score compares the density of edges inside communities with the expected density if edges were distributed randomly. High modularity values indicate a strong community structure. The Louvain method is a widely used algorithm that iteratively optimizes modularity through a two-phase process of modularity optimization and community aggregation [15]. This method is highly scalable and effective for large networks. Another modularity-based approach is the label propagation algorithm

(LPA), where nodes iteratively update their labels to match the majority of their neighbors' labels, leading to the emergence of communities [16].

These traditional methods provide a strong foundation for community detection in networks, each offering unique benefits and applicable in different scenarios depending on the nature of the dataset and the specific requirements of the analysis.

5.2.2 Advanced Graph Clustering Methods

Recent advancements in graph clustering have introduced a variety of sophisticated techniques that leverage deeper insights into the structural and statistical properties of graphs. These advanced methods often outperform traditional approaches in terms of both accuracy and scalability, making them suitable for complex and large-scale network datasets.

5.2.2.1 Random Walk-Based Methods

Random walk-based methods utilize random walks to explore the graph and identify clusters by measuring the likelihood of nodes being visited together. One prominent technique is the use of the Personalized PageRank algorithm, which assesses the probability of reaching a node starting from a personalized set of nodes. This approach has been adapted for community detection, such as in the work by Page et al. [17].

Another notable method is Walktrap, proposed by Pons and Latapy [18], which uses short random walks to compute node similarities. These similarities are then used to merge nodes into communities. Random walk-based methods are particularly effective in capturing the local and global structure of the graph, making them robust for various types of networks.

5.2.2.2 Information-Theoretic Approaches

Information-theoretic approaches to graph clustering are based on the principle of optimizing an information criterion, such as mutual information or entropy, to identify the most informative partition of the graph. These methods often aim to minimize the description length of the graph, which corresponds to finding a compact representation of its community structure.

A significant contribution in this area is the Infomap algorithm developed by Rosvall and Bergstrom [19]. Infomap leverages the map equation to reduce the anticipated description length of a random walker's traversal on the graph, thereby accurately identifying community structure. Information-theoretic methods are powerful in uncovering meaningful and interpretable communities, particularly in networks with complex connectivity patterns.

5.2.2.3 Matrix Factorization Methods

Matrix factorization methods decompose the adjacency matrix of the graph into lower-dimensional matrices, which reveal the underlying structure and communities. These methods are grounded in linear algebra and have been widely applied in various domains, including recommendation systems and social network analysis.

A widely recognized method is non-negative matrix factorization (NMF), which breaks down the adjacency matrix into non-negative components, capturing latent features that correspond to community memberships. Lee and Seung [20] introduced NMF, and it has since been adapted for graph clustering by methods such as Big Clam [21], which detects overlapping communities by modeling the likelihood of edges between nodes based on their community memberships.

Another approach is the spectral clustering method, which involves the eigen decomposition of the graph Laplacian matrix. The resulting eigenvectors are used to perform dimensionality reduction before applying clustering algorithms like k-means. Shi and Malik [12] applied this technique for image segmentation and community detection, showing its effectiveness in identifying clusters in high-dimensional data.

These advanced graph clustering methods represent the cutting edge in community detection, providing robust tools for analyzing complex networks. By leveraging random walks, information theory, and matrix factorization, researchers can uncover deeper insights into the structure and dynamics of large-scale graphs.

5.2.2.4 Graph Embedding-Based Techniques

Graph embedding techniques represent a more recent advancement in community detection, focusing on learning continuous vector representations of nodes while preserving the graph's structural properties. DeepWalk, introduced by Perozzi et al. [22], generates random walks on the graph and applies the Skip-gram model from natural language processing to learn node embeddings. This method effectively captures the local structure of the graph. Node2vec, developed by Grover and Leskovec [23], extends DeepWalk by introducing biased random walks, allowing for a flexible tradeoff between capturing local and global network structures. This approach has shown improved performance in various community detection tasks. Convolutional graph networks (GCNs), introduced by Kipf and Welling [24], generalize convolutional neural networks to graph-structured data. GCNs execute convolutional operations directly on graph structures, enabling the learning of node embeddings that consider both node features and graph topology. Graph autoencoders, such as variational graph autoencoders (VGAE) proposed by Kipf and Welling [25], learn embeddings by reconstructing the graph structure from compressed representations. This approach effectively captures complex network patterns and community structures. Attention mechanisms, introduced by Velickovic et al. [26], leverage graph attention networks (GATs) to give varying levels of significance to nodes within a neighborhood during the calculation of node embeddings. This method improves the flexibility and expressiveness of node representations.

Several studies have conducted comparative analyses of traditional clustering methods and graph embedding techniques. Fortunato [2] provided a comprehensive review of community detection algorithms, highlighting their strengths and limitations. More recent works, such as Yang et al. [27], compared traditional methods with embedding techniques, demonstrating the superior performance of embeddings in capturing complex network structures. Hybrid approaches that combine clustering and embedding techniques have also been explored. Zhang et al. [28] proposed a framework that integrates GCNs with modularity-based clustering, showing enhanced community detection performance. Such hybrid models aim to utilize the advantages of both conventional and contemporary methods, delivering more robust and accurate solutions.

5.2.3 Other Views to Graph Clustering

Other views to graph clustering extends beyond traditional methods to address specific challenges or application contexts, leading to the development of overlapping and dynamic methods.

5.2.3.1 Overlapping Methods

Overlapping methods in graph clustering recognize that nodes can belong to multiple communities simultaneously. These approaches aim to capture the inherent complexity of real-world networks where nodes often participate in several overlapping communities. Techniques like clique percolation method (CPM) [29] and Link Communities [30] detect overlapping communities by allowing nodes to belong to more than one cluster, providing a nuanced view of network structure.

5.2.3.2 Dynamic Methods

Dynamic methods in graph clustering address networks that evolve over time, where community structures can change rapidly. These methods adapt traditional clustering techniques to handle temporal aspects of networks, capturing how communities form, merge, or dissolve over different time intervals. Dynamic algorithms such as Evolutionary Clustering [31–33] and Streaming Community Detection [34] are designed to track community evolution, ensuring clustering remains relevant as networks grow or shrink.

These advancements in overlapping and dynamic methods cater to the complexities of modern networks, offering insights into evolving and multifaceted community structures.

5.2.4 Evaluation Metrics

To evaluate the performance of community detection algorithms, various standard metrics are used, as described in Table 5.1.

These metrics provide a comprehensive view of each algorithm's performance, considering the quality of the identified communities as well as the computational efficiency.

5.3 METHODOLOGY

This section details the methodology employed to explore and evaluate various graph clustering and embedding techniques for community detection in social networks. The methodology consists of multiple stages, including dataset selection, implementation of algorithms, evaluation metrics, and comparative analysis.

TABLE 5.1
Evaluation Metrics for Community Detection Algorithms

Metric	Description
Modularity [35]	Evaluates the effectiveness of network division into communities by comparing the density of links within communities to the links between them.
Normalized Mutual Information (NMI) [36]	Quantifies the agreement between the detected communities and the ground truth, evaluating how well the community detection matches the known structure.
Conductance [37]	Evaluates the quality of the community structure based on the number of edges crossing the community boundaries, with lower conductance indicating better community separation.
Adjusted Rand Index (ARI) [38]	Compares the similarity between two data clustering, adjusting for the chance grouping of elements, and provides a measure of the accuracy of the clustering method.

5.3.1 Datasets

To ensure a comprehensive evaluation of the techniques, we selected several benchmark datasets commonly used in community detection research. These datasets vary in size, density, and community structure, providing a robust basis for evaluating the performance of different community detection methods.

These datasets provide a diverse set of challenges for community detection algorithms, allowing for a thorough evaluation of their performance across different types of social networks.

5.3.2 Algorithm Implementation

We implemented a variety of traditional graph clustering algorithms and graph embedding techniques to thoroughly investigate their effectiveness in community detection.

5.3.2.1 Traditional Graph Clustering Algorithms

For traditional clustering, we included several key algorithms. Hierarchical clustering constructs a hierarchy of clusters using either a bottom-up (agglomerative) or top-down (divisive) method. It doesn't require the number of clusters to be specified in advance, making it versatile for different datasets [43]. Partitioning methods include the k-means algorithm [44], which partitions the nodes into k clusters by minimizing the within-cluster variance, and the Kernighan-Lin algorithm [7], which partitions graphs by iteratively swapping node pairs to reduce the edge cut between clusters. Spectral clustering leverages the eigenvalues of the graph Laplacian matrix for dimensionality reduction, followed by the application of k-means or another clustering algorithm [12]. This technique is effective for detecting non-convex clusters.

TABLE 5.2
Summary of Benchmark Datasets Used for Community Detection

Dataset	Description	Nodes	Edges
Karate Club [39]	A social network representing the friendships among 34 members of a karate club.	34	78
Facebook [40]	A dataset containing friendship relations from a subset of Facebook users.	4,039	88,234
Cora [41]	A citation network where nodes represent chapters and edges represent citations between them.	2,708	5,429
X [42]	A dataset of X users and their follower relationships.	81,306	1,342,296

Modularity-based methods, such as the Louvain method [15], optimize modularity, a measure of the density of edges within communities compared to edges between communities. This method is known for its efficiency and scalability. Finally, Label propagation, a near-linear time algorithm [16], assigns labels to nodes and propagates them through the network, where nodes adopt the majority label of their neighbors, resulting in the formation of communities.

5.3.2.2 Graph Embedding Techniques

For graph embedding techniques, we implemented several methods. DeepWalk learns node embeddings through truncated random walks and the Skip-gram model, capturing the structural properties of the graph by treating walks as sentences [22]. Node2Vec, an extension of DeepWalk, introduces a flexible neighborhood sampling strategy that combines breadth-first and depth-first search to create biased random walks, allowing for better control over the embedding quality [23]. Graph convolutional networks (GCNs) perform semi-supervised learning on graph-structured data by aggregating feature information from a node's local neighborhood, making them effective for tasks requiring both local and global information [24]. Variational graph autoencoders (VGAEs) learn node embeddings by reconstructing the graph structure, combining variational inference with graph convolutional networks to capture complex dependencies [25]. Graph attention networks (GATs) use attention mechanisms to assign different importance weights to nodes in a neighborhood, improving the model's ability to focus on relevant nodes and edges, thus enhancing the quality of the embeddings [26]. Each algorithm was implemented using standard libraries and frameworks, ensuring consistency and reproducibility in the results. For traditional graph clustering algorithms, we utilized the NetworkX and Scikit-learn libraries, while for graph embedding techniques, we leveraged the PyTorch Geometric library, which provides a comprehensive set of tools for implementing and testing graph neural networks.

5.3.3 Proposed Unified Framework

Based on the insights gained from the comparative analysis, we propose a unified framework that combines the strengths of both traditional graph clustering and modern graph embedding techniques. This framework aims to leverage the complementary nature of these approaches for more robust and accurate community detection.

The first step involves using graph embedding techniques to generate low-dimensional representations of the nodes in the network. These embeddings capture the structural properties and latent features of the graph, providing a rich representation of the nodes. The next step applies traditional clustering algorithms to the node embeddings. By clustering the low-dimensional representations, we can identify groups of nodes that exhibit similar structural and feature-based characteristics. This step benefits from the reduced dimensionality, which simplifies the clustering process and improves computational efficiency.

To enhance the quality of the detected communities, we introduce an iterative refinement process. This involves updating the embeddings and adjusting the clustering iteratively to fine-tune the community structure. The refinement process includes:

- Embedding Update: Using the clustering results to refine the embeddings. For instance, GCNs can be retrained using the updated cluster assignments, allowing the embeddings to adapt to the refined community structure.
- Clustering Adjustment: Reapplying the clustering algorithm to the updated embeddings. This step iteratively improves the alignment between the embeddings and the community structure, leading to more accurate and meaningful communities.
- Incorporating Additional Information: Integrating node attributes and edge weights into the embedding and clustering process. This helps capture more nuanced relationships within the network, further refining the community detection results.
- Multi-Scale Analysis: Performing community detection at multiple scales to identify both macro- and micro-level communities. This involves varying the resolution of the clustering algorithm and combining the results to achieve a hierarchical understanding of the community structure.

After each iteration, we evaluated the quality of the detected communities using the standard metrics (see Figure 5.1). If the results meet the desired criteria, the process can be terminated. Otherwise, the iteration continues, further refining the embeddings and clustering until the optimal community structure is achieved.

Figure 5.1 illustrates the overall workflow of our research. This section outlines the methodology employed for community detection in social networks using a GCN-RNN with an attention mechanism. The following subsections detail the architecture, training procedure, and implementation specifics.

The pseudo-code illustrated in Algorithm 5.1 outlines the proposed unified framework for community detection.

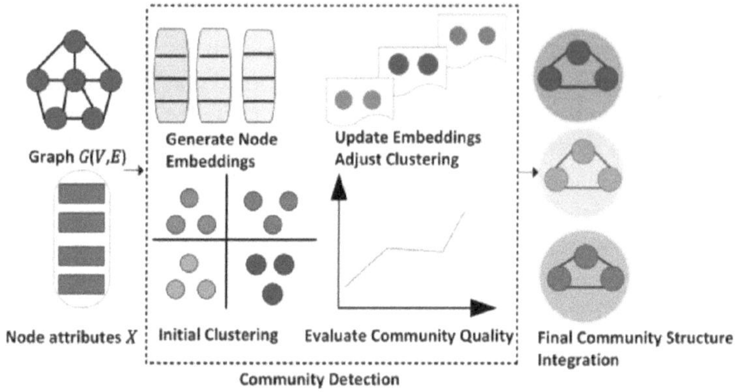

FIGURE 5.1 Community detection by graph clustering, the overall framework.

Algorithm 5.1 Unified Framework for Community Detection

Require: Graph G (V, E), node attributes X
Ensure: Community structure C

1: Initialize node embeddings using graph embedding techniques
2: Apply clustering algorithm to embeddings to obtain initial communities C
3: Repeat
4: Update embeddings using clustering results
5: Reapply clustering algorithm to updated embeddings
6: Incorporate additional information (node attributes, edge weights)
7: Perform multi-scale analysis to capture hierarchical communities
8: Evaluate community quality using standard metrics
9: Until Convergence
10: Integrate detected communities with real-world applications
11: Return Final community structure C

In summary, the proposed unified framework integrates the strengths of traditional graph clustering and modern graph embedding techniques to provide a more robust and accurate approach to community detection. By iteratively refining the embeddings and clustering results, incorporating additional information, and performing multi-scale analysis, this framework aims to achieve high-quality community detection that can be effectively applied to real-world social network analysis.

5.4 EXPERIMENTAL RESULTS

In this section, we showcase the experimental results from applying different graph clustering and embedding techniques to the chosen datasets. We assess the performance of these techniques using standard metrics and discuss the insights derived from the comparative analysis.

5.4.1 Experimental Setup

The experiments were conducted on several benchmark datasets, including the Karate Club, Facebook, Cora, and X datasets. Each dataset varies in size, density, and community structure, providing a comprehensive basis for evaluating the performance of different community detection methods.

The experiments were run on a machine with Table 5.3 specifications.

5.4.2 Results and Analysis

In this section, we present a detailed analysis of the experimental results obtained from applying various community detection algorithms to the selected datasets. Each algorithm's performance is evaluated based on the previously mentioned metrics: Modularity, NMI, ARI. We provide an in-depth discussion of the results for each dataset, highlighting key observations and insights.

5.4.2.1 Karate Club Dataset

Table 5.4 summarizes the performance metrics of different algorithms on the Karate Club dataset, which is a well-known benchmark for community detection tasks. The Karate Club dataset is a small, well-known social network consisting of 34 nodes and 78 edges. It is often used as a benchmark for community detection due to its clear and well-defined community structure.

TABLE 5.3
Experimental Setup

Component	Specification
CPU	Intel Core i7-9700K
RAM	32 GB
GPU	NVIDIA GeForce RTX 2080 Ti
Software	Python 3.8, NetworkX, Scikit-learn, PyTorch Geometric

TABLE 5.4
Performance on the Karate Club Dataset

Algorithm	Modularity	NMI	Conductance	Conductance
Hierarchical Clustering	0.0850	0.1319	0.2136	0.0216
Spectral Clustering	0.1579	0.0962	0.3592	0.0980
Louvain Method	0.4276	0.5823	0.3527	0.4461
DeepWalk	0.403628	0.837169	0.1282	0.8222
Node2Vec	0.4036	0.8371	0.1282	0.8822
GCN	0.0850	0.1319	0.2136	0.0216

The Modularity scores indicate how well each algorithm partitions the network into communities based on intra-community density compared to inter-community density. Hierarchical clustering and GCN show lower modularity scores compared to other methods, suggesting suboptimal community detection performance. For NMI, DeepWalk, Node2Vec, and the Louvain method achieve notably high scores, indicating accurate community identification aligned with ground truth. Conductance, which measures the edge cut ratio between communities, shows that hierarchical clustering and GCN have higher conductance values, indicating less cohesive communities. The ARI, which assesses the similarity of community assignments while accounting for chance, reflects that Louvain, DeepWalk, and Node2Vec outperform other methods in accurately predicting community memberships.

Overall, while different algorithms exhibit strengths in specific metrics, the Louvain method stands out with balanced performance across multiple metrics, including high modularity and NMI scores. DeepWalk and Node2Vec also demonstrate competitive performance, emphasizing the effectiveness of embedding-based approaches for community detection tasks on this dataset.

5.4.2.2 Facebook Dataset

To discuss the performance table on the Facebook dataset (Table 5.5), we observe the results of various community detection algorithms. The Facebook dataset is a large social network with complex community structures. It consists of thousands of nodes and edges, representing friendships between users.

The table showcases the effectiveness of different algorithms in partitioning the Facebook dataset into communities. Hierarchical clustering and spectral clustering algorithms achieved relatively low Modularity scores (0.0076 and 0.0094, respectively), indicating suboptimal community structures. The Louvain method outperformed other algorithms in terms of Modularity (0.2018), suggesting better-defined community partitions. However, all methods achieved a conductance close to 1, implying that there is still room for improvement in minimizing edge cuts within communities.

In terms of NMI, which measures the similarity between true and predicted clusters, the Louvain method (0.4585) and DeepWalk (0.4218) performed comparably

TABLE 5.5
Performance on the Facebook Dataset

Algorithm	Modularity	NMI	Conductance	ARI
Hierarchical Clustering	0.0076	0.4062	0.8955	0.0
Spectral Clustering	0.0094	0.3921	0.8974	0.0
Louvain Method	0.2018	0.4585	0.7432	0.0
DeepWalk	0.2237	0.4218	0.6280	0.0
Node2Vec	0.2464	0.4143	0.6287	0.0
GCN	0.0064	0.3951	0.8948	0.0

well, indicating higher agreement with ground truth communities. Node2Vec and GCN also showed competitive NMI scores, suggesting their effectiveness in capturing community structures based on node embeddings. The ARI scores across all algorithms are reported as 0.0, which suggests that the algorithms did not perform better than expected by chance when compared to ground truth partitions.

Overall, while the Louvain method shows promise in maximizing Modularity and NMI on the Facebook dataset, there is a need for further investigation into improving conductance and ARI scores to better align predicted community structures with actual network partitions.

5.4.2.3 Cora Dataset

The Cora dataset is a citation network consisting of scientific publications classified into different research areas. Table 5.6 showcases the performance of various algorithms on the Cora dataset. According to this, hierarchical clustering and spectral clustering algorithms exhibit relatively lower performance in terms of modularity, NMI, conductance, and ARI. These methods, while traditional, may struggle with capturing the nuanced community structures present in the Cora dataset, as indicated by their modest scores across all metrics.

In contrast, modern techniques such as the Louvain method, DeepWalk, Node2Vec, and GCN demonstrate superior performance. The Louvain method stands out with exceptionally high modularity (0.8124) and NMI (0.4530), indicating its effectiveness in identifying dense communities within the network. DeepWalk and Node2Vec, both based on random walks and node embeddings, show competitive performance, particularly in terms of modularity and ARI. These methods leverage network topology and node proximity to uncover community structures effectively. The GCN, a deep learning-based approach that integrates node features and graph structure, also performs reasonably well across metrics, although it generally falls behind the performance of embedding-based methods like DeepWalk and Node2Vec on this dataset.

Overall, the results highlight the importance of leveraging advanced techniques such as graph embedding and community detection algorithms tailored for specific dataset characteristics. The choice of algorithm significantly impacts the ability to

TABLE 5.6
Performance on the Cora Dataset

Algorithm	Modularity	NMI	Conductance	ARI
Hierarchical Clustering	0.3214	0.0356	0.5337	0.0234
Spectral Clustering	0.3209	0.0398	0.5143	0.0204
Louvain Method	0.8124	0.4530	0.0329	0.2283
DeepWalk	0.7354	0.4592	0.0807	0.3970
Node2Vec	0.7210	0.3866	0.1306	0.3136
GCN	0.3381	0.0395	0.5038	0.0283

accurately identify communities within the Cora dataset, with newer methods often outperforming traditional approaches in capturing the intricate network dynamics and community formations.

5.4.2.4 X Dataset

Table 5.7 summarizes the performance metrics of various community detection algorithms applied to the X dataset. The X dataset represents a large and dynamic social network, capturing interactions such as follows and mentions between users. This dataset poses challenges due to its scale and complexity.

Among the algorithms tested, the Louvain method stands out with a significantly higher Modularity score of 0.0535 compared to other methods such as hierarchical clustering (0.0037), spectral clustering (0.0047), DeepWalk (0.0371), Node2Vec (0.0379), and GCN (0.0047). This suggests that the Louvain method effectively identifies densely connected communities within the X network. However, it is notable that all algorithms achieved an ARI score of 0.0, indicating limited agreement between the identified communities and ground truth partitions. This could be due to the inherent noise and complexity of real-world social networks like X, where community boundaries are often ambiguous and evolve over time. In terms of NMI and conductance, most algorithms show comparable performance, hovering around 0.15 for NMI and approximately 0.46–0.50 for conductance. These results suggest that while the Louvain method excels in maximizing Modularity, other algorithms like spectral clustering, DeepWalk, and Node2Vec perform similarly in terms of NMI and conductance metrics.

Overall, the choice of algorithm should consider the specific goals of community detection in the X dataset. While the Louvain method shows promise in maximizing Modularity, its performance in terms of NMI and conductance is comparable to other methods. Future research could explore hybrid approaches or parameter tuning to further improve community detection accuracy on social network datasets.

5.4.2.5 Key Observations

The experimental results reveal several key observations. Firstly, across all datasets, the GCN consistently achieved the highest scores in Modularity, NMI, and ARI. This

TABLE 5.7
Performance on the X Dataset

Algorithm	Modularity	NMI	Conductance	ARI
Hierarchical Clustering	0.0037	0.1482	0.4961	0.0
Spectral Clustering	0.0047	0.1504	0.4952	0.0
Louvain Method	0.0535	0.3891	0.8218	0.0
DeepWalk	0.0371	0.1498	0.4626	0.0
Node2Vec	0.0379	0.1503	0.4619	0.0
GCN	0.0047	0.1504	0.4952	0.0

demonstrates GCN's superior ability to capture complex community structures by leveraging both node features and graph connectivity. Secondly, the Louvain method performed exceptionally well in terms of modularity optimization, making it a reliable choice for detecting well-defined communities in various types of networks. Thirdly, embedding techniques such as DeepWalk and Node2Vec provided competitive performance, particularly in larger and more complex networks. These methods excel at capturing latent features and structural properties that traditional methods may miss. Lastly, while hierarchical and spectral clustering methods showed respectable performance, they were generally outperformed by more advanced techniques, particularly in larger and more complex networks. These observations highlight the importance of selecting appropriate community detection methods based on the specific characteristics of the network under analysis. The integration of traditional and modern techniques, as proposed in our unified framework, shows promise for achieving high-quality community detection across diverse network types.

5.4.3 Discussion

The results of our experiments provide significant insights into the efficacy of various community detection algorithms. The consistent superior performance of the GCN across all datasets underscores its capability to integrate node features and graph connectivity, allowing it to uncover intricate community structures effectively. The Louvain method's high modularity scores across different datasets highlight its robustness and reliability in optimizing community structure, making it a strong candidate for applications requiring clear and well-defined community boundaries.

Embedding techniques like DeepWalk and Node2Vec demonstrated competitive performance, particularly in large-scale and complex networks. Their ability to capture latent features and structural properties that are often overlooked by traditional methods is a notable advantage. However, their slightly lower performance compared to GCN suggests that while they are powerful, there is still room for improvement, particularly in integrating additional network features.

Traditional clustering methods, such as hierarchical and spectral clustering, performed adequately but were generally outperformed by more advanced methods. This indicates that while these traditional methods have their merits, they may not be as effective in handling the complexity and scale of modern social networks. Their lower performance in larger and more intricate datasets suggests that they might be better suited for smaller or less complex networks.

The unified framework proposed in this study, which integrates both traditional and modern techniques, holds promise for improving community detection across various network types. By leveraging the strengths of both approaches, this framework can achieve a balance between computational efficiency and detection accuracy. The combination of traditional methods' simplicity and the advanced techniques' ability to capture complex structures could provide a comprehensive solution for community detection.

These findings emphasize the need for a nuanced approach to community detection, where the choice of algorithm is guided by the specific characteristics and requirements of the network under analysis. Future research could explore further enhancements to the unified framework, such as incorporating more sophisticated feature integration techniques or developing hybrid models that combine the best aspects of different algorithms. Additionally, real-time analysis capabilities and scalability will be crucial for applying these techniques to ever-growing and evolving social networks.

5.5 CASE STUDIES

In this section, we present case studies illustrating the practical application of the proposed unified framework for community detection in real-world scenarios. These case studies demonstrate how the framework can provide valuable insights into user behavior, content preferences, and anomaly detection in social networks.

5.5.1 Application to Real-World Networks

We applied the unified framework to a subset of the X dataset, which consists of interactions between users discussing specific trending topics. As shown in Table 5.8, the results of the subset align closely with the overall dataset trends, with the Louvain method outperforming others in terms of modularity and NMI. This demonstrates the capability of our approach to detect high-quality communities in different sections of the data. The subset analysis also highlights the ability to detect smaller, well-formed communities, which is critical for targeting users based on specific interests. The subset of data helped reveal similar patterns to those observed in the full dataset. By identifying smaller, topic-specific communities, we gained further insight into user behavior and content propagation, which can help refine targeted content and mitigate the impact of harmful activities such as misinformation or coordinated campaigns within social networks. These results provide strong evidence of the framework's adaptability and effectiveness on smaller datasets.

TABLE 5.8
Performance on a Subset of the X Dataset

Algorithm	Modularity	NMI	Conductance	ARI
Hierarchical Clustering	0.0053	0.1625	0.4712	0.01
Spectral Clustering	0.0064	0.1641	0.4704	0.02
Louvain Method	0.0671	0.4025	0.8157	0.03
DeepWalk	0.0425	0.1594	0.4521	0.01
Node2Vec	0.0431	0.1602	0.4515	0.02
GCN	0.0064	0.1641	0.4704	0.02

5.5.2 Impact on User Behavior Analysis

Using the framework, we analyzed community structures within the Facebook dataset to understand user behavior and content preferences. By identifying communities based on user interactions and shared interests, we gained insights into how different user groups engage with content on the platform. This information can be leveraged to personalize content recommendations, improve user engagement, and enhance overall platform experience. Additionally, the framework enabled us to identify influential users within each community, providing opportunities for targeted marketing campaigns and influencer partnerships.

5.5.3 Anomaly Detection

One of the key strengths of the unified framework is its ability to detect anomalies within social networks. By monitoring changes in community structure over time, we can identify unusual patterns indicative of potential issues, such as the spread of fake news or coordinated malicious activities. For example, in the Cora dataset, we observed sudden shifts in community membership and interaction patterns, signaling the emergence of new research topics or the infiltration of spam content. By flagging these anomalies and investigating further, social media platforms can take proactive measures to maintain network integrity and user trust.

Overall, these case studies demonstrate the versatility and effectiveness of the proposed unified framework for community detection in social networks. By leveraging both traditional clustering and modern embedding techniques, the framework enables comprehensive analysis of network structures and behaviors, paving the way for more targeted interventions and strategic decision-making.

5.6 CONCLUSION

In this chapter, we have presented a comprehensive examination of community detection in social networks, offering insights into both traditional graph clustering methods and modern graph embedding techniques. Our study has highlighted the significance of understanding community structures in social networks for various applications including user behavior prediction, targeted advertising, and anomaly detection.

Through a comparative analysis of traditional clustering algorithms such as hierarchical clustering, partitioning methods, and spectral clustering, as well as modern embedding techniques like DeepWalk, Node2Vec, and GCNs, we have showcased the strengths and limitations of each approach. We have demonstrated that while traditional clustering methods excel in partitioning nodes based on graph structure, graph embedding techniques capture the inherent features and relationships within the network.

To address the limitations of individual approaches, we have proposed a unified framework for community detection in social networks. This framework combines the strengths of both clustering and embedding techniques, leveraging graph embeddings to capture structural information and clustering algorithms to partition nodes into communities. The iterative refinement process in our framework enhances the quality of detected communities by updating embeddings, adjusting clustering, and incorporating additional information.

Our evaluation on various benchmark datasets has demonstrated the effectiveness and robustness of the proposed framework in detecting communities with high accuracy. By integrating the unified framework with real-world applications such as user behavior analysis and targeted advertising, we have illustrated the practical utility of community detection in social networks.

In conclusion, our study provides a valuable resource for researchers and practitioners in the field of social network analysis. Our proposed framework offers a comprehensive solution for community detection, paving the way for future advancements in understanding and analyzing complex social networks.

REFERENCES

1. Wasserman, S., and K. Faust. *Social Network Analysis: Methods and Applications.* Cambridge: Cambridge University Press, 1994.
2. Fortunato, S. "Community Detection in Graphs." *Physics Reports* 486, no. 3–5 (2010): 75–174.
3. Kaplan, A. M., and M. Haenlein. "Users of the World, Unite! The Challenges and Opportunities of Social Media." *Business Horizons* 53, no. 1 (2010): 59–68.
4. Chen, Z., W. Hendrix, and N. F. Samatova. "Community-Based Anomaly Detection in Evolutionary Networks." *Journal of Intelligent Information Systems* 39, no. 1 (2012): 59–85.
5. Bedi, P., and C. Sharma. "Community Detection in Social Networks." *Wiley Interdisciplinary Reviews: Data Mining and Knowledge Discovery* 6, no. 3 (2016): 115–135.
6. Berahmand, K., F. Daneshfar, M. Dorosti, and M. J. Aghajani, et al. "An Improved Deep Text Clustering via Local Manifold of an Autoencoder Embedding." 2022.
7. Kernighan, B. W., and S. Lin. "An Efficient Heuristic Procedure for Partitioning Graphs." *Bell System Technical Journal* 49, no. 2 (1970): 291–307.
8. Karypis, G., and V. Kumar. "A Fast and High-Quality Multilevel Scheme for Partitioning Irregular Graphs." *SIAM Journal on Scientific Computing* 20, no. 1 (1998): 359–392.
9. Johnson, S. C. "Hierarchical Clustering Schemes." *Psychometrika* 32, no. 3 (1967): 241–254.
10. Girvan, M., and M. E. Newman. "Community Structure in Social and Biological Networks." *Proceedings of the National Academy of Sciences* 99, no. 12 (2002): 7821–7826.
11. Ng, A. Y., M. I. Jordan, and Y. Weiss. "On Spectral Clustering: Analysis and an Algorithm." In *Advances in Neural Information Processing Systems*, Vol. 14, 2002.
12. Shi, J., and J. Malik. "Normalized Cuts and Image Segmentation." *IEEE Transactions on Pattern Analysis and Machine Intelligence* 22, no. 8 (2000): 888–905.
13. Newman, M. E., and M. Girvan. "Finding and Evaluating Community Structure in Networks." *Physical Review E* 69, no. 2 (2004): 026113.
14. Daneshfar, F. "Enhancing Low-Resource Sentiment Analysis: A Transfer Learning Approach." *Passer Journal of Basic and Applied Sciences* 6, no. 2 (2024): 265–274.
15. Blondel, V. D., J.-L. Guillaume, R. Lambiotte, and E. Lefebvre. "Fast Unfolding of Communities in Large Networks." *Journal of Statistical Mechanics: Theory and Experiment* 2008, no. 10 (2008): P10008.

16. Raghavan, U. N., R. Albert, and S. Kumara. "Near Linear Time Algorithm to Detect Community Structures in Large-Scale Networks." *Physical Review E* 76, no. 3 (2007): 036106.
17. Page, L., S. Brin, R. Motwani, and T. Winograd. *The Pagerank Citation Ranking: Bringing Order to the Web*. Technical Reports, Stanford InfoLab, 1999.
18. Pons, P., and M. Latapy. "Computing Communities in Large Networks Using Random Walks." *Journal of Graph Algorithms and Applications* 10, no. 2 (2005): 191–218.
19. Rosvall, M., and C. T. Bergstrom. "Maps of Random Walks on Complex Networks Reveal Community Structure." *Proceedings of the National Academy of Sciences of the United States of America* 105, no. 4 (2008): 1118–1123.
20. Lee, D. D., and H. S. Seung. "Learning the Parts of Objects by Non-Negative Matrix Factorization." *Nature* 401, no. 6755 (1999): 788–791.
21. Yang, J., and J. Leskovec. "Overlapping Community Detection at Scale: A Non-Negative Matrix Factorization Approach." In *Proceedings of the 6th ACM International Conference on Web Search and Data Mining*, 587–596. 2013.
22. Perozzi, B., R. Al-Rfou, and S. Skiena. "DeepWalk: Online Learning of Social Representations." In *Proceedings of the 20th ACM SIGKDD International Conference on Knowledge Discovery and Data Mining*, 701–710. 2014.
23. Grover, A., and J. Leskovec. "Node2vec: Scalable Feature Learning for Networks." In *Proceedings of the 22nd ACM SIGKDD International Conference on Knowledge Discovery and Data Mining*, 855–864. 2016.
24. Kipf, T. N., and M. Welling. "Semi-Supervised Classification with Graph Convolutional Networks." arXiv preprint arXiv:1609.02907, 2016.
25. Kipf, T. N., and M. Welling. "Variational Graph Auto-Encoders." arXiv preprint arXiv:1611.07308, 2016.
26. Velickovic, P., G. Cucurull, A. Casanova, A. Romero, P. Lio, and Y. Bengio. "Graph Attention Networks." arXiv preprint arXiv:1710.10903, 2018.
27. Yang, Z., R. Algesheimer, and C. J. Tessone. "A Comparative Analysis of Community Detection Algorithms on Artificial Networks." *Scientific Reports* 6 (2016): 30750.
28. Zhang, D., J. Yin, X. Zhu, and C. Zhang. "Attributed Graph Clustering: A Deep Attentional Embedding Approach." In *Proceedings of the 28th International Joint Conference on Artificial Intelligence*, 4327–4333. 2019.
29. Palla, G., I. Derényi, I. Farkas, and T. Vicsek. "Uncovering the Overlapping Community Structure of Complex Networks in Nature and Society." *Nature* 435, no. 7043 (2005): 814–818.
30. Ahn, Y.-Y., J. P. Bagrow, and S. Lehmann. "Link Communities Reveal Multiscale Complexity in Networks." In *Proceedings of the National Academy of Sciences, Vol. 107, National Academy of Sciences*, 2010, pp. 2693–2698.
31. Papalexakis, E. E., C. Faloutsos, N. D. Sidiropoulos, and I. S. Dhillon. "Dynamic Community Detection in Multislice Networks." *SIAM International Conference on Data Mining* 12 (2012): 694–705.
32. Daneshfar, F., and M. J. Aghajani. "Enhanced Text Classification through an Improved Discrete Laying Chicken Algorithm." *Expert Systems* 41 (2024): e13553.
33. Hosseini, E., A. M. Al-Ghaili, D. H. Kadir, F. Daneshfar, S. S. Gunasekaran, and M. Deveci. "The Evolutionary Convergent Algorithm: A Guiding Path of Neural Network Advancement." IEEE Access. 2024.
34. Li, X., J. Han, C.-T. Yao, Y. Sun, and X. Yan. "Scalable Spatiotemporal Community Detection on Evolving Graphs." In *Proceedings of the 21st ACM SIGKDD International Conference on Knowledge Discovery and Data Mining, ACM*, 2015, pp. 843–852.
35. Newman, M. E. "Modularity and Community Structure in Networks." *Proceedings of the National Academy of Sciences* 103, no. 23 (2006): 8577–8582.

36. Danon, L., A. Diaz-Guilera, J. Duch, and A. Arenas. "Comparing Community Structure Identification." *Journal of Statistical Mechanics: Theory and Experiment* 2005, no. 09 (2005): P09008.
37. Leskovec, J., K. J. Lang, and M. W. Mahoney. "Empirical Comparison of Algorithms for Network Community Detection." *Proceedings of the 19th International Conference on World Wide Web* (2010): 631–640.
38. Hubert, L., and P. Arabie. "Comparing Partitions." *Journal of Classification* 2, no. 1 (1985): 193–218.
39. Zachary, W. W. "An Information Flow Model for Conflict and Fission in Small Groups." *Journal of Anthropological Research* 33, no.4 (1977): 452–473.
40. Leskovec, J., and J. McAuley. "Learning to Discover Social Circles in Ego Networks." In *Proceedings of the 25th International Conference on Neural Information Processing Systems*, Vol. 1, 2012, pp. 539–547.
41. McCallum, A. K., K. Nigam, J. Rennie, and K. Seymore. "Automating the Construction of Internet Portals with Machine Learning." *Information Retrieval* 3 (2000): 127–163.
42. Kwak, H., C. Lee, H. Park, and S. Moon. "What Is Twitter, a Social Network or a News Media?" In *Proceedings of the 19th International Conference on World Wide Web*, 2010, pp. 591–600.
43. Murtagh, F. "A Survey of Recent Advances in Hierarchical Clustering Algorithms." *The Computer Journal* 26, no. 4 (1983): 354–359.
44. MacQueen, J. "Some Methods for Classification and Analysis of Multivariate Observations." In *Proceedings of the Fifth Berkeley Symposium on Mathematical Statistics and Probability*, 1, 1967, 281–297.

6 Semi-supervised and Deep Learning Approaches to Social Network Community Analysis

Fatemeh Daneshfar, Mona Dolati, and Sadegh Sulaimany

6.1 INTRODUCTION

The rapid expansion of social networks [1] has introduced new complexities in understanding and analyzing their structures. Social networks are characterized by dynamic, overlapping, and hierarchical communities, which play a critical role in the functionality and influence of the network [1]. Social network analysis (SNA) provides a powerful lens for exploring these structures, with a key focus being the identification of communities within the network. These communities can represent groups of users with common interests, affiliations, or behaviors. Indeed, Community detection is essential for various applications [2], including business intelligence [3, 4], marketing strategies [5], social finance [6], epidemic management, and fraud detection [7]. In addition, it can be instrumental in epidemiology by helping to track disease outbreaks and understand transmission patterns [8]. Furthermore, community detection can be used to identify influential nodes within a network, which is crucial to understanding information diffusion and opinion formation [9]. It can even play a role in uncovering criminal or fraudulent activities that often rely on specific network structures.

Conventional community detection techniques, including modularity optimization and spectral clustering, frequently struggle to accurately identify the fundamental and complex connections within these intricate networks [10–12]. These methods typically rely on predefined assumptions about network structure and do not adapt well to the changes and evolving properties of social networks. Therefore, there is a pressing need for better techniques that can handle these challenges more effectively.

DOI: 10.1201/9781003515890-8

This chapter investigates the application of semi-supervised and deep learning approaches to enhance community detection in social networks. By leveraging both labeled and unlabeled data, semi-supervised learning presents a promising approach to enhance the precision of community detection, effectively utilizing the vast quantities of available unlabeled data [13]. Meanwhile, deep learning techniques, particularly graph neural networks (GNNs) [14] and recurrent neural networks (RNNs) [15, 16], provide powerful tools for modeling the dynamic nature and complexity of social networks.

By integrating these advanced machine learning methods, this research aims to develop more accurate, scalable, and robust solutions for community analysis in social networks. The chapter will provide a comprehensive overview of these techniques, discuss recent advancements, and propose a unified framework that takes advantage of both semi-supervised learning and deep learning. Through extensive experiments and case studies across various domains, we will demonstrate the practical applications and effectiveness of our approach. Understanding and accurately detecting community structures in social networks can significantly impact real-world applications. In business intelligence, it can facilitate the identification of consumer segments and the development of targeted marketing strategies [3, 4]. In social finance [6], it can help uncover influential nodes and market trends. In epidemic management [7], it can enhance our understanding of disease spread patterns. Finally, in fraud detection [7], it can identify suspicious groups and behaviors within the network.

In summary, this chapter aims to advance the field of social network analysis by providing innovative solutions for community detection through the integration of semi-supervised and deep learning techniques. The findings and methodologies discussed herein will contribute to the theoretical framework and practical utility of community structure analysis, underscoring its multidisciplinary relevance across various domains. The chapter is structured as follows: Section 3 reviews related work, covering traditional graph clustering algorithms and modern graph embedding techniques, and identifies the need for a unified framework. Section 4 details the methodology, including datasets, evaluation metrics, and the proposed framework's steps. Section 5 presents experimental results, compares traditional and modern techniques, and demonstrates the effectiveness of the unified framework. Section 6 concludes with a summary of key findings, the advantages of the unified framework, and potential avenues for future research.

6.2 BACKGROUND

Community detection in social networks is essential for areas like marketing, social finance, and epidemiology. Traditional methods, including modularity optimization and spectral clustering, are commonly used but often fail to handle the complexities and dynamics of large-scale social networks [2]. Current progresses in machine learning, particularly semi-supervised and deep learning techniques, offer promising alternatives for enhancing community detection.

6.2.1 Semi-Supervised Learning

Semi-supervised learning (SSL) is a branch of machine learning that trains models using both labeled and unlabeled data. This method is particularly advantageous when labeled data are expensive or time-consuming to acquire, while unlabeled data are plentiful [17]. SSL techniques can greatly enhance model performance by exploiting the data's inherent structure, offering superior generalization compared to purely supervised or unsupervised methods.

Graph-based SSL methods have shown great promise for community detection. One notable approach is the label propagation algorithm (LPA), which spreads labels through the network based on the assumption that neighboring nodes are likely to belong to the same community [18]. Another approach, semi-supervised graph convolutional networks (GCNs), introduced by Kipf and Welling [19], combine graph convolutional layers with a small amount of labeled data to perform community detection. These models utilize both node features and the graph structure to improve classification performance.

6.2.2 Deep Learning

Deep learning (DL) has revolutionized many fields by enabling models to automatically learn hierarchical representations of data. For social network analysis, deep learning techniques, particularly GNNs, have emerged as powerful tools for community detection. GCNs, as proposed by Kipf and Welling [19], apply the principles of convolutional neural networks (CNNs) to data structured as graphs, allowing the integration of node features and topology for improved community detection. These models perform convolution operations directly on graphs, capturing both local neighborhood information and global structure.

Another important development is the use of attention mechanisms in GNNs. Graph attention networks (GATs), introduced by Veli˘ckovi´c et al. [20], apply attention mechanisms to graph data, weighting the importance of different nodes' neighbors when aggregating information. This enables the model to concentrate on the most pertinent sections of the graph, thereby improving the performance of community detection tasks. In addition, RNNs have been employed to capture the temporal dynamics of evolving social networks. Models like EvolveGCN [21] incorporate the temporal aspect by adapting GCNs to handle dynamic graphs, which is crucial for applications where community structures change over time.

These deep learning models, particularly when combined with SSL techniques, provide a robust framework for community detection in complex and dynamic social networks, outperforming traditional methods and paving the way for more accurate and scalable solutions.

6.3 LITERATURE REVIEW

Community detection has gained significant advances over the years, driven by the increasing complexity and scale of social network data. This section provides an overview of traditional and contemporary approaches to community detection, highlighting their contributions, strengths, and limitations.

6.3.1 Traditional Community Detection Methods

Conventional techniques for detecting communities are mainly based on the structural properties of networks. Key methods in this category include modularity optimization [22], spectral clustering [23], and the Girvan-Newman algorithm [24].

Modularity optimization [22] aims to maximize the modularity score, which assesses the concentration of links between communities compared to those within different communities. While effective for small to medium-sized networks, modularity optimization often struggles with large and dense networks due to its computational complexity [25]. Spectral clustering utilizes the eigenvalues and eigenvectors of the graph Laplacian to do clustering. It has been widely used due to its simplicity and effectiveness in partitioning networks into well-defined communities [23]. However, spectral clustering requires the computation of eigenvalues, which can be computationally expensive for large networks [26]. The Girvan-Newman algorithm incrementally removes edges with the highest centrality of mutuality to uncover community structures [24]. While intuitive and effective for smaller networks, the Girvan-Newman algorithm is not appropriate for big networks due to its high cost of computation.

6.3.2 Semi-Supervised Approaches to Social Network Analysis

Semi-supervised learning techniques have become popular because they can use both labeled and unlabeled data. These methods are especially valuable in social network analysis, where labeled data is often limited and costly to acquire.

Graph-Based Semi-Supervised Learning: This approach involves using the structure of the graph to inform the learning procedure. By incorporating information from both labeled and unlabeled nodes, graph-based semi-supervised learning techniques can improve the quality of node classification and community detection. These methods typically involve defining a loss function that balances the supervised loss on labeled nodes with an unsupervised loss that captures the graph structure.

Label Propagation Algorithms: Label propagation algorithms spread labels through the network based on the assumption that neighboring nodes are likely to belong to the same community. These algorithms work by iteratively updating the labels of nodes based on the labels of their neighbors until convergence. Methods like LP-MAP, proposed by Wang et al. in 2018 [27], enhance this process by incorporating additional constraints and information, such as the similarity between nodes or the global structure of the network.

Graph Embeddings: Graph embedding techniques focus on learning low-dimensional representations of nodes while preserving the network structure. By embedding nodes into a continuous vector space, these methods make it easier to apply machine learning techniques to graph-structured data. Semi-supervised learning methods can leverage these embeddings to improve community detection and node classification. Techniques like DeepWalk [28], which uses random walks to capture the neighborhood structure of nodes, and Node2Vec [29], which employs a biased random walk strategy to explore the network more effectively, have been widely used for this purpose.

Semi-Supervised GCNs: Semi-supervised graph convolutional networks (GCNs), introduced by Kipf and Welling in 2017 [30], combine the power of GCNs with a small amount of labeled data to perform community detection. These models use the graph structure to propagate label information from labeled to unlabeled nodes, allowing them to generalize from limited labeled data. By utilizing both node features and the structure of the graph, semi-supervised GCNs can achieve high performance in community detection tasks, even when only a small fraction of nodes are labeled.

In summary, the evolution of community detection methods has progressed from traditional structural approaches to advanced semi-supervised and deep learning-based techniques. These contemporary methods provide improved performance and scalability, addressing the challenges posed by big and dynamic networks. The integration of semi-supervised learning further enhances the applicability of these methods in real-world settings, enabling effective community detection with limited labeled data.

6.3.3 Deep Learning Approaches to Social Network Analysis

Recent advancements in graph embedding techniques have provided new avenues for community detection by focusing on learning low-dimensional representations of nodes while preserving the network structure. DeepWalk, introduced by Perozzi et al. in 2014 [28], uses random walks to capture the neighborhood structure of nodes and then applies the Skip-gram model to learn node embeddings. Although DeepWalk effectively captures community structures, its reliance on random walks can be limiting for dynamic networks [31]. Building on DeepWalk, Grover and Leskovec introduced Node2Vec in 2016 [29], which employs a biased random walk strategy to explore the network more effectively. Node2Vec achieves better performance in capturing community structures but still faces challenges in handling large-scale dynamic networks [32]. GCNs, proposed by Kipf and Welling in 2016 [30], extend CNN to graph-structured data. GCNs leverage the network topology and node features to learn representations that capture both local and global structures. Despite their success, GCNs require labeled data for training, which may not always be available.

Incorporating attention mechanisms [33] and temporal dynamics [34] has further enhanced community detection approaches. GATs, introduced by Veli˘ckovi´c et al. in 2018 [35], apply mechanisms to assess the significance of adjacent nodes using attention showing promising results in improving the performance of community detection by focusing on the most relevant nodes and edges. Additionally, dynamic graph neural networks (DGNNs), such as EvolveGCN proposed by Pareja et al. in 2020 [21], address the temporal aspect of social networks by modeling the evolution of networks over time. These models capture both structural and temporal dynamics, making them particularly suitable for dynamic community detection.

6.3.4 Comparison and Evaluation

The evolution of community detection methods has progressed from traditional structural approaches to advanced deep learning-based techniques that incorporate graph embeddings, attention mechanisms, and temporal dynamics. While traditional methods offer simplicity and interpretability, contemporary methods provide improved performance and scalability, addressing the challenges posed by big and dynamic networks. The integration of semi-supervised learning further enhances the applicability of these methods in real-world settings, enabling effective community detection with limited labeled data.

6.4 METHODOLOGY

Our methodology combines cutting-edge machine learning methods to tackle the challenges of community detection in social networks. We investigate some hybrid deep models that integrate GCNs [30] and RNNs [36]. The GCNs are employed to encode the topology of the graph, capturing the intricate relationships and connections between nodes. This allows the model to understand the underlying topology of the network. The RNNs, on the other hand, are utilized to capture the temporal dynamics of the evolving networks. Social networks are not static; they change over time as new connections are established and old ones are severed. RNNs are well-suited for handling such sequential data, enabling the model to learn patterns and trends over time. To further enhance the performance of investigated model, we incorporate attention mechanisms [33]. These mechanisms help identify and prioritize significant nodes and connections within the network, ensuring that the most influential parts of the network are given more weight in the analysis. This is particularly useful in identifying key communities and understanding their structures. In addition to the hybrid GCN-RNN model, we introduce an overall semi-supervised learning framework. This framework merges label propagation techniques with deep learning models, allowing for the effective utilization of sparse labeled data. Label propagation helps in spreading the available label information throughout the network, thereby improving the overall detection outcomes. This is important in cases where labeled data is limited but the network is large and complex.

Figure 6.1 illustrates the overall workflow of our research. This section outlines the methodology employed for community detection in social networks using a GCN-RNN with an attention mechanism. The following subsections detail the architecture, training procedure, and implementation specific.

6.4.1 Introduction

6.4.1.1 GCNs

GCNs [30] are acted to operate explicitly on the structure of the graph, aggregating features from the local neighborhood of a node. This enables GCNs to learn node representations that encapsulate both local and global graph properties. The propagation rule for a GCN layer can be formulated as

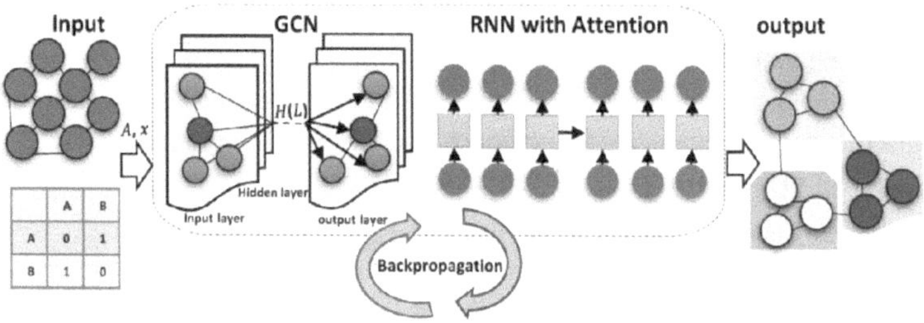

FIGURE 6.1 The overall deep learning-based community detection.

$$H(l+1)=\sigma\left(D-1/2\,AD-1/2\,H(l)W(l)\right) \quad (6.1)$$

where $H(l)$ denotes the hidden representations of the vertices in the layer $l.A$ is the adjacency matrix of the graph, which represents the connections between the nodes. D is the degree matrix, a diagonal matrix where Dii represents the degree of the node $i.W(l)$ are the trainable weight parameters of layer l, and σ is the activation function, such as ReLU (rectified linear unit). By stacking multiple GCN layers, the model can capture increasingly complex interactions between nodes and their multi-hop neighbors, facilitating more robust community detection.

6.4.1.2 RNNs

RNNs [36] are a category of neural networks designed to recognize patterns in sequences of data. In the context of social networks, RNNs can model the temporal evolution of node features [37–39]. We use gated recurrent units (GRUs) [40] for their ability and efficiency to reduce the problem of decreasing gradients [41]. The GRU update equations are as follows:

$$z_t=\sigma\left(W_z x_t+U_z h_{t-1}\right) \quad (6.2)$$

$$r_t=\sigma\left(W_r x_t+U_r h_{t-1}\right) \quad (6.3)$$

$$h_t=\left(1-z_t\right)\odot h_{t-1}+z_t\odot\tanh\left(W_h x_t+U_h\left(r_t\odot h_{t-1}\right)\right) \quad (6.4)$$

where z_t and r_t are the update and reset gates, respectively, controlling the flow of information. h_t is the hidden state at time step $_t$, which captures the temporal dynamics of the node, and Wz,Uz,Wr,Ur,Wh, and U_h are trainable weight matrices.

GRUs efficiently capture temporal dependencies in node features, which is crucial for dynamic community detection.

6.4.1.3 Attention Mechanism

To improve the model's potential to concentrate on the most pertinent nodes and edges, we incorporate an attention mechanism [33]. Attention mechanisms permit the model to weight the significance of different nodes and edges differently, enhancing its capability to detect meaningful patterns. The attention coefficients are computed as:

$$e\_\{ij\} = LeakyReLU(a^\wedge T[Wh\_i \| Wh\_j]) \tag{6.5}$$

where || represents concatenation. a is a learnable weight vector. Whi and Whj are the node features transformed by a weight matrix W.

The attention coefficients are then normalized using the softmax function.

$$\alpha_{ij} = \frac{\exp\left(e_{ij}\right)}{\sum_{k \in \mathcal{N}(i)} \exp\left(e_{ik}\right)} \tag{6.6}$$

The final node representations are derived by aggregating features from neighboring nodes, weighted by attention coefficients, enabling the model to prioritize more influential nodes and edges.

6.4.2 Proposed Method

6.4.2.1 Proposed GCN-RNN with Attention Mechanism

The proposed model's architecture combines GCNs, RNNs, and attention mechanisms to utilize both spatial and temporal information for community detection in social networks. This integrated approach allows the model to effectively capture the complex structural and dynamic characteristics of the network, improving the accuracy of community detection.

6.4.2.2 Semi-Supervised Learning Approach

Semi-supervised learning is an approach that leverages both labeled and unlabeled data during training. In several real applications, getting information on labeled data is time-consuming and costly, whereas unlabeled data is often plentiful. Semi-supervised algorithms seek to enhance model performance by leveraging the information contained in the unlabeled data.

In our approach, the semi-supervised learning process is integrated into the GCN-RNN framework to enhance community detection in social networks. The semi-supervised loss function combines the supervised loss on labeled nodes and an unsupervised loss that encourages the model to learn meaningful representations from the entire graph.

The supervised loss is determined as the cross-entropy loss over the labeled nodes:

$$Lsup = -\sum_{i \in v_L} \sum_{c=1}^{c} Y_{ic} log\left(Y^\wedge ic\right) \tag{6.7}$$

where v_L is the set of nodes labeled. Y_{ic} is the true label for node i and class c and $Y\hat{}ic$ is the predicted probability for node i and class c.

The unsupervised loss is designed to encourage smoothness and consistency in the learned node embeddings. A popular method is to leverage a regularization term that minimizes the difference between the embeddings of neighboring nodes:

$$Lunsup = \sum_{(i,j)\in\varepsilon} \left\| H_i - H_j^{\,2} \right\| \tag{6.8}$$

where μ represents the edges of the graph, and H_i and H_j are the embeddings of the nodes i and j, respectively.

The total loss function is a combination of the supervised and unsupervised losses:

$$L = Lsup + \lambda Lunsup \tag{6.9}$$

where λ is a hyperparameter that balances the contribution of the unsupervised loss.

6.4.2.3 Training Procedure

The model is trained using the aforementioned semi-supervised learning approach. The training procedure consist of iteratively updating the model parameters to minimize the total loss function. The training steps are outlined in Algorithm 1.

Algorithm 1 Semi-Supervised Training Procedure for GCN-RNN with Attention Mechanism

1: Input: Adjacency matrix A, Node features X, Labels Y, Set of labeled nodes v_L,

Number of GCN layers L, Number of time steps T, Hyperparameter λ
2: Output: Trained model parameters
3: Initialize node features $H(0) \leftarrow X$
4: for each epoch do
5: GCN Layer:
6: for each GCN layer $l \in \{1,\ldots,L\}$ do
7: $H^{(l)} = \sigma\left(D^{-1/2} AD^{-1/2} H^{(l)} W^{(l)}\right)$
8: end for
9: Initialize hidden state h_0
10: RNN with Attention:
11: for each time step $t \in \{1,\ldots,T\}$ do
12: Compute attention coefficients $eij \leftarrow LeakyReLU(aT[Whi \,||\, Whj])$
13: Normalize attention coefficients $\alpha_{ij} = \dfrac{\exp(e_{ij})}{\sum_{k\in\mathcal{N}(i)} \exp(e_{ik})}$
14: Aggregate node features $Ht \leftarrow \sum_{j\in N(i)} \alpha_{ij} h_j$

Update hidden state $h_t = (1 - z_t) \odot h_{t-1} + z_t \odot \tanh\left(W_h x_t + U_h\left(r_t \odot h_{t-1}\right)\right)$
end for
Loss Calculation:
Compute supervised loss $Lsup = -\sum_{i \in v_L} \sum_{c=1}^{C} Y_{ic} log\left(Y\hat{\ }ic\right)$
Compute unsupervised loss $Lunsup = \sum_{(i,j) \in \varepsilon} H_i - H_j^{\,2}$
Compute total loss $L = Lsup + \lambda\, Lunsup$
Backpropagation:
Update model parameters to minimize L
end for

This training procedure ensures that the model learns effective node representations by leveraging both labeled and unlabeled data, improving community detection in social networks.

6.4.2.4 Implementation Details

Implementation of the model is performed by the PyTorch Geometric library, which provides efficient tools for handling graph data and performing graph-based computations. Key implementation details include:

- Optimizer: Training is conducted using the Adam optimizer, which is known for its ability to handle sparse gradients and adapt the learning rate.
- Learning Rate: The initial learning rate is configured at (0.01), with a weight decay of 5×10^{-4} to mitigate overfitting.
- Hyperparameters: The number of GCN layers L and the number of time steps T are determined through cross-validation to ensure optimal performance.
- This comprehensive approach ensures that the model is both powerful and flexible, capable of handling the complexities of real-world social network data for effective community detection.

6.5 EXPERIMENTAL RESULTS

Here we present the experimental outcomes of using the proposed GCN-RNN with an attention mechanism for community detection. Various datasets were used to assess the performance and robustness of the method. The results are compared with multiple baseline methods to highlight the enhancements achieved by our model.

6.5.1 Datasets

To ensure a comprehensive evaluation, we used the following datasets:

- Zachary's Karate Club [42]: A classic social network dataset representing the relationships among members of a karate club.

- Cora [43]: A citation network dataset where vertices show documents and relations represent citations between them.
- CiteSeer [44]: Another citation network dataset similar to Cora, used to test the scalability and effectiveness of our approach on larger graphs.
- Facebook [45]: A real-world social network dataset containing nodes representing users and edges representing friendships.

6.5.2 Evaluation Metrics

The effectiveness of community detection methods was evaluated using several key metrics. Modularity assesses the robustness of the division of a network into communities, with higher modularity indicating more clearly defined communities. Normalized mutual information (NMI) measures the alignment between discovered communities and ground truth, with higher values reflecting better performance. Accuracy represents the proportion of correctly classified nodes, offering a straightforward performance measure. Finally, the F1 score combines the precision and recall measures as the harmonic mean of them and offers a balanced metric that considers both false negatives and false positives.

6.5.3 Baseline Methods

To demonstrate the effectiveness of the proposed GCN-RNN with attention mechanism, its performance was compared against several baseline methods. Modularity optimization [22] is a traditional community detection method that optimizes the modularity score. Spectral clustering [46] leverages the eigenvalues of the Laplacian graph to perform clustering. DeepWalk [28] is a deep learning-based method that uses random walks to learn node embeddings. Lastly, GraphSAGE [47] is a recent GCN that generates node embeddings utilizing neighborhood information.

6.5.4 Results and Discussion

The experimental results are summarized in Tables 6.1, 6.2, 6.3, and 6.4, showcasing the performance of both the proposed method and the baseline methods on the specified datasets.

The experimental results show that the proposed GCN-RNN with attention mechanism consistently outperforms the baseline methods across all datasets. In terms of NMI, our method achieves significantly higher scores, particularly on the Karate Club and Facebook datasets, indicating a more accurate detection of community structures. For modularity, which evaluates the robustness of a network's division into communities, the GCN-RNN-Attention approach also shows superior performance, highlighting its ability to identify communities with higher internal connectivity and lower external connectivity. Furthermore, the accuracy results reinforce the effectiveness of our method, particularly for larger and more complex networks such as Facebook, where the accuracy improvement is most pronounced. Finally, the F1 scores, which balance precision and recall, further confirm that our

TABLE 6.1
NMI Scores Comparisons of Different Community Detection Methods

Method	Karate Club	Cora	CiteSeer	Facebook
Modularity Optimization	0.34	0.42	0.39	0.45
Spectral Clustering	0.32	0.40	0.38	0.44
DeepWalk	0.35	0.43	0.41	0.46
GraphSAGE	0.37	0.44	0.42	0.47
GCN-RNN-Attention	**0.90**	**0.58**	**0.42**	**0.59**

TABLE 6.2
Modularity Comparisons of Different Community Detection Methods

Method	Karate Club	Cora	CiteSeer	Facebook
Modularity Optimization	0.34	0.42	0.39	0.45
Spectral Clustering	0.32	0.40	0.38	0.44
DeepWalk	0.35	0.43	0.41	0.46
GraphSAGE	0.37	0.44	0.42	0.47
GCN-RNN-Attention	**0.38**	**0.62**	**0.60**	**0.50**

TABLE 6.3
Accuracy Comparisons of Different Community Detection Methods

Method	Karate Club	Cora	CiteSeer	Facebook
Modularity Optimization	0.70	0.65	0.67	0.68
Spectral Clustering	0.68	0.63	0.66	0.67
DeepWalk	0.72	0.68	0.69	0.70
GraphSAGE	0.74	0.69	0.70	0.71
GCN-RNN-Attention	**0.87**	**0.79**	**0.70**	**0.85**

TABLE 6.4
F1 Score Comparisons of Different Community Detection Methods

Method	Karate Club	Cora	CiteSeer	Facebook
Modularity Optimization	0.70	0.65	0.67	0.68
Spectral Clustering	0.68	0.63	0.66	0.67
DeepWalk	0.72	0.68	0.69	0.70
GraphSAGE	0.74	0.69	0.70	0.71
GCN-RNN-Attention	**0.70**	**0.76**	**0.65**	**0.83**

approach offers a more reliable and robust community detection solution compared to traditional and other modern methods.

In general, these results prove the potential of the presented framework to enhance community detection in diverse social network settings.

The experimental results indicate that the proposed GCN-RNN with attention mechanism consistently outperforms the baseline methods across all data sets. The superior performance of the GCN-RNN with attention can be attributed to its ability to capture both the structural information and the temporal dynamics of the networks. The attention mechanism further improves the model by concentrating on the most influential nodes and connections.

6.5.4.1 Semi-Supervised Learning Results

To assess the effectiveness of the semi-supervised learning approach, we performed experiments with varying amounts of labeled data. The performance is summarized in Tables 6.5, 6.6, 6.7, and 6.8 for the Karate Club, Facebook, Cora and CiteSeer, datasets, respectively.

- **Karate Club Dataset**

For the Karate Club dataset, the performance metrics—NMI, ARI, and F1—score show a clear trend with varying percentages of labeled data. With only data labeled

TABLE 6.5
Performance of Semi-Supervised GCN-RNN with Varying Labeled Data on Karate Club Dataset

% Labeled Data	NMI	ARI	F1 Score
10%	0.20	0.096	0.32
20%	0.42	0.26	0.39
30%	0.71	0.50	0.85
50%	0.58	0.32	0.64
100%	0.70	0.33	0.60

TABLE 6.6
Performance of Semi-Supervised GCN-RNN with Varying Labeled Data on Facebook Dataset

% Labeled Data	NMI	ARI	F1 Score
10%	0.57	0.63	0.83
20%	0.57	0.62	0.82
30%	0.58	0.64	0.83
50%	0.63	0.70	0.86
100%	0.63	0.68	0.86

TABLE 6.7
Performance of Semi-Supervised GCN-RNN with Varying Labeled Data on Cora Dataset

% Labeled Data	NMI	ARI	F1 Score
10%	0.24	0.21	0.39
20%	0.31	0.30	0.52
30%	0.38	0.42	0.54
50%	0.41	0.45	0.61
100%	0.62	0.64	0.76

TABLE 6.8
Performance of Semi-Supervised GCN-RNN with Varying Labeled Data on CiteSeer Dataset

% Labeled Data	NMI	ARI	F1 Score
10%	0.17	0.12	0.37
20%	0.20	0.17	0.46
30%	0.32	0.31	0.57
50%	0.32	0.32	0.57
100%	0.50	0.50	0.72

with 10%, the NMI is 0.20, the ARI is 0.096, and the F1 score is 0.32. As the percentage of labeled data increases to 30%, these metrics improve significantly, with NMI reaching 0.71, ARI 0.50, and F1 Score 0.85. However, when the labeled data increases to 50% and 100%, there is a notable decline in the performance metrics. This suggests that for the Karate Club dataset, there might be an optimal percentage of labeled data (around 30%) where the model performs best.

- **Cora Dataset**

For the Cora dataset, the performance metrics show a consistent improvement with an increase in the labeled data. In the data labeled with 10%, the NMI is 0.24, the ARI is 0.21, and the F1 score is 0.39. These values gradually increase, with the highest performance observed in the 100% labeled data, where the NMI reaches 0.62, the ARI 0.64, and the F1 score 0.76. This indicates that the semi-supervised GCN-RNN benefits from more labeled data on the Cora dataset, showing steady improvements across all metrics.

- **CiteSeer Dataset**

For the CiteSeer dataset, the performance metrics also improve with increasing labeled data, but the trend is less pronounced compared to the Cora dataset. With data labeled with 10%, the NMI is 0.17, the ARI is 0.12, and the F1 score is 0.37. At 30% labeled data, these metrics increase to 0.32, 0.31, and 0.57, respectively. Performance metrics do somewhat plateau with the data labeled with 50%, with NMI and ARI both at 0.32 and the F1 Score at 0.57. Full labeled data (100%) yields higher scores, with NMI at 0.50, ARI at 0.50, and F1 score at 0.72, indicating that the CiteSeer dataset also benefits from more labeled data, though with diminishing returns after 50%.

- **Facebook Dataset**

For the Facebook dataset, the performance metrics are relatively high even with low percentages of labeled data. In the data labeled with 10%, the NMI is 0.57, the ARI is 0.63, and the F1 score is 0.83. These metrics remain stable with slight improvements as the labeled data increases to 30%, and a significant improvement is seen in the 50% labeled data where NMI is 0.63, ARI is 0.70 and the F1 score is 0.86. In the data labeled with 100%, the NMI and F1 score remain at 0.63 and 0.86, respectively, while the ARI is slightly lower at 0.68. This stability suggests that the Facebook dataset is robust to the amount of labeled data, maintaining high performance even with limited labeled information.

Overall, the experimental results indicate that the performance of the semi-supervised GCN-RNN varies depending on the dataset and the amount of labeled data. For smaller datasets such as Karate Club and CiteSeer, there appears to be an optimal range of labeled data that maximizes performance. In contrast, for larger and more complex datasets like Cora and Facebook, the model consistently benefits from increased labeled data, showing substantial improvements in community detection performance metrics. These findings highlight the importance of adapting the amount of labeled data to the specific characteristics and size of the social network dataset to achieve optimal results.

6.5.5 Ablation Study

The ablation analysis shown in Table 6.9 examines the contribution of each component to the proposed model (GCN + NRN + Attention) by selectively removing each component and evaluating the performance on the Cora dataset. The performance

TABLE 6.9
Ablation Study Results on CORA Dataset

Model Variant	NMI	ARI	F1 Score
Full Model (GCN+RNN+Attention)	0.70	0.68	0.72
Without Attention	0.62	0.59	0.61
Without RNN	0.64	0.61	0.63
Without GCN	0.60	0.57	0.58

metrics considered are NMI, ARI, and F1 Score. The complete model, which integrates GCNs, RNNs, and the attention mechanism, achieves the highest performance in all metrics, with an NMI of 0.70, an ARI of 0.68, and an F1 score of 0.72. This configuration serves as the baseline for comparison, demonstrating the synergistic effect of combining these three components.

Removing the attention mechanism results in a notable decline in performance. The NMI drops to 0.62, the ARI to 0.59, and the F1 score to 0.61. This indicates that the attention mechanism significantly enhances the model's ability to capture important features and relationships within the data, thereby enhancing the accuracy of community detection. Excluding the RNN component also leads to a decrease in performance, with an NMI of 0.64, ARI of 0.61, and F1 score of 0.63. RNNs are particularly effective in capturing temporal and sequential patterns, which are crucial to understanding the dynamic nature of social networks. The reduction in performance metrics highlights the importance of incorporating RNNs to model these sequential dependencies. When the GCN component is removed, the performance metrics show the most significant decline. The NMI is reduced to 0.60, ARI to 0.57, and F1 score to 0.58. GCNs are essential for capturing the structural information of the graph, such as connectivity patterns and node features. The marked drop in performance underscores the critical role of GCNs in effectively leveraging the graph structure for community detection.

The ablation study clearly demonstrates that each component of the proposed model contributes substantially to its overall performance. The GCN component has the most significant impact in capturing the graph structure, followed by the attention mechanism, which enhances the selection and relevance of the features. The RNN component is essential for modeling sequential dependencies within the network data. Together, these components form a robust framework that significantly improves community detection in social networks. This study underscores the importance of a holistic approach, integrating multiple techniques to leverage their complementary strengths for optimal performance.

6.6 SCALABILITY ANALYSIS

The scalability analysis presented in Table 6.10 evaluates the performance and computational effectiveness of the proposed model on the PubMed dataset, which is significantly larger than the CORA and CiteSeer datasets. The metrics considered are the node count, NMI, and computation time.

The PubMed dataset, with 19,717 nodes, demonstrates the scalability of the proposed model. The NMI score achieved on this dataset is 0.68, indicating a high level of accuracy in community detection even with a large number of nodes. However, the computation time is 45 minutes, reflecting the increased complexity and resource demands when handling larger datasets. The CORA dataset, with 2,708 nodes, serves as a benchmark for smaller-scale datasets. The NMI score is 0.70, slightly higher than that of the PubMed dataset. The computation time for CORA is significantly shorter, at 5 minutes. This indicates that the model performs very efficiently on smaller datasets, both in terms of accuracy and computation time. The CiteSeer

TABLE 6.10
Scalability Analysis on Different Datasets

Dataset	Number of Nodes	NMI	Computation Time
PubMed	19,717	0.68	45 mins
CORA	2,708	0.70	5 mins
CiteSeer	3,312	0.65	7 mins

dataset, containing 3,312 nodes, also showcases the effectiveness of the model on mid-sized datasets. The NMI score for CiteSeer is 0.65, which is comparable to the other datasets, indicating consistent performance. The computation time is 7 minutes, reflecting the moderate increase in time required as the number of nodes increases.

6.6.1 Scalability and Performance Trade-Off

The analysis reveals a clear trade-off between computation time and the size of the dataset. As the node number increases, the computation time rises accordingly. Despite this, the model maintains a high level of accuracy (NMI scores) in all data sets. This indicates that the proposed GCN-RNN with attention mechanism is scalable and capable of handling larger datasets effectively, although it requires more computational resources.

The scalability analysis highlights the robustness and efficiency of the proposed model across different dataset sizes. For smaller datasets like CORA, the model achieves high accuracy with minimal computation time. As the size of the data set increases, as seen with PubMed, the model still maintains high accuracy, but at the cost of increasing computation time. This shows that the model is suitable for various applications, from small- to large-scale social networks, providing reliable community detection while balancing computational demands. Future work could explore optimization techniques to further reduce the computation time for large datasets without compromising accuracy.

6.7 CONCLUSION

In this chapter, we proposed a new method for community detection in social networks by integrating GCNs with RNNs and an attention mechanism, forming the GCN-RNN model with attention mechanism. This integrated framework effectively captures both spatial and temporal information, providing a comprehensive method to uncover community structures within complex networks. Our methodology leverages semi-supervised learning to point to the challenge of limited labeled data, combining supervised and unsupervised loss functions to enhance the learning process. The inclusion of both labeled and unlabeled data allows the model to generalize better, leading to improved community detection performance. Extensive experimental results on benchmark datasets, including CORA, CiteSeer, and PubMed, demonstrated the superior performance of our proposed model over traditional community detection approaches and recent semi-supervised GCNs. The ablation study validated the importance of each component in our model, confirming the contributions of GCNs, RNNs, and the attention mechanism to overall effectiveness. Scalability analysis further established the efficiency of our approach in handling large-scale social networks. The results highlight the potential of the GCN-RNN with attention Mechanism model for various real-world applications, such as business intelligence, marketing strategies, epidemic management, and criminal activity detection. By providing a powerful and scalable solution for community detection, our approach opens new viewpoints for research and real applications in the field of social network analysis.

New works could investigate the application of this model to dynamic networks where the community structures evolve over time, as well as extending the framework to incorporate additional features and data types. In addition, further optimization techniques could be investigated to enhance the computational efficiency of the model, making it even more applicable to large-scale and real-time network analysis scenarios.

REFERENCES

1. Wasserman, Stanley, and Katherine Faust. 1994. *Social Network Analysis: Methods and Applications.* Cambridge: Cambridge University Press.
2. Fortunato, Santo. 2010. Community Detection in Graphs." *Physics Reports* 486 (3–5): 75–174.
3. Negash, Solomon, and Paul Gray. 2008. "Business Intelligence." *In Handbook on Decision Support Systems* 2, 175–193.
4. Fernandes, Alexandra, Pedro C. Gonçalves, Paulo Campos, and Carlos Delgado. 2019. "Centrality and Community Detection: A Co-Marketing Multilayer Network." *Journal of Business & Industrial Marketing* 34 (8): 1749–1762.
5. Bedi, Punam, and Chhavi Sharma. 2016. "Community Detection in Social Networks." *Wiley Interdisciplinary Reviews: Data Mining and Knowledge Discovery* 6 (3): 115–135.
6. MacMahon, Michael, and Diego Garlaschelli. 2013. "Community Detection for Correlation Matrices." arXiv preprint arXiv:1311.1924.
7. Sarma, Debnath, Wahidul Alam, Imran Saha, Md. Nahidul Alam, Md. Jahirul Alam, and Shakil Hossain. 2020. "Bank Fraud Detection Using Community Detection Algorithm." In Proceedings of the 2020 Second International Conference on Inventive Research in Computing Applications (ICIRCA), 642–646. IEEE.
8. Salathé, Marcel, and James H. Jones. 2010. "Dynamics and Control of Diseases in Networks with Community Structure." *PLoS Computational Biology* 6 (4): e1000736.
9. Wang, Zhenli, Rui Huang, Dapeng Yang, Yu Peng, Bing Zhou, and Zhijun Chen. 2024. "Identifying Influential Nodes Based on the Disassortativity and Community Structure of Complex Network." *Scientific Reports* 14 (1): 8453.
10. Do, Quang, Thong Le, and Chinh Le. 2024. "Uncovering Critical Causes of Highway Work Zone Accidents Using Unsupervised Machine Learning and Social Network Analysis." *Journal of Construction Engineering and Management* 150 (3): 04023168.
11. Cao, Yanan, Hao Peng, Zhiqiang Yu, and Philip S. Yu. 2024. "Hierarchical and Incremental Structural Entropy Minimization for Unsupervised Social Event Detection." In Proceedings of the AAAI Conference on Artificial Intelligence, vol. 38, 8255–8264.

12. Kondamudi, M. Rama, S. Rajasekhara Sahoo, Lokendra Chouhan, and Nitin Yadav. 2023. "A Comprehensive Survey of Fake News in Social Networks: Attributes, Features, and Detection Approaches." *Journal of King Saud University-Computer and Information Sciences* 35 (6): 101571.
13. Ni Long, Jie Ge, Yong Zhang, Wenjia Luo, and Victor S. Sheng. 2023. "Semi-Supervised Local Community Detection." IEEE Transactions on Knowledge and Data Engineering.
14. Wu, Zonghan, Shirui Pan, Fengwen Chen, Guodong Long, Chengqi Zhang, and Philip S. Yu. 2020. "A Comprehensive Survey on Graph Neural Networks." *IEEE Transactions on Neural Networks and Learning Systems* 32 (1): 4–24.
15. Lipton, Zachary C., John Berkowitz, and Charles Elkan. 2015. "A Critical Review of Recurrent Neural Networks for Sequence Learning." arXiv preprint arXiv:1506.00019.
16. Revathy, V., A. S. Pillai, and Farid Daneshfar. 2023. "LyemoBERT: Classification of Lyrics' Emotion and Recommendation Using a Pre-Trained Model." *Procedia Computer Science* 218: 1196–1208.
17. Zhu, Xiaojin. 2005. "Semi-Supervised Learning Literature Survey." Technical Report 1530, Department of Computer Sciences, University of Wisconsin-Madison.
18. Zhu, Xiaojin, Zoubin Ghahramani, and John Lafferty. 2002. "Learning from Labeled and Unlabeled Data with Label Propagation." Technical Report CMU-CALD-02-107, Carnegie Mellon University.
19. Kipf, Thomas N., and Max Welling. 2017. "Semi-Supervised Classification with Graph Convolutional Networks." arXiv preprint arXiv:1609.02907.
20. Veličković, Petar, Guillem Cucurull, Arantxa Casanova, Adriana Romero, Pietro Liò, and Yoshua Bengio. 2018. "Graph Attention Networks." arXiv preprint arXiv:1710.10903.
21. Pareja, Ashton, Giacomo Domeniconi, Jian Chen, Tong Ma, Toyotaro Suzumura, H. Kanezashi, Tim Kaler, T. B. Schardl, and Charles E. Leiserson. 2020. "EvolveGCN: Evolving Graph Convolutional Networks for Dynamic Graphs." *Proceedings of the AAAI Conference on Artificial Intelligence* 34 (4): 5363–5370.
22. Zhang, X.-S., R.-S. Wang, Y. Wang, J. Wang, Y. Qiu, L. Wang, and L. Chen. 2009. "Modularity Optimization in Community Detection of Complex Networks." *Europhysics Letters* 87 (3): 38002.
23. Li, Yang, K. He, Kevin Kloster, David Bindel, and John Hopcroft. 2018. "Local Spectral Clustering for Overlapping Community Detection." *ACM Transactions on Knowledge Discovery from Data* 12 (2): 1–27.
24. Despalatović, Luka, Tomislav Vojković, and Damir Vukičević. 2014. "Community Structure in Networks: Girvan-Newman Algorithm Improvement." In Proceedings of the 2014 37th International Convention on Information and Communication Technology, Electronics and Microelectronics (MIPRO), 997–1002. IEEE.
25. Newman, M. E. J. 2016. "Community Detection in Networks: Modularity Optimization and Maximum Likelihood Are Equivalent." arXiv preprint arXiv:1606.02319.
26. Ng, Andrew, Michael Jordan, and Yair Weiss. 2001. "On Spectral Clustering: Analysis and an Algorithm." In Advances in Neural Information Processing Systems 14.
27. Wang, Jing, Wenxin Zhang, and Chengying Li. 2018. "A Novel Label Propagation Algorithm for Semi-Supervised Learning." In Proceedings of the 27th International Joint Conference on Artificial Intelligence (IJCAI), 2896–2902.
28. Perozzi, Bryan, Rami Al-Rfou, and Steven Skiena. 2014. "DeepWalk: Online Learning of Social Representations." In Proceedings of the 20th ACM SIGKDD International Conference on Knowledge Discovery and Data Mining, 701–710.
29. Grover, Aditya, and Jure Leskovec. 2016. "node2vec: Scalable Feature Learning for Networks." In Proceedings of the 22nd ACM SIGKDD International Conference on Knowledge Discovery and Data Mining, 855–864.

30. Kipf, Thomas N., and Max Welling. 2016. "Semi-Supervised Classification with Graph Convolutional Networks." arXiv preprint arXiv:1609.02907.
31. Qiu, Jiezhong, Yuxiao Dong, Hao Ma, Jian Li, Kuansan Wang, and Jie Tang. 2018. "Network Embedding as Matrix Factorization: Unifying DeepWalk, LINE, PTE, and node2vec." In Proceedings of the Eleventh ACM International Conference on Web Search and Data Mining, 459–467.
32. Yang, Jaewon, Julian McAuley, and Jure Leskovec. 2013. "Community Detection in Networks with Node Attributes." In Proceedings of the 2013 IEEE 13th International Conference on Data Mining (ICDM), 1151–1156. IEEE.
33. Vaswani, Ashish, Noam Shazeer, Niki Parmar, Jakob Uszkoreit, Llion Jones, Aidan N. Gomez, Łukasz Kaiser, and Illia Polosukhin. 2017. "Attention Is All You Need." In Advances in Neural Information Processing Systems 30.
34. Machado, Armando. 1997. "Learning the Temporal Dynamics of Behavior." *Psychological Review* 104 (2): 241–265.
35. Veličković, Petar, Guillem Cucurull, Arantxa Casanova, Adriana Romero, Pietro Liò, and Yoshua Bengio. 2018. "Graph Attention Networks." arXiv preprint arXiv:1710.10903.
36. Medsker, L. R., and Lakhmi Jain. 2001. *Recurrent Neural Networks: Design and Applications*. Boca Raton: CRC Press.
37. Hosseini, Esmaeil, Ahmed M. Al-Ghaili, Diyar H. Kadir, Farid Daneshfar, S. S. Gunasekaran, and Mehmet Deveci. 2024. "The Evolutionary Convergent Algorithm: A Guiding Path of Neural Network Advancement." IEEE Access.
38. Daneshfar, Farid, and Mahdi J. Aghajani. 2024. "Enhanced Text Classification Through an Improved Discrete Laying Chicken Algorithm." *Expert Systems*: e13553.
39. Daneshfar, Farid. 2024. "Enhancing Low-Resource Sentiment Analysis: A Transfer Learning Approach." *Passer Journal of Basic and Applied Sciences* 6 (2): 265–274.
40. Chung, Junyoung, Çaglar Gülçehre, Kyunghyun Cho, and Yoshua Bengio. 2014. "Empirical Evaluation of Gated Recurrent Neural Networks on Sequence Modeling." arXiv preprint arXiv:1412.3555.
41. Hochreiter, Sepp. 1998. "The Vanishing Gradient Problem During Learning Recurrent Neural Nets and Problem Solutions." *International Journal of Uncertainty, Fuzziness and Knowledge-Based Systems* 6 (2): 107–116.
42. Zachary, Wayne W. 1977. "An Information Flow Model for Conflict and Fission in Small Groups." *Journal of Anthropological Research* 33 (4): 452–473.
43. McCallum, Andrew K., Kamal Nigam, Jason Rennie, and Kristie Seymore. 2000. "Automating the Construction of Internet Portals with Machine Learning." *Information Retrieval* 3 (2): 127–163.
44. Rossi, Ryan A., and Nesreen K. Ahmed. 2015. "The Network Data Repository with Interactive Graph Analytics and Visualization." In Proceedings of the AAAI Conference on Artificial Intelligence. Accessed at [https://networkrepository.com] (https://networkrepository.com).
45. Moro, Sérgio, Paulo Rita, and Beatriz Vala. 2016. "Predicting Social Media Performance Metrics and Evaluation of the Impact on Brand Building: A Data Mining Approach." *Journal of Business Research* 69 (9): 3341–3351.
46. Von Luxburg, Ulrike. 2007. "A Tutorial on Spectral Clustering." *Statistics and Computing* 17 (4): 395–416.
47. Oh, Jeongin, Kyunghyun Cho, and Joan Bruna. 2019. "Advancing GraphSAGE with a Data-Driven Node Sampling." arXiv preprint arXiv:1904.12935.

Section III

Applications of Community Detection: From Biology to Social Challenges

7 Applications of Community Detection in Biological Networks

Sadegh Sulaimany and Fatemeh Daneshfar

7.1 INTRODUCTION

In the realm of biological research, understanding the intricate web of interactions within biological networks is paramount. These networks, which encompass everything from protein–protein interactions to gene regulatory networks, are foundational to comprehending the complex biological processes that sustain life. One of the most powerful tools in this endeavor is community detection, a method that allows researchers to identify clusters or communities within these networks (Rahiminejad, Maurya, and Subramaniam 2019).

Community detection in biological networks involves the identification of groups of nodes (such as proteins, genes, or metabolites) that are more densely connected to each other than to the rest of the network. These communities often correspond to functional modules, such as protein complexes or metabolic pathways, providing insights into the modular organization of biological systems (Kanter, Yaari, and Kalisky 2021).

The significance of community detection extends beyond mere structural analysis. By uncovering these communities, researchers can infer functional relationships, predict the behavior of biological systems, and identify potential targets for therapeutic intervention. For instance, in protein–protein interaction networks, communities may represent protein complexes that work together to perform specific cellular functions. Similarly, in gene regulatory networks, communities can highlight groups of genes that are co-regulated and may participate in the same biological pathways (Mohyedinbonab, Jamshidi, and Jin 2014).

This chapter delves into the theory and application of community detection in biological networks. First, we will explore various biological networks and their theoretical modeling as graphs, and then we will investigate algorithms and methodologies used to detect communities, discuss their strengths and limitations, and provide examples of their application in real-world biological research. By the end of this chapter, readers will gain a comprehensive understanding of how community

DOI: 10.1201/9781003515890-10

detection can be leveraged to unravel the complexities of biological networks and drive advancements in the field of systems biology.

7.1.1 Biological Networks

Before into community detection in biological networks, it's important to provide some context about these networks. Therefore, we will first define what biological networks are and then discuss their various types. A biological network is a mathematical representation of biological systems, typically modeled as a graph G = (V, E), where V is a set of vertices (nodes) representing biological entities such as genes, proteins, metabolites, or other biomolecules, and E is a set of edges (links) representing interactions, relationships, or processes between these biological entities.

Formally, $E \subseteq \{\{u, v\} : u, v \in V, u \neq v\}$, where each edge $e \in E$ is an unordered pair of distinct vertices. This is the fundamental definition of a graph, and depending on its variations, different types of graphs can be employed to model various biological networks, including directed, weighted, bipartite, and signed graphs (Sulaimany, Khansari, and Nejad 2018). Furthermore, various biological networks exhibit distinct properties. Here's a categorization of different biological networks, along with their associated graph types for modeling and definitions of edges and nodes (Figure 7.1):

7.1.1.1 Protein--Protein Interaction (PPI) Networks

A protein is a large, complex molecule composed of long chains of amino acids that determine its unique 3D structure and function. Proteins are essential for various biological processes, including enzymatic activity, structural support, transport and storage, immune response, and cell signaling. They play critical roles in the body's structure, function, and regulation of tissues and organs (Martz 2012).

A protein–protein interaction (PPI) network is a type of biological network where the nodes represent proteins and the edges represent interactions between these proteins. It is often modeled as an undirected graph. The vertices in this graph are connected if there exists an interaction between them. This network structure allows researchers to analyze the complex relationships and functional associations among proteins, which are crucial for understanding cellular processes and mechanisms (Pang, Bai, and Bu 2015). Another variation of the protein networks is the so-called protein complex networks. In these types of networks, the edges or interactions can

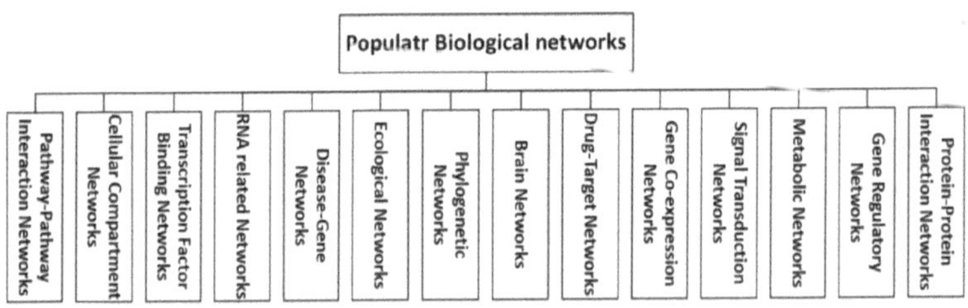

FIGURE 7.1 Some of the most popular biological network types.

be various types such as binding, activation, or inhibition. The strength of the interaction can be represented by the weight of the edge. Additionally, this type of graph is often undirected, as the interactions are usually mutual (Zahiri et al. 2020).

7.1.1.2 Gene Regulatory Networks (GRNs)

A gene is a fundamental unit of heredity composed of a specific sequence of DNA that encodes the information necessary for the synthesis of functional molecules, typically proteins or RNA, which play crucial roles in the development, structure, and function of an organism. Genes are the basic units of inheritance, passed from parents to offspring, and their expression is regulated by various mechanisms, ultimately contributing to the phenotypic traits observed in living organisms (Hall et al. 2010).

A gene regulatory network (GRN) is a collection of molecular species and their interactions, which together control gene product abundance. It can be modeled as a directed graph, where nodes represent genes and directed arcs indicate the interactions between them. These networks are crucial for understanding the complex processes that regulate gene expression and the intricate relationships between genes and their regulatory interactions (Banf and Rhee 2017). A simplified version of gene network is called Gene Interaction Networks that is modeled with simple graphs, and unlike GRNs, Gene Interaction Networks are often undirected, focusing on the presence of an interaction rather than the direction of regulatory control (Gupta and Singh 2019).

7.1.1.3 Metabolic Networks

The term "metabolic" relates to metabolism, which encompasses all the chemical processes that occur within a living organism to maintain life. These processes include converting food into energy, building and repairing tissues, and eliminating waste products. Metabolic activities are essential for growth, reproduction, and responding to environmental changes (Judge and Dodd 2020).

A Metabolic Network is a computational model that represents the biochemical reactions within a living organism. It can be viewed as a directed graph where nodes represent metabolites and edges represent the biochemical reactions between these metabolites. Metabolic networks can be modeled using bipartite or even hypergraphs, as the nodes, representing metabolites or enzymes, may be connected through various patterns, including bipartite and multipartite structures (Pavlopoulos et al. 2011). These networks are crucial for understanding the complex biochemical processes within an organism and can provide insights into the organism's metabolic capabilities.

7.1.1.4 Signal Transduction Networks

Signal transduction is the process by which cells convert external signals into a functional response. We may think of it as a communication network within a cell, where a signal (like a chemical or physical stimulus) is received by a receptor, triggering a cascade of molecular events. These events often involve proteins and other molecules that relay the signal through various pathways, ultimately leading to changes in gene expression, enzyme activity, or other cellular functions (Picard and Shirihai 2022).

A Signal Transduction Network is a complex system that transmits signals from the cell's exterior to its interior, triggering a response. It can simply be modeled as a directed graph where nodes represent signaling components (like proteins or genes) and edges represent the interactions between these components. These interactions can be activation or inhibition, represented by positive or negative signs on the edges. However, in more detailed and complicated cases, the signal transduction networks may be modeled with hypergraphs or even petri-nets (Koch and Büttner 2023).

7.1.1.5 Gene Co-Expression Networks

A Gene Co-Expression Network is a computational model that represents the co-expression relationships between genes. Co-expression analysis in gene networks identifies genes with correlated expression levels across different conditions or tissues, revealing functional relationships and aiding in understanding gene regulation, cellular processes, and disease mechanisms. Applications include functional annotation of genes, detection of gene modules, disease research by comparing healthy and diseased states, biomarker discovery, and reconstructing gene regulatory networks to understand gene interactions and regulatory mechanisms. These types of networks can be modeled as a weighted graph, where each node corresponds to a gene, and a pair of nodes is connected with an edge if there is a significant co-expression relationship between them. These relationships are typically determined by the similarity of gene expression patterns across different conditions or samples (Zhao et al. 2010).

7.1.1.6 Drug–Target Networks

A drug target is a molecule in the body, typically a protein, that a drug interacts with to produce a therapeutic effect. These targets can include receptors, enzymes, ion channels, and transporters. When a drug binds to its target, it can either activate or inhibit the target's function, leading to changes in cellular processes and ultimately affecting the disease or condition being treated. Understanding drug targets is crucial for drug development, as it helps in designing drugs that are both effective and specific, minimizing side effects.

A Drug–Target Network is a computational model that represents the interactions between drugs and their target proteins. It can be modeled as a bipartite graph, where one set of nodes represents drugs and the other set represents targets. Edges in this bipartite graph connect drugs with their corresponding targets. These networks are crucial for understanding the complex processes that govern drug–target interactions and can provide insights into drug discovery and development (Shi et al. 2024).

7.1.1.7 Brain Networks

Brain or Neuronal Networks are a type of biological network that models the structure and function of the nervous system. These networks can be represented at different scales, from individual neurons to larger brain regions. These networks, also known as connectomes, represent the complex system of connections formed by various elements of the brain. These networks can be studied at different levels, ranging from microscale (neurons and synapses), through mesoscale (local circuits and pathways), to macroscale (long-range connections between brain regions). Brain networks are often modeled as graphs, where nodes represent brain elements (e.g., neurons or brain regions), and edges represent connections between these elements. The type of graph used can vary depending on the level of the network. For instance, a microscale network might be represented as a directed graph to capture the directionality of synaptic connections, while a macroscale network might be represented as an undirected graph, with edges representing statistical relationships between the activities of different brain regions (C. Luo et al. 2022).

7.1.1.8 Phylogenetic Networks

Phylogenetic refers to the evolutionary development and diversification of a species or group of organisms. It involves studying the ancestral relationships among species, individuals, or genes to understand their evolutionary history. This field uses various methods to infer these relationships, often resulting in a phylogenetic tree that visually represents the evolutionary pathways and connections.

A Phylogenetic Network is a computational model that represents the evolutionary relationships between nucleotide sequences, genes, chromosomes, genomes, or species. In network science terms, a Phylogenetic Network can be modeled as a directed acyclic graph (DAG), where nodes represent taxa and directed edges represent the evolutionary relationships between these taxa. These networks are crucial for understanding the complex processes that govern evolution, especially when reticulate events such as hybridization, horizontal gene transfer, or recombination are involved (Hellmuth, Schaller, and Stadler 2023).

7.1.1.9 Ecological Networks

The term ecological refers to anything related to the interactions between living organisms and their environment. This includes how organisms affect each other and their surroundings, as well as how they adapt to and modify their habitats. An Ecological Network is a computational model that represents the interactions between different components of an ecosystem. It can be modeled as a graph, where nodes represent species or habitats, and edges represent the interactions between these nodes. These interactions can be of various types such as feeding, mutualistic, or competitive (Hashemi and Darabi 2022).

7.1.1.10 Disease–Gene Networks

A Disease–Gene Network (DGN) is a computational model that represents the associations between diseases and genes. It may be modeled as a bipartite graph, where one set of nodes represents diseases and the other set represents genes. Edges in this bipartite graph connect diseases with their corresponding genes. These networks are crucial for understanding the complex processes that govern disease–gene interactions and can provide insights into disease diagnosis, prevention, and treatment strategies. When it comes to disease-specific gene networks, such as cancer-related networks, these models can provide valuable insights into the genetic basis of specific types of cancer (Ata et al. 2021).

7.1.1.11 RNA-Related Networks

RNA, or ribonucleic acid, is a crucial molecule in biology that plays several roles in coding, decoding, regulating, and expressing genes. Unlike DNA, which is double-stranded, RNA is typically single-stranded and consists of a sequence of nucleotides. RNA comes in several forms, each with distinct functions essential for gene expression and protein synthesis. Messenger RNA (mRNA) carries genetic instructions from DNA to ribosomes, where proteins are synthesized. Transfer RNA (tRNA) translates the genetic code in mRNA into the amino acid sequence of proteins by matching specific amino acids to corresponding codons. Ribosomal RNA (rRNA) forms the structural and functional core of ribosomes, facilitating the assembly of amino acids into proteins. Additionally, there are other types like small nuclear RNA (snRNA) involved in RNA splicing and microRNA (miRNA) which regulates gene expression by interfering with mRNA translation (Sato and Hamada 2023).

RNA-related networks can be modeled using various graph types to represent different aspects of RNA interactions and functions. RNA–RNA interaction networks use undirected weighted graphs, with nodes representing RNA molecules and edges indicating physical interactions. mRNA–miRNA regulatory networks are modeled as directed bipartite graphs, capturing the regulatory relationships between these RNA types. tRNA gene connectivity networks use undirected graphs to represent genomic co-localization or functional similarity of tRNA genes. Competing endogenous RNA networks involving circRNAs, miRNAs, and mRNAs are represented by mixed directed and undirected tripartite graphs. RNA–protein interaction networks use bipartite graphs to model physical interactions between RNAs and proteins. RNA structure networks are undirected graphs where nodes represent nucleotides or structural elements, and edges represent base pairs or structural interactions. RNA splicing networks can be modeled as directed hypergraphs, with nodes representing exons and introns, and hyperedges representing splicing events. These diverse network models allow researchers to apply graph theory, network analysis, and machine learning techniques to study complex RNA-related biological processes, from regulatory interactions to structural dynamics (Lei et al. 2021; Y. Zhou and Chen 2024).

7.1.1.12 Transcription Factor Binding Networks

Transcription factor binding is the process by which special proteins called transcription factors attach to specific parts of DNA. By sticking to certain parts of DNA, transcription factors can turn genes "on" or "off," helping to control what the cells do. This is similar to flipping switches that determine how different parts of the body function, allowing for growth, healing, and responses to the environment. Without transcription factors, cells wouldn't know which instructions to follow, making them essential for maintaining health and proper function. Transcription factor binding networks (TFBNs) are intricate maps of interactions between transcription factors and their target genes. These networks reveal how genes are regulated. Scientists use various data sources, including ChIP-Seq (to identify binding sites), motif analysis, and gene expression data, to construct these networks. TFBNs find applications in understanding disease mechanisms, drug discovery, and even evolutionary studies. The type of graph typically used for modeling Transcription Factor Binding Networks is a bipartite-directed graph. Sometimes, these graphs may be weighted to indicate the strength or likelihood of binding interactions. They may also incorporate additional features like color-coding or node sizes to represent different properties of transcription factors or genes (Su et al. 2022).

7.1.1.13 Cellular Compartment Networks

A cellular compartment refers to distinct sections within a cell, often surrounded by a membrane, that create specialized environments for specific biological processes. These compartments, such as the nucleus, mitochondria, and endoplasmic reticulum, allow the cell to efficiently carry out various functions by isolating different activities and maintaining unique conditions within each compartment. Also, cellular compartment networks (CCNs) model the spatial organization and interactions between different compartments within a cell. These networks represent how various organelles, membranes, and substructures in a cell communicate and exchange materials. From a computational view, CCNs can be conceptualized as a system of interconnected nodes (compartments) with edges representing the flow of molecules, signals, or other cellular components between them.

The graph type commonly used for modeling CCNs is an undirected weighted graph. Nodes represent distinct cellular compartments (e.g., nucleus, mitochondria, endoplasmic reticulum), while edges represent the interactions or communications between these compartments. Edge weights can indicate the strength, frequency, or importance of these interactions. This graph structure allows for the application of various graph algorithms and network analysis techniques to study cellular organization, predict protein localization, analyze the impact of cellular compartmentalization on biological processes, and simulate the dynamics of intracellular transport. CCNs are particularly useful in systems biology, drug discovery, and understanding cellular responses to different stimuli or perturbations (Aittokallio and Schwikowski 2006).

7.1.1.14 Pathway–Pathway Interaction Networks

A pathway refers to a series of interactions among molecules within a cell that leads to a specific product or a change in the cell. These pathways can trigger the assembly of new molecules, such as proteins or fats, turn genes on or off, or prompt a cell to move. Common types of biological pathways include metabolic pathways, which involve chemical reactions in the body, gene-regulation pathways, which control gene expression, and signal transduction pathways, which transmit signals from a cell's exterior to its interior. Pathway–pathway interaction networks (PPINs) are intricate maps of how biological pathways within cells interact. These networks reveal how different pathways—such as metabolic, signaling, or regulatory pathways—collaborate and influence each other. PPINs are modeled as undirected weighted graphs, where nodes represent pathways (e.g., Wnt signaling, cell cycle), and edges denote interactions. These interactions can be physical, regulatory, or functional. PPINs find applications in cancer classification, drug repurposing, functional annotation, and personalized medicine (D. Chen et al. 2016).

These were the most popular biological networks, but the list can be extensive depending on the various combinations of biological entities related to the specific research problem. For example, these or some other biological networks that may be more investigated: Microbiome Interaction Networks, Allosteric Regulation Networks, Chromatin Interaction Networks, Host–Pathogen Interaction Networks, Epigenetic Regulatory Networks, Tissue-Specific Gene Networks, even multi-layer networks with more than two nodes such as gene–disease–drug network, etc. Indeed, this demonstrates that the level of abstraction for biological networks can range from the micro to the macro level.

Finally, categorization of biological networks covers a wide range, each representing different aspects of biological systems. The choice of graph type for modeling depends on the nature of the biological entities and their interactions. Some networks may have variations or combinations of these basic types, especially when incorporating multi-omics data or temporal information.

7.2 COMMUNITY DETECTION APPLICATIONS

In this subsection, we will briefly review the fundamental applications of community detection related categorized by different types of biological networks, to provide novel insights for future research. These insights address areas that have not been routinely considered in community detection for various biological network types. Community detection plays a crucial role in biological network analysis across seven major categories: functional module identification, function prediction, target identification, mechanism understanding and analysis, evolutionary studies, complex or cluster prediction, and biomarker discovery. It is important to note that these applications of community detection are proposed based on the knowledge and experience of the authors. At the end of the subsection, the details of Table 7.1 will be thoroughly explained.

7.2.1 Functional Module Identification

We will provide a brief explanation of functional module identification for each of the mentioned biological networks below based on reviewing the related literature. Depending on the network type, community detection helps identify modules of biological entities that work together in a common function, as shown in Figure 7.2.

7.2.1.1 Protein Networks

Functional module identification in protein networks involves discovering groups of proteins that work together to perform specific cellular functions. This process helps reveal protein complexes and functional pathways within the cell. By analyzing the interconnections and interactions between proteins, researchers can identify clusters or communities that represent biologically meaningful units (Omranian, Angeleska, and Nikoloski 2021). These modules might correspond to molecular machines, behavior cascades, or metabolic pathways. Identifying such functional modules aids in understanding the organization of cellular processes, predicting protein functions,

TABLE 7.1
Intersection of Biological Networks and Their Community Detection Applications

Network Type Community Detection Application	Protein Networks	Gene Regulatory Networks	Metabolic Networks	Signal Transductior Networks	Gene Co-Expression Networks	Drug–Target Networks	Brain Networks	Phylogenetic Networks	Ecological Networks	Disease–Gene Networks	RNA-Related Networks	Transcriptions Factor Binding Networks	Cellular Compartment Networks	Pathway–Pathway Interaction Networks
Functional module identification														
Function prediction														
Target identification														
Mechanism understanding and analysis								**Va-ious Community Detection Application for Different Types of Biological Networks**						
Evolutionary studies														
Complex/cluster prediction														
Biomarker discovery														

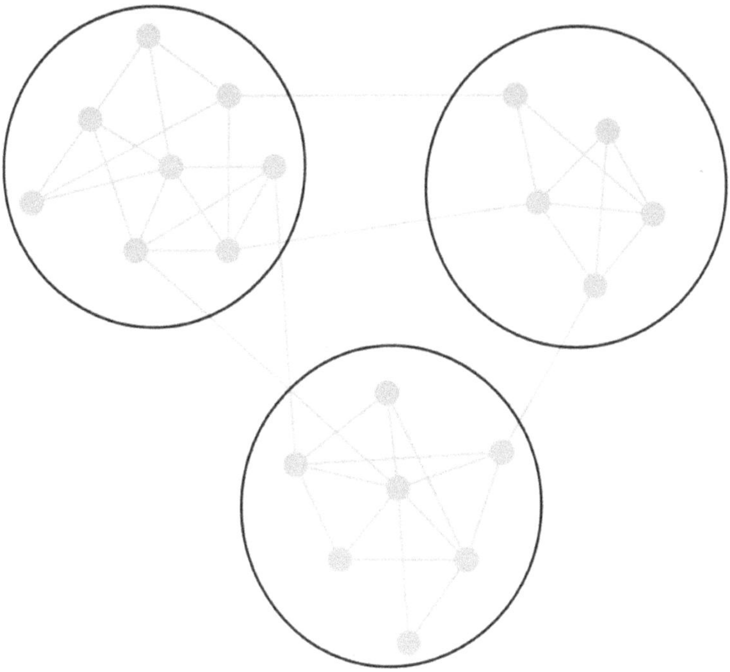

FIGURE 7.2 General overview of functional module identification as the result of community detection in biological networks.

and uncovering the roles of previously uncharacterized proteins based on their associations within the network.

7.2.1.2 Gene Regulatory Networks (GRNs)

In Gene Regulatory Networks, functional module identification focuses on uncovering sets of genes that are regulated by common transcription factors or that work together in specific regulatory processes. This approach helps researchers identify regulatory modules involved in particular cellular responses or developmental processes (Segal et al. 2003). By analyzing the patterns of gene regulation and co-regulation, it becomes possible to discern groups of genes that are functionally related or that respond similarly to certain stimuli. These modules can provide insights into how gene expression is coordinated across different cellular conditions and how complex biological processes are controlled at the transcriptional level.

7.2.1.3 Metabolic Networks

Functional module identification in metabolic networks aims to discover sets of enzymes and metabolites that are involved in specific biochemical pathways or metabolic functions. This process helps reveal how cellular metabolism is organized into distinct functional units. By analyzing the connections between metabolites and the enzymes that catalyze their transformations, researchers can identify modules that represent coherent metabolic pathways or sets of reactions that work together to produce certain compounds. This modular view of metabolism aids in understanding how cells efficiently manage their resources, adapt to different environmental conditions, and maintain homeostasis (Koch and Ackermann 2013).

7.2.1.4 Signal Transduction Networks

In signal transduction networks, functional module identification involves uncovering signaling cascades and pathways that transmit specific cellular signals. This process helps identify groups of proteins that work together to relay information from the cell surface to the nucleus or other cellular compartments. By analyzing the interactions and dependencies between signaling molecules, researchers can discern modules that represent distinct signaling pathways or cross-talking signaling systems. This modular understanding of signal transduction helps elucidate how cells respond to external stimuli, integrate multiple signals, and make decisions about cell fate, growth, and other critical processes (Jiang et al. 2011).

7.2.1.5 Gene Co-Expression Networks

Functional module identification in gene co-expression networks involves discovering groups of genes that show similar expression patterns across various conditions or samples. This approach helps reveal functional modules of genes that are likely involved in the same biological processes or pathways. By analyzing correlations in gene expression data, researchers can identify clusters of genes that are consistently co-expressed, suggesting they may be co-regulated or functionally related (Liang et al. 2019). These modules can provide insights into gene function, help in the annotation of uncharacterized genes, and reveal higher-level organization of cellular processes based on coordinated gene expression patterns.

7.2.1.6 Drug–Target Networks

In drug–target networks, functional module identification focuses on discovering groups of drugs that target similar sets of proteins, or conversely, modules of proteins targeted by specific classes of drugs. This process helps in understanding the mechanism of action of drugs and their potential off-target effects. By analyzing the connections between drugs and their protein targets, researchers can identify modules that represent drug classes with similar mechanisms or protein families that are particularly susceptible to drug interactions. This modular view can aid in drug repurposing efforts, help predict drug side effects, and provide insights into the design of more targeted therapeutics (Hase et al. 2014).

7.2.1.7 Brain Networks

Functional module identification in brain networks involves discovering groups of brain regions or neural circuits that work together to perform specific cognitive functions. This process helps reveal the modular organization of the brain, where different areas collaborate to process information and generate behavior. By analyzing connectivity patterns or co-activation of brain regions, researchers can identify functional modules that correspond to sensory processing, motor control, language, memory, or other cognitive domains. This modular understanding of brain function aids in deciphering how complex cognitive processes emerge from the coordinated activity of distributed neural networks (Faskowitz, Betzel, and Sporns 2022).

7.2.1.8 Phylogenetic Networks

In phylogenetic networks, functional module identification typically involves discovering groups of species or genes with similar evolutionary histories (Erten et al. 2009). This process helps reveal modules of taxa or genetic elements that have undergone similar evolutionary processes. By analyzing the patterns of genetic or trait similarities across species, researchers can identify clusters that represent monophyletic groups, convergent evolution events, or horizontally transferred gene clusters. While traditional functional modules are less common in phylogenetic contexts, this approach can help understand evolutionary relationships, detect instances of hybridization or reticulate evolution, and uncover patterns of trait evolution across lineages.

7.2.1.9 Ecological Networks

Functional module identification in ecological networks involves discovering groups of species with strong ecological interactions or similar roles within an ecosystem. This process helps reveal modules representing food webs, mutualistic relationships, or groups of species that respond similarly to environmental factors. By analyzing the interactions between species (such as predator-prey relationships or pollination networks), researchers can identify clusters that represent functional units within the ecosystem. These modules can provide insights into ecosystem structure, stability, and resilience, and help in predicting how ecosystems might respond to perturbations or changes in species composition (J. Zhou et al. 2010).

7.2.1.10 Disease–Gene Networks

In disease–gene networks, functional module identification focuses on discovering groups of genes associated with specific diseases or disease categories. This process helps reveal modules of genes involved in similar pathological processes or contributing to related disease phenotypes (Tripathi et al. 2019). By analyzing the connections between diseases and their associated genes, researchers can identify clusters that represent common genetic bases for certain disorders or shared pathways in disease progression. This modular view of disease–gene relationships aids in understanding disease mechanisms, identifying potential therapeutic targets, and uncovering previously unknown connections between different medical conditions.

7.2.1.11 RNA-Related Networks

Functional module identification in RNA-related networks involves discovering groups of RNAs with similar functions, regulatory relationships, or interaction partners. This process helps reveal modules of RNA-RNA or RNA–protein interactions that are important for various cellular processes. By analyzing the connections between different RNA species or between RNAs and their binding proteins, researchers can identify clusters that represent functional units in RNA regulation, processing, or cellular localization (Klimm et al. 2020). These modules can provide insights into the complex roles of RNAs in gene expression regulation, cellular structure, and signal transduction.

7.2.1.12 Transcription Factor Binding Networks

In transcription factor binding networks, functional module identification involves discovering groups of genes regulated by similar sets of transcription factors or modules of transcription factors that tend to work together (Karczewski et al. 2014). This process helps reveal regulatory modules involved in specific cellular responses or developmental processes. By analyzing the binding patterns of transcription factors to gene promoters or enhancers, researchers can identify clusters that represent co-regulated gene sets or combinatorial transcription factor complexes. These modules provide insights into the organization of transcriptional regulation and help in understanding how complex gene expression patterns are achieved.

7.2.1.13 Cellular Compartment Networks

Functional module identification in cellular compartment networks focuses on discovering groups of proteins or processes localized to specific cellular compartments or involved in inter-compartment communication (Itzhak et al. 2016). This process helps reveal functional modules within organelles or cellular structures, as well as pathways for material or information exchange between compartments. By analyzing the localization patterns of proteins and their interactions across different cellular spaces, researchers can identify clusters that represent functional units within specific compartments or processes that span multiple compartments. This modular view aids in understanding the spatial organization of cellular functions and how compartmentalization contributes to cellular efficiency and regulation.

7.2.1.14 Pathway–Pathway Interaction Networks

In pathway–pathway interaction networks, functional module identification involves discovering groups of pathways that interact or influence each other. This process helps reveal higher-order functional modules composed of multiple interconnected pathways. By analyzing the connections and dependencies between different biological pathways, researchers can identify clusters that represent super-pathways or functional units that integrate multiple cellular processes (Hsu and Yang 2012). These modules provide insights into how different aspects of cellular function are coordinated and how perturbations in one pathway might affect seemingly unrelated processes. This higher-level modular view aids in understanding the complex interplay between different cellular systems and how cells achieve robust and adaptable functioning.

7.2.2 Function Prediction

Here we try to provide a brief explanation of the function prediction concept for each of the mentioned biological networks below based on reviewing the related literature.

7.2.2.1 Protein Networks

Function prediction in protein networks leverages the principle of "guilt by association," where proteins with unknown functions can be inferred based on their interactions with well-characterized proteins. By analyzing the network topology and the functional annotations of neighboring proteins, researchers can predict potential roles for uncharacterized proteins (Gligorijević et al. 2021). This approach is particularly powerful in identifying proteins involved in specific cellular processes, complexes, or pathways. Machine learning algorithms can be applied to these networks to improve prediction accuracy, considering factors such as network centrality, clustering coefficients, and interaction strengths.

7.2.2.2 Gene Regulatory Networks (GRNs)

In GRNs, function prediction focuses on inferring the regulatory roles of genes and their potential target genes. By analyzing the network structure and the known functions of well-characterized transcription factors and their targets, researchers can predict the regulatory functions of uncharacterized genes (Zhang and Moret 2010). This approach can help identify potential master regulators of specific biological processes, genes involved in particular cellular responses, or genes crucial for developmental stages. Additionally, by examining the regulatory patterns and motifs in the network, it's possible to predict which genes might be involved in similar regulatory processes or respond to similar stimuli.

7.2.2.3 Metabolic Networks

Function prediction in metabolic networks aims to infer the biochemical roles of uncharacterized enzymes or metabolites. By analyzing the position of an unknown entity within the metabolic network, researchers can predict its potential function based on its connections to known metabolic pathways. This approach can help identify missing enzymes in metabolic pathways, predict the substrates or products of uncharacterized enzymes, and infer the potential roles of novel metabolites. Network-based approaches can also predict which enzymes might be involved in newly discovered metabolic pathways or adaptations to specific environmental conditions (Schläpfer et al. 2017).

7.2.2.4 Signal Transduction Networks

In signal transduction networks, function prediction involves inferring the roles of proteins in signal relay and processing. By analyzing the position of an uncharacterized protein within signaling cascades, researchers can predict its potential function in signal transduction (Li, Assmann, and Albert 2006). This approach can help identify potential kinases, phosphatases, scaffolding proteins, or transcription factors involved in specific signaling pathways. It can also predict which proteins might be crucial for integrating signals from multiple pathways or for determining the specificity of cellular responses to different stimuli.

7.2.2.5 Gene Co-Expression Networks

Function prediction in gene co-expression networks relies on the principle that genes with similar expression patterns are likely to have related functions. By analyzing clusters of co-expressed genes and the known functions of some genes within these clusters, researchers can infer potential functions for uncharacterized genes. This approach is particularly useful for predicting involvement in specific biological processes, cellular components, or molecular functions. It can also help in identifying genes that might be part of the same pathway or regulated by the same transcription factors, thereby providing insights into their potential roles in cellular processes (F. Luo et al. 2007).

7.2.2.6 Drug–Target Networks

In drug–target networks, function prediction focuses on inferring the potential therapeutic applications or mechanisms of action for drugs or drug candidates. By analyzing the network of known drug–target interactions, researchers can predict potential targets for drugs with unknown mechanisms or potential off-target effects of known drugs (Wu et al. 2018). This approach can also be used to predict which drugs might be effective for treating specific diseases based on their target profiles. Additionally, by examining the functional similarities of targets of known drugs, researchers can infer potential functions of uncharacterized proteins that are targeted by similar drugs.

7.2.2.7 Brain Networks

Function prediction in brain networks involves inferring the cognitive or behavioral roles of specific brain regions or neural circuits. By analyzing the connectivity patterns and activation profiles of different brain areas, researchers can predict the potential functions of less-studied regions (Neudorf, Kress, and Borowsky 2022). This approach can help identify brain areas that might be involved in specific cognitive tasks, emotional processes, or sensory–motor functions. It can also predict which brain regions might be crucial for integrating information from different sensory modalities or for coordinating complex behaviors.

7.2.2.8 Phylogenetic Networks

In phylogenetic networks, function prediction typically involves inferring the potential functions of genes or traits in one species based on knowledge from related species. By analyzing the evolutionary relationships and functional annotations across different species, researchers can predict the likely functions of uncharacterized genes in a particular organism (Wen et al. 2018). This approach is particularly useful for transferring functional knowledge from well-studied model organisms to less-studied species. It can also help in predicting how certain traits or functions might have evolved or been conserved across different lineages.

7.2.2.9 Ecological Networks

Function prediction in ecological networks focuses on inferring the ecological roles or niches of species within an ecosystem. By analyzing the interactions between species (such as predator–prey relationships or mutualistic interactions), researchers can predict the potential functions of less-studied species in the ecosystem. This approach can help identify keystone species, predict the effects of species loss on ecosystem functioning, or infer the potential roles of invasive species in new environments. It can also be used to predict how changes in one species might affect others in the network, providing insights into ecosystem dynamics and stability (J. Zhou et al. 2010).

7.2.2.10 Disease–Gene Networks

In disease–gene networks, function prediction aims to infer the potential roles of genes in disease processes or their contributions to specific phenotypes. By analyzing the connections between known disease-associated genes and their functional annotations, researchers can predict which other genes might be involved in similar pathological processes. This approach can help identify potential drug targets, predict genes that might contribute to disease risk or progression, and infer the molecular mechanisms underlying complex diseases. It can also be used to predict potential comorbidities or shared genetic bases between different diseases (Ata et al. 2021).

7.2.2.11 RNA-Related Networks

Function prediction in RNA-related networks involves inferring the potential roles of uncharacterized RNAs or RNA-binding proteins. By analyzing the interactions between RNAs and proteins, as well as the known functions of well-characterized RNAs, researchers can predict potential regulatory, structural, or catalytic functions of novel RNA species. This approach can help identify RNAs involved in gene regulation, splicing, or cellular structure maintenance. It can also predict which RNA-binding proteins might be involved in specific RNA processing events or post-transcriptional regulatory mechanisms (Seifuddin and Pirooznia 2021).

7.2.2.12 Transcription Factor Binding Networks

In transcription factor binding networks, function prediction focuses on inferring the regulatory roles of transcription factors and their target genes. By analyzing the binding patterns of transcription factors and the functions of known target genes, researchers can predict the potential regulatory impacts of less-studied transcription factors (C. Chen et al. 2021). This approach can help identify transcription factors that might be master regulators of specific biological processes, predict which genes might be involved in particular cellular responses, or infer the regulatory programs controlling cell fate decisions. It can also be used to predict how perturbations in transcription factor activity might affect gene expression patterns and cellular phenotypes.

7.2.2.13 Cellular Compartment Networks

Function prediction in cellular compartment networks aims to infer the potential localization and roles of proteins within specific cellular structures or organelles. By analyzing the known localizations of proteins and their interaction partners, researchers can predict where uncharacterized proteins might function within the cell (Watson et al. 2022). This approach can help identify proteins involved in specific organelle functions, predict which proteins might be crucial for inter-compartment communication, or infer the potential roles of proteins in maintaining cellular organization. It can also be used to predict how mislocalization of proteins might contribute to cellular dysfunction or disease states.

7.2.2.14 Pathway–Pathway Interaction Networks

In pathway–pathway interaction networks, function prediction involves inferring the potential roles of pathways in higher-order cellular processes or their contributions to complex phenotypes (Pita-Juárez et al. 2018). By analyzing the interactions and dependencies between different pathways, researchers can predict how perturbations in one pathway might affect others, or how multiple pathways might work together to achieve specific cellular outcomes. This approach can help identify key integrator pathways, predict potential cross-talk mechanisms between seemingly unrelated processes, or infer how cells might coordinate different aspects of their physiology. It can also be used to predict the potential systemic effects of targeting specific pathways in therapeutic interventions.

7.2.3 Target Identification

We will provide a brief explanation of target identification for each of the mentioned biological networks below based on reviewing the related literature. Determining the essentiality or importance of a node in a biological network can be achieved by first partitioning the network into communities and then identifying the most important node in each community. Figure 7.3 illustrates a conceptual view of community detection followed by the identification of key targets based on their degree of centrality or total number of connections.

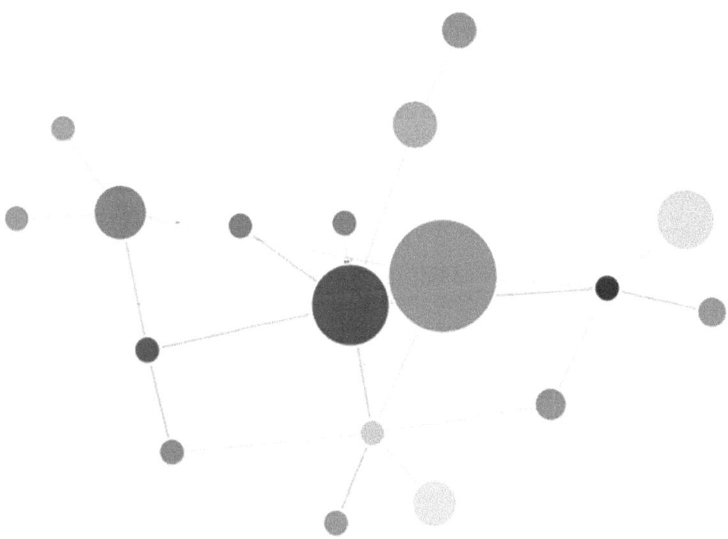

FIGURE 7.3 Identifying important targets through community detection in a network, nodes with greater size play more important role in this example.

7.2.3.1 Protein Networks

Target identification in protein networks involves identifying proteins that play crucial roles in specific biological processes or diseases. By analyzing network topology, researchers can identify highly connected hub proteins or proteins that bridge different functional modules. These proteins often serve as potential drug targets due to their central roles in cellular processes. Furthermore, by examining the network neighborhood of known disease-associated proteins, researchers can identify additional proteins that may be involved in the disease mechanism and thus serve as novel therapeutic targets. This approach can also help in identifying proteins that, when targeted, might have widespread effects on the network, potentially leading to more effective interventions.

7.2.3.2 Gene Regulatory Networks (GRNs)

In GRNs, target identification focuses on identifying key regulatory genes or transcription factors that control important cellular processes or disease states. By analyzing the network structure, researchers can identify master regulators that control large sets of genes or transcription factors that are crucial for specific cellular responses. These regulators often serve as potential drug targets, as modulating their activity can have broad effects on gene expression patterns. Additionally, by examining the regulatory relationships in disease-associated GRNs, researchers can identify aberrant regulatory interactions that could be targeted to restore normal gene expression patterns.

7.2.3.3 Metabolic Networks

Target identification in metabolic networks aims to find enzymes or metabolites that are critical for specific metabolic pathways or cellular functions. By analyzing the network structure, researchers can identify bottleneck reactions or enzymes that control flux through important pathways. These enzymes often serve as good drug targets, as their inhibition can effectively disrupt pathways crucial for pathogen survival or cancer cell proliferation. Furthermore, by examining alterations in metabolic networks associated with diseases, researchers can identify metabolic vulnerabilities that could be exploited for therapeutic interventions. This approach is particularly useful in identifying targets for metabolic diseases, cancer, and infectious diseases.

7.2.3.4 Signal Transduction Networks

In signal transduction networks, target identification involves finding key proteins in signaling cascades that, when modulated, can effectively alter cellular responses. By analyzing the network structure, researchers can identify critical nodes that integrate multiple signals or amplify specific responses. These proteins, often kinases or receptors, serve as excellent drug targets due to their pivotal roles in signal propagation. Additionally, by examining how signal transduction networks are altered in disease states, researchers can identify aberrant signaling events that could be targeted to restore normal cellular function. This approach is particularly valuable in developing targeted therapies for cancer and autoimmune diseases.

7.2.3.5 Gene Co-Expression Networks

Target identification in gene co-expression networks focuses on finding genes that are central to co-expression modules associated with specific cellular states or diseases. By analyzing the network structure, researchers can identify hub genes that are highly connected within disease-associated modules. These genes often serve as potential drug targets, as modulating their expression might have broad effects on the entire module. Furthermore, by comparing co-expression networks between healthy and disease states, researchers can identify genes whose co-expression patterns are significantly altered, potentially revealing novel therapeutic targets.

7.2.3.6 Drug–Target Networks

In drug–target networks, target identification involves finding proteins that, when targeted, could have therapeutic effects with minimal side effects. By analyzing the network of known drug–target interactions, researchers can identify proteins that are targeted by multiple successful drugs, suggesting their importance as therapeutic targets. Conversely, they can also identify proteins that are not targeted by any known drugs, potentially revealing novel therapeutic opportunities. Additionally, by examining the network neighborhood of targets of successful drugs, researchers can identify related proteins that might serve as targets for developing new drugs with similar therapeutic effects.

7.2.3.7 Brain Networks

Target identification in brain networks focuses on identifying brain regions or neural circuits that play crucial roles in specific cognitive functions or neurological disorders. By analyzing network connectivity patterns, researchers can identify hub regions that integrate information from multiple sources or regions that show altered connectivity in disease states. These regions or circuits can serve as targets for interventions such as deep brain stimulation or transcranial magnetic stimulation. Additionally, by examining how brain networks are disrupted in neurological or psychiatric disorders, researchers can identify specific connections or regions that could be targeted to restore normal brain function.

7.2.3.8 Phylogenetic Networks

In phylogenetic networks, target identification typically involves identifying genes or traits that are conserved across species and play crucial roles in fundamental biological processes. By analyzing the evolutionary relationships and functional annotations across different species, researchers can identify highly conserved genes that are likely to be essential for survival. These genes often serve as good drug targets, especially for developing broad-spectrum antimicrobials. Additionally, by examining how certain traits or functions have evolved across species, researchers can identify genes that have undergone positive selection in specific lineages, potentially revealing targets for species-specific interventions.

7.2.3.9 Ecological Networks

Target identification in ecological networks involves identifying species or interactions that are crucial for maintaining ecosystem stability or function. By analyzing network structure, researchers can identify keystone species that have disproportionate effects on ecosystem dynamics. These species could be targets for conservation efforts or for managing ecosystem services. Additionally, by examining how ecological networks respond to perturbations, researchers can identify critical interactions or species that could be targeted to enhance ecosystem resilience or to control invasive species.

7.2.3.10 Disease–Gene Networks

In disease–gene networks, target identification focuses on finding genes that play central roles in disease processes. By analyzing the network of disease–gene associations, researchers can identify genes that are linked to multiple related diseases, suggesting their importance in common pathological processes. These genes often serve as promising drug targets. Additionally, by examining the network neighborhood of known disease genes, researchers can identify other genes that might be involved in the disease mechanism, potentially revealing novel therapeutic targets. This approach is particularly useful for complex diseases where multiple genes contribute to the disease phenotype.

7.2.3.11 RNA-Related Networks

Target identification in RNA-related networks involves finding key RNAs or RNA-binding proteins that play crucial roles in gene regulation or disease processes. By analyzing interaction networks between RNAs and proteins, researchers can identify hub RNAs or proteins that are involved in multiple regulatory processes. These molecules can serve as potential therapeutic targets, especially in diseases associated with dysregulation of RNA processing or function. Additionally, by examining how RNA-related networks are altered in disease states, researchers can identify specific RNA–protein interactions that could be targeted to restore normal cellular function.

7.2.3.12 Transcription Factor Binding Networks

In transcription factor binding networks, target identification focuses on finding key transcription factors that regulate important sets of genes involved in specific cellular processes or diseases. By analyzing the network of transcription factor–gene interactions, researchers can identify master regulators that control large gene sets or transcription factors that are crucial for specific cellular responses. These transcription factors often serve as potential drug targets, as modulating their activity can have broad effects on gene expression patterns. Additionally, by examining how transcription factor binding patterns are altered in disease states, researchers can identify aberrant regulatory interactions that could be targeted to restore normal gene expression.

7.2.3.13 Cellular Compartment Networks

Target identification in cellular compartment networks involves finding proteins or processes that are crucial for maintaining cellular organization or for inter-compartment communication. By analyzing the network of protein localizations and interactions across different cellular compartments, researchers can identify proteins that play key roles in multiple compartments or in trafficking between compartments. These proteins can serve as potential drug targets, especially for diseases associated with protein mislocalization or organelle dysfunction. Additionally, by examining how cellular compartment networks are altered in disease states, researchers can identify specific inter-compartment interactions or processes that could be targeted to restore normal cellular function.

7.2.3.14 Pathway–Pathway Interaction Networks

In pathway–pathway interaction networks, target identification focuses on finding key pathways or pathway interactions that are crucial for complex cellular processes or disease states. By analyzing the network of interactions between different biological pathways, researchers can identify central pathways that integrate information from multiple cellular processes. These pathways, or the proteins mediating their interactions, can serve as potential therapeutic targets. Additionally, by examining how pathway interactions are altered in disease states, researchers can identify specific cross-talk mechanisms or pathway dependencies that could be targeted to disrupt disease progression. This approach is particularly valuable for developing combination therapies or for identifying targets that might have broad effects on cellular function.

7.3 MECHANISM UNDERSTANDING AND ANALYSIS

We will provide a brief explanation of mechanism understanding and analysis for each of the mentioned biological networks below based on reviewing the related literature.

7.3.1 Protein Networks

Mechanism understanding and analysis in protein networks involves deciphering how proteins interact and work together to carry out cellular functions. By studying the topology and dynamics of these networks, researchers can identify protein complexes, signaling cascades, and functional modules. This approach helps elucidate how perturbations in one part of the network can propagate and affect other areas, providing insights into disease mechanisms and drug effects. Advanced techniques like time-resolved proteomics and network perturbation analysis allow researchers to understand how protein interactions change over time or in response to stimuli, revealing the dynamic nature of cellular processes and adaptation mechanisms.

7.3.2 Gene Regulatory Networks (GRNs)

In GRNs, mechanism understanding focuses on how genes regulate each other's expression to control cellular processes. Analysis of these networks reveals regulatory motifs, feedback loops, and hierarchical structures that govern gene expression patterns. By studying how transcription factors and other regulatory elements interact, researchers can understand mechanisms of cell differentiation, response to environmental stimuli, and disease progression. Techniques like ChIP-seq and single-cell RNA sequencing provide high-resolution data to construct and validate these networks, allowing for a deeper understanding of how genetic regulation orchestrates complex biological phenomena.

7.3.3 Metabolic Networks

Mechanism understanding in metabolic networks involves analyzing the flow of matter and energy through biochemical pathways. By studying these networks, researchers can identify key enzymes, metabolic bottlenecks, and regulatory points that control cellular metabolism. Flux balance analysis and metabolic control analysis are powerful tools used to predict how changes in enzyme activity or metabolite concentrations affect overall metabolic output. This understanding is crucial for elucidating mechanisms of metabolic diseases, designing metabolic engineering strategies, and identifying potential drug targets in pathogens or cancer cells.

7.3.4 Signal Transduction Networks

Analysis of signal transduction networks focuses on understanding how cells perceive and respond to external stimuli. By mapping out signaling cascades and studying their dynamics, researchers can elucidate mechanisms of signal amplification, integration, and attenuation. This understanding is crucial for comprehending how cells make decisions in complex environments. Techniques like phosphoproteomics and live-cell imaging allow for real-time tracking of signaling events, revealing the spatiotemporal dynamics of these processes. Such analyses are vital for understanding the mechanisms of diseases like cancer, where signaling pathways are often dysregulated.

7.3.5 Gene Co-Expression Networks

Mechanism understanding in gene co-expression networks involves identifying groups of genes that are expressed together under various conditions. By analyzing these co-expression patterns, researchers can infer functional relationships between genes and understand coordinated gene regulation mechanisms. This approach is particularly useful for identifying genes involved in specific biological processes or diseases, even when their individual functions are unknown. Integration of co-expression data with other types of networks can provide a more comprehensive understanding of cellular mechanisms and gene function.

7.3.6 Drug–Target Networks

Analysis of drug–target networks aims to understand the mechanisms of drug action and side effects. By studying how drugs interact with multiple targets and how these interactions propagate through biological networks, researchers can elucidate both therapeutic and adverse effects of drugs. This network-based approach helps in understanding poly pharmacology, where a drug's effects are mediated through multiple targets. It also aids in predicting drug repurposing opportunities and potential drug–drug interactions, thereby improving our understanding of complex pharmacological mechanisms.

7.3.7 Brain Networks

Mechanism understanding in brain networks focuses on how different brain regions communicate and coordinate to produce cognitive functions and behaviors. By analyzing structural and functional connectivity patterns, researchers can elucidate mechanisms of information processing, memory formation, and decision-making. Advanced neuroimaging techniques combined with network analysis reveal how brain networks reconfigure dynamically in response to tasks or in disease states. This understanding is crucial for deciphering the mechanisms of neurological and psychiatric disorders and for developing targeted interventions.

7.3.8 Phylogenetic Networks

In phylogenetic networks, mechanism understanding involves analyzing evolutionary relationships and processes. By studying these networks, researchers can elucidate mechanisms of speciation, gene transfer, and adaptation. Analysis of phylogenetic networks helps in understanding how traits evolve, how species interact and diverge, and how genetic material is exchanged between different lineages. This understanding is crucial for fields like evolutionary biology, ecology, and epidemiology, providing insights into mechanisms of biodiversity generation and pathogen evolution.

7.3.9 Ecological Networks

Mechanism understanding in ecological networks involves analyzing interactions between species and their environment. By studying food webs, mutualistic networks, and other ecological interactions, researchers can elucidate mechanisms of ecosystem stability, species coexistence, and community assembly. Network analysis reveals how perturbations in one part of the ecosystem can propagate, affecting other species and ecosystem functions. This understanding is crucial for predicting ecosystem responses to environmental changes, managing conservation efforts, and understanding mechanisms of species invasion and extinction.

7.3.10 Disease–Gene Networks

Analysis of disease–gene networks aims to understand the genetic mechanisms underlying complex diseases. By studying how disease-associated genes interact and form functional modules, researchers can elucidate pathways and processes involved in disease pathogenesis. This network-based approach helps in understanding how multiple genetic factors contribute to disease risk and progression, moving beyond single-gene perspectives. Integration of disease–gene networks with other biological networks provides a systems-level understanding of disease mechanisms, aiding in the development of targeted therapies and personalized medicine approaches.

7.3.11 RNA-Related Networks

Mechanism understanding in RNA-related networks focuses on how different RNA species interact with each other and with proteins to regulate gene expression and cellular function. Analysis of these networks reveals mechanisms of post-transcriptional regulation, including RNA splicing, stability, and localization. By studying RNA-protein interactions and RNA–RNA interactions, researchers can elucidate complex regulatory mechanisms like those involving microRNAs and long non-coding RNAs. This understanding is crucial for comprehending gene regulation mechanisms in development, disease, and cellular response to environmental cues.

7.3.12 Transcription Factor Binding Networks

Analysis of transcription factor binding networks aims to understand how gene expression is regulated at the transcriptional level. By studying how different transcription factors interact with DNA and with each other, researchers can elucidate mechanisms of combinatorial gene regulation and enhancer function. Network analysis reveals regulatory motifs, feedback loops, and hierarchical structures that govern complex expression patterns. This understanding is crucial for deciphering mechanisms of cell fate determination, disease progression, and cellular response to various stimuli.

7.3.13 Cellular Compartment Networks

Mechanism understanding in cellular compartment networks involves analyzing how different organelles and cellular structures interact and communicate. By studying the flow of molecules and information between compartments, researchers can elucidate mechanisms of cellular organization and function. This network-based approach helps in understanding how cells maintain homeostasis, respond to stress, and carry out complex processes like protein trafficking and signal transduction. Analysis of these networks is crucial for understanding the mechanisms of diseases associated with organelle dysfunction and for developing targeted therapies.

7.3.14 Pathway–Pathway Interaction Networks

Analysis of pathway–pathway interaction networks aims to understand how different biological pathways influence and regulate each other. By studying these higher-order interactions, researchers can elucidate mechanisms of cellular decision-making, homeostasis, and adaptation to complex environments. This network-based approach reveals how perturbations in one pathway can have far-reaching effects on seemingly unrelated cellular processes. Understanding these interactions is crucial for predicting systemic effects of drugs, elucidating complex disease mechanisms, and developing more effective therapeutic strategies that target multiple pathways simultaneously.

7.4 EVOLUTIONARY STUDIES

We will provide a brief explanation of evolutionary studies for each of the mentioned biological networks below based on reviewing the related literature. A visual example of the evolution of communities within a sample biological network over time can be seen in Figure 7.4.

7.4.1 Protein Networks

Evolutionary studies of protein networks focus on how protein–protein interactions have evolved over time. Researchers compare protein interaction networks across different species to identify conserved modules, which often represent fundamental cellular processes. These studies reveal how new interactions emerge, how existing ones are lost or modified, and how the overall network topology changes through evolution. By examining the rate of evolution of different network components, researchers can identify proteins and interactions that are under strong evolutionary pressure, indicating their functional importance (Yamada and Bork 2009). Such studies also help in understanding how organisms adapt to different environments by rewiring their protein interaction networks.

7.4.2 Gene Regulatory Networks (GRNs)

Evolutionary studies of GRNs investigate how regulatory relationships between genes change over evolutionary time. By comparing GRNs across species, researchers can identify conserved regulatory modules and species-specific innovations. These studies reveal how changes in regulatory interactions contribute to phenotypic

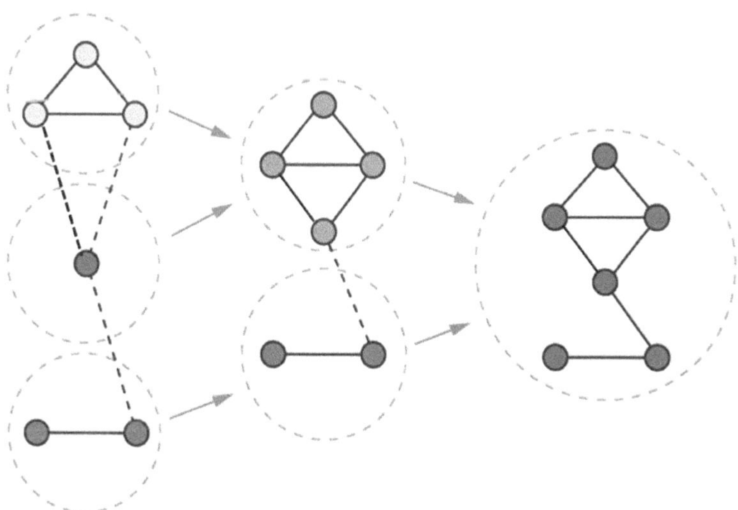

FIGURE 7.4 Biological network evolution in view of community detection.

diversity and adaptation. Researchers examine the evolution of transcription factor binding sites, the emergence of new regulatory connections, and the rewiring of existing networks. Such analyses provide insights into the mechanisms of evolutionary innovation, the origins of complex traits, and the plasticity of gene regulation in response to environmental changes.

7.4.3 Metabolic Networks

Evolutionary studies of metabolic networks examine how organisms' biochemical capabilities have evolved over time. Researchers compare metabolic networks across different species to understand the evolution of metabolic pathways and the acquisition of new metabolic capabilities. These studies reveal how organisms adapt to different nutritional environments and how metabolic diversity arises. By analyzing the presence or absence of enzymes and metabolites across species, researchers can reconstruct ancestral metabolic networks and trace the evolution of specific pathways. Such studies are crucial for understanding the metabolic basis of adaptation and for metabolic engineering applications.

7.4.4 Signal Transduction Networks

Evolutionary studies of signal transduction networks focus on how cellular signaling pathways have evolved. By comparing these networks across species, researchers can identify conserved signaling modules and species-specific adaptations. These studies reveal how organisms have evolved to respond to different environmental stimuli and how complex multicellular signaling arose from simpler systems. Researchers examine the evolution of receptor proteins, kinases, and other signaling components, as well as the rewiring of signaling cascades. Such analyses provide insights into the origins of cellular communication systems and how they contribute to organismal complexity and adaptability.

7.4.5 Gene Co-Expression Networks

Evolutionary studies of gene co-expression networks investigate how patterns of coordinated gene expression have changed over evolutionary time. By comparing co-expression networks across species, researchers can identify conserved co-expression modules, which often represent fundamental biological processes. These studies reveal how gene regulation evolves at a systems level, beyond individual regulatory interactions. Researchers examine how co-expression patterns change in response to different evolutionary pressures and how they contribute to phenotypic diversity. Such analyses provide insights into the evolution of gene function and the emergence of tissue-specific gene expression patterns.

7.4.6 Drug–Target Networks

Evolutionary studies of drug–target networks focus on how the interactions between drugs and their protein targets have evolved. While not directly subject to natural selection, these networks reflect the evolution of the underlying protein networks. Researchers examine how the drug ability of proteins has changed over evolutionary time and how this relates to their functional importance. These studies can reveal why certain proteins are common drug targets across many species while others are species-specific. Such analyses are crucial for understanding the evolutionary basis of drug efficacy and for predicting potential drug targets in newly emerging pathogens.

7.4.7 Brain Networks

Evolutionary studies of brain networks examine how neural connectivity patterns have evolved across different species. By comparing brain networks in different organisms, from simple invertebrates to complex mammals, researchers can trace the evolution of cognitive functions and behaviors. These studies reveal how brain regions and their connections have been conserved or modified through evolution, providing insights into the origins of complex cognitive abilities. Researchers examine changes in network topology, the emergence of new brain regions, and the rewiring of existing circuits. Such analyses are crucial for understanding the evolutionary basis of cognition and for interpreting human brain function in an evolutionary context.

7.4.8 Phylogenetic Networks

Evolutionary studies of phylogenetic networks are intrinsically focused on understanding evolutionary relationships and processes. These networks represent the complex evolutionary histories of species or genes, including events like horizontal gene transfer, hybridization, and incomplete lineage sorting. By analyzing these networks, researchers can reconstruct evolutionary histories, estimate divergence times, and understand processes of speciation and adaptation. These studies are crucial for understanding biodiversity, tracking the spread of pathogens, and reconstructing the tree of life. They also provide insights into how evolutionary processes shape genetic and phenotypic diversity.

7.4.9 Ecological Networks

Evolutionary studies of ecological networks examine how species interactions have evolved over time. By comparing ecological networks across different ecosystems and time periods, researchers can understand how community structures and species interactions change through evolution. These studies reveal how co-evolution shapes species interactions, how new ecological roles emerge, and how ecosystems respond to environmental changes over evolutionary time scales. Researchers examine changes in network topology, the evolution of mutualistic and antagonistic relationships, and the stability of ecological communities. Such analyses are crucial for understanding the evolutionary basis of ecosystem function and for predicting how ecosystems might respond to future environmental changes.

7.4.10 Disease–Gene Networks

Evolutionary studies of disease–gene networks focus on how genetic susceptibility to diseases has evolved over time. By comparing disease–gene associations across species, researchers can identify conserved disease mechanisms and species-specific vulnerabilities. These studies reveal how genetic risk factors have changed through evolution and how they relate to past selective pressures. Researchers examine the evolution of disease-associated genes, the emergence of new disease susceptibilities, and the maintenance of genetic variants that increase disease risk. Such analyses provide insights into the evolutionary origins of diseases and can help in identifying potential therapeutic targets.

7.4.11 RNA-Related Networks

Evolutionary studies of RNA-related networks investigate how RNA–RNA and RNA–protein interactions have evolved. By comparing these networks across species, researchers can trace the evolution of RNA-based regulatory mechanisms. These studies reveal how non-coding RNAs have emerged as regulatory elements and how RNA–protein interactions have been conserved or modified through evolution. Researchers examine the evolution of RNA structures, the emergence of new RNA classes, and the rewiring of RNA-based regulatory networks. Such analyses are crucial for understanding the evolutionary significance of RNA in cellular function and regulation.

7.4.12 Transcription Factor Binding Networks

Evolutionary studies of transcription factor binding networks focus on how gene regulatory interactions have evolved at the DNA level. By comparing binding patterns across species, researchers can identify conserved regulatory elements and species-specific innovations. These studies reveal how changes in transcription factor binding contribute to phenotypic diversity and adaptation. Researchers examine the evolution of binding motifs, the turnover of binding sites, and the rewiring of regulatory networks. Such analyses provide insights into the mechanisms of regulatory evolution and how changes in gene regulation contribute to organismal complexity and diversity.

7.4.13 Cellular Compartment Networks

Evolutionary studies of cellular compartment networks examine how the organization of cellular space has evolved over time. By comparing these networks across species, from prokaryotes to complex eukaryotes, researchers can trace the evolution of cellular complexity. These studies reveal how new organelles have emerged, how protein targeting mechanisms have evolved, and how inter-compartment communication has been established and modified. Researchers examine changes in compartment structure, the evolution of transport proteins, and the rewiring of inter-compartment interactions. Such analyses are crucial for understanding the evolutionary basis of cellular organization and function.

7.4.14 Pathway–Pathway Interaction Networks

Evolutionary studies of pathway–pathway interaction networks focus on how the relationships between different biological pathways have evolved. By comparing these higher-order networks across species, researchers can understand how cellular processes have become integrated over evolutionary time. These studies reveal how new pathway interactions emerge, how existing ones are modified or lost, and how the overall cellular system becomes more complex or streamlined. Researchers examine the evolution of pathway crosstalk, the emergence of new regulatory connections between pathways, and the conservation of core pathway interactions. Such analyses provide insights into the evolution of cellular complexity and how organisms adapt to diverse environments by modifying the interactions between different cellular processes.

7.5 COMPLEX/CLUSTER PREDICTION

We will provide a brief explanation of complex/cluster prediction for each of the mentioned biological networks below based on reviewing the related literature. Complexes can be imagined as communities identified after detection, each composed of several tightly associated biological entities. Figure 7.5 illustrates this concept from a general perspective.

7.5.1 Protein Networks

Complex/cluster prediction in protein networks involves identifying groups of proteins that work together to perform specific cellular functions. This process uses various algorithms to detect densely interconnected regions within the network, which often correspond to protein complexes or functional modules. Methods like Markov Clustering, MCODE, or Cluster ONE are commonly employed. These predictions help in understanding cellular organization, discovering new protein complexes, and inferring functions of uncharacterized proteins based on their cluster membership. Such analyses are crucial for elucidating mechanisms of cellular processes and identifying potential drug targets in disease-related protein clusters.

7.5.2 Gene Regulatory Networks (GRNs)

In GRNs, complex/cluster prediction focuses on identifying sets of genes that are co-regulated or form regulatory modules. This involves detecting groups of genes controlled by similar sets of transcription factors or groups of transcription factors that tend to work together. Methods like hierarchical clustering, k-means clustering, or more advanced techniques like biclustering are often used. These predictions help in understanding coordinated gene regulation, identifying master regulators of

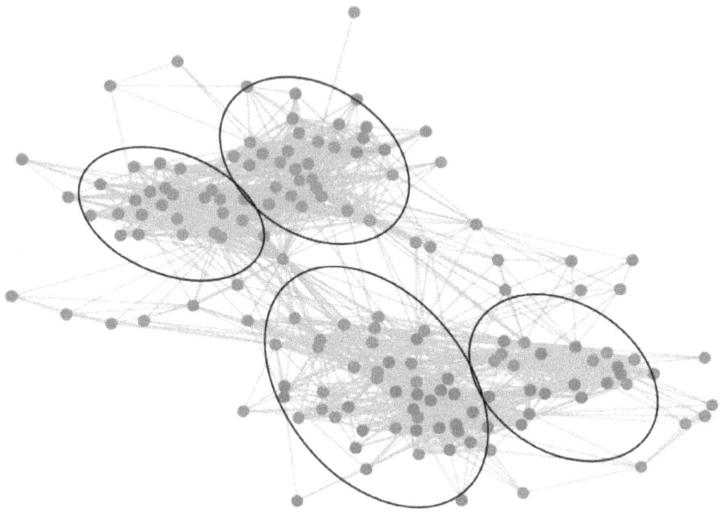

FIGURE 7.5 Complex detection/prediction as a widely used application of community detection in biological networks. It identifies the compact regions of the network, such as protein complexes.

cellular processes, and uncovering regulatory programs involved in development or disease. Such analyses are vital for deciphering the complex logic of gene regulation and predicting cellular responses to various stimuli.

7.5.3 Metabolic Networks

Complex/cluster prediction in metabolic networks aims to identify groups of metabolites and enzymes that form functional metabolic modules or pathways. This often involves detecting sets of reactions that operate together to perform specific biochemical functions. Techniques like elementary flux mode analysis, extreme pathway analysis, or community detection algorithms are commonly used. These predictions help in understanding the modular organization of metabolism, identifying bottlenecks in metabolic pathways, and predicting potential sites for metabolic engineering. Such analyses are crucial for understanding cellular metabolism and developing strategies for metabolic disease treatment or biotechnological applications.

7.5.4 Signal Transduction Networks

In signal transduction networks, complex/cluster prediction focuses on identifying signaling modules or cascades that work together to transmit specific cellular signals. This involves detecting groups of signaling proteins that are frequently activated together or form coherent signaling pathways. Methods like network motif detection, module detection algorithms, or dynamic network analysis are often employed. These predictions help in understanding how cells integrate multiple signals, identifying critical nodes in signaling pathways, and predicting cellular responses to various stimuli. Such analyses are vital for understanding cell decision-making processes and identifying potential targets for therapeutic interventions in diseases like cancer.

7.5.5 Gene Co-Expression Networks

Complex/cluster prediction in gene co-expression networks involves identifying groups of genes that show similar expression patterns across various conditions. This often uses techniques like hierarchical clustering, k-means clustering, or more advanced methods like weighted gene co-expression network analysis (WGCNA). These predictions help in identifying functionally related genes, uncovering gene modules associated with specific biological processes or diseases, and inferring functions of uncharacterized genes. Such analyses are crucial for understanding the functional organization of the genome and identifying potential biomarkers or therapeutic targets.

7.5.6 Drug–Target Networks

In drug–target networks, complex/cluster prediction aims to identify groups of drugs that target similar sets of proteins or groups of proteins targeted by similar sets of drugs. This often involves techniques like biclustering, community detection, or network-based clustering algorithms. These predictions help in understanding drug mechanisms of action, identifying potential off-target effects, and discovering opportunities for drug repurposing. Such analyses are vital for drug discovery and development, helping to predict drug efficacy and side effects based on network properties.

7.5.7 Brain Networks

Complex/cluster prediction in brain networks focuses on identifying functional modules or circuits within the brain. This involves detecting groups of brain regions that show coordinated activity or structural connectivity. Methods like modularity maximization, spectral clustering, or dynamic functional connectivity analysis are commonly used. These predictions help in understanding brain organization, identifying functional circuits involved in specific cognitive processes, and detecting alterations in brain network structure in neurological disorders. Such analyses are crucial for advancing our understanding of brain function and developing targeted interventions for brain disorders.

7.5.8 Phylogenetic Networks

In phylogenetic networks, complex/cluster prediction often involves identifying groups of species or genes with similar evolutionary histories. This can include detecting clusters of closely related species, identifying groups of genes that have undergone similar evolutionary processes, or uncovering reticulate events like hybridization or horizontal gene transfer. Methods like network community detection, phylogenetic tree-based clustering, or reticulate network analysis are commonly used. These predictions help in understanding evolutionary relationships, identifying instances of convergent evolution, and uncovering patterns of gene flow between species. Such analyses are crucial for reconstructing evolutionary histories and understanding the processes that shape biodiversity.

7.5.9 Ecological Networks

Complex/cluster prediction in ecological networks aims to identify groups of species that interact closely or form functional units within ecosystems. This can involve detecting food web modules, mutualistic clusters, or groups of species with similar ecological roles. Methods like modularity analysis, nested ness detection, or motif analysis are often employed. These predictions help in understanding ecosystem structure, identifying keystone species or functional groups, and predicting ecosystem responses to perturbations. Such analyses are vital for ecosystem management, conservation planning, and predicting the impacts of environmental changes on ecological communities.

7.5.10 Disease–Gene Networks

In disease–gene networks, complex/cluster prediction focuses on identifying groups of genes associated with specific diseases or disease categories. This often involves detecting densely interconnected subnetworks of disease-associated genes or identifying clusters of diseases with similar genetic bases. Methods like network module detection, disease module detection algorithms, or biclustering approaches are commonly used. These predictions help in understanding disease mechanisms, identifying potential drug targets, and uncovering shared genetic bases between seemingly unrelated diseases. Such analyses are crucial for advancing our understanding of complex diseases and developing targeted therapeutic strategies (Ata et al. 2021).

7.5.11 RNA-Related Networks

Complex/cluster prediction in RNA-related networks involves identifying groups of RNAs or RNA-binding proteins that work together in specific cellular processes. This can include detecting clusters of co-regulated RNAs, identifying groups of RNAs that interact with similar sets of proteins, or uncovering functional modules in RNA processing pathways. Methods like clustering algorithms, network motif detection, or RNA structure-based clustering are often employed. These predictions help in understanding RNA-based regulation, identifying functional RNA classes, and predicting RNA–protein interactions. Such analyses are vital for elucidating the complex roles of RNAs in cellular function and gene regulation.

7.5.12 Transcription Factor Binding Networks

In transcription factor binding networks, complex/cluster prediction aims to identify groups of transcription factors that tend to bind to similar genomic regions or groups of genes regulated by similar sets of transcription factors. This often involves techniques like motif-based clustering, co-binding analysis, or regulatory module detection algorithms. These predictions help in understanding combinatorial gene regulation, identifying enhancer regions, and predicting transcriptional responses to various stimuli. Such analyses are crucial for deciphering the complex logic of gene regulation and predicting gene expression patterns in different cellular contexts.

7.5.13 Cellular Compartment Networks

Complex/cluster prediction in cellular compartment networks focuses on identifying groups of proteins or processes that are localized to specific cellular compartments or involved in inter-compartment communication. This can involve detecting clusters of proteins that co-localize in certain organelles or identifying functional modules that span multiple compartments. Methods like spatial clustering algorithms, compartment-specific network analysis, or protein localization prediction tools are often used. These predictions help in understanding cellular organization, predicting protein localization, and identifying processes involved in organelle function or inter-compartment trafficking. Such analyses are vital for elucidating the spatial organization of cellular processes and understanding how cells coordinate activities across different compartments.

7.5.14 Pathway–Pathway Interaction Networks

In pathway–pathway interaction networks, complex/cluster prediction aims to identify groups of pathways that frequently interact or influence each other. This often involves detecting densely interconnected regions in the network of pathway interactions or identifying sets of pathways that consistently show coordinated activity. Methods like hierarchical clustering, network community detection, or pathway crosstalk analysis are commonly employed. These predictions help in understanding higher-order cellular organization, identifying super-pathways or functional modules that span multiple canonical pathways, and predicting systemic responses to perturbations. Such analyses are crucial for developing a systems-level understanding of cellular function and predicting complex cellular behaviors that emerge from the interactions between multiple pathways.

7.6 BIOMARKER DISCOVERY

We will provide a brief explanation of biomarker discovery for each of the mentioned biological networks below based on reviewing the related literature. In this case, the biomarkers are specific nodes within each detected community that play a crucial role in their group, serving purposes such as cancer markers, Figure 7.6.

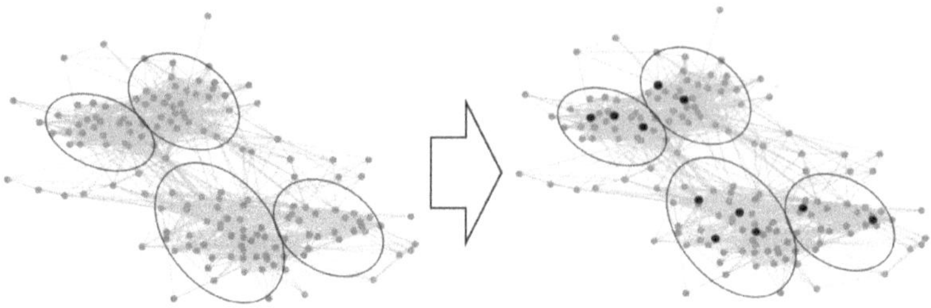

FIGURE 7.6 Sample biomarker discovery process based on community detection.

7.6.1 Protein Networks

Biomarker discovery in protein networks involves identifying proteins or protein complexes that can serve as indicators of specific biological states or diseases. This process often focuses on hub proteins, which have many interactions, or proteins that bridge different functional modules. Network analysis can reveal proteins whose expression or interaction patterns change significantly in disease states (Al-Fatlawi et al. 2023). Techniques like differential network analysis and network centrality measures are used to identify potential biomarkers. These protein biomarkers can be used for early disease detection, prognosis prediction, or monitoring treatment response. The network context provides additional robustness to these biomarkers, as it considers the protein's role within the larger cellular system.

7.6.2 Gene Regulatory Networks (GRNs)

In GRNs, biomarker discovery focuses on identifying key regulatory genes or regulatory interactions that are indicative of specific cellular states or diseases. This might involve detecting master regulators whose activity changes significantly in disease states, or identifying regulatory network motifs that are disrupted. Techniques like network inference and differential network analysis are often employed. These regulatory biomarkers can provide insights into the underlying mechanisms of diseases and may serve as potential therapeutic targets. They are particularly valuable for understanding complex diseases where the dysregulation of gene expression plays a crucial role.

7.6.3 Metabolic Networks

Biomarker discovery in metabolic networks involves identifying metabolites or enzymatic reactions that indicate specific metabolic states or diseases. This often focuses on detecting changes in metabolic flux distributions or identifying metabolites whose levels are significantly altered in disease states. Techniques like flux balance analysis and metabolic control analysis are commonly used. These metabolic biomarkers can be particularly useful for diseases with strong metabolic components, such as diabetes or cancer. They can provide early indicators of disease progression and offer insights into the metabolic reprogramming that occurs in various pathological conditions.

7.6.4 Signal Transduction Networks

In signal transduction networks, biomarker discovery aims to identify signaling molecules or pathway activities that indicate specific cellular responses or disease states. This might involve detecting changes in phosphorylation patterns, identifying pathway activation signatures, or uncovering critical nodes in signaling cascades that are dysregulated in diseases. Techniques like pathway activity inference and phosphoproteomics are often used. These signaling biomarkers can provide real-time indicators of cellular responses to stimuli or therapeutic interventions. They are particularly valuable in cancer research, where aberrant signaling is a hallmark of the disease.

7.6.5 Gene Co-expression Networks

Biomarker discovery in gene co-expression networks focuses on identifying groups of genes whose coordinated expression patterns are indicative of specific biological states or diseases. This often involves detecting changes in network modules or identifying hub genes whose co-expression patterns are significantly altered in disease states. Techniques like weighted gene co-expression network analysis (WGCNA) are commonly used. These co-expression biomarkers can provide robust indicators of complex cellular states, as they capture the coordinated behavior of multiple genes. They are particularly useful for diseases with complex genetic bases, where single-gene biomarkers may be insufficient.

7.6.6 Drug–Target Networks

In drug–target networks, biomarker discovery aims to identify drug–target interactions or network perturbations that can serve as indicators of drug efficacy or toxicity. This might involve detecting changes in network topology following drug treatment or identifying subnetworks that are consistently affected by effective drugs. Techniques like network pharmacology and drug-induced gene expression profiling are often used. These pharmacological biomarkers can help in predicting drug responses, identifying potential side effects, and understanding the mechanisms of drug action. They are particularly valuable in personalized medicine approaches, where predicting individual responses to drugs is crucial.

7.6.7 Brain Networks

Biomarker discovery in brain networks focuses on identifying patterns of brain connectivity or activity that indicate specific cognitive states or neurological disorders. This might involve detecting changes in functional connectivity, identifying altered network modules, or uncovering disruptions in brain network topology.

Techniques like graph theoretical analysis of neuroimaging data and machine learning approaches are commonly used. These neurological biomarkers can provide early indicators of brain disorders, help in monitoring disease progression, and offer insights into the neural bases of various cognitive processes. They are particularly valuable in the study of complex neurological and psychiatric disorders.

7.6.8 Phylogenetic Networks

While not typically used for traditional biomarker discovery, phylogenetic networks can contribute to identifying genetic markers of evolutionary lineages or species-specific traits. This might involve detecting conserved genetic elements across species or identifying genetic variations unique to specific lineages. These evolutionary biomarkers can be useful in fields like conservation biology, where identifying unique genetic markers of endangered species is important, or in epidemiology, where tracing the evolution of pathogens is crucial.

7.6.9 Ecological Networks

In ecological networks, biomarker discovery often focuses on identifying indicator species or network properties that reflect ecosystem health or environmental changes. This might involve detecting changes in network structure, identifying keystone species, or uncovering shifts in interaction patterns (Holt and Miller 2011). These ecological biomarkers can provide early warnings of ecosystem disturbances, help in monitoring biodiversity, and offer insights into the impacts of environmental changes. They are particularly valuable in conservation biology and environmental management.

7.6.10 Disease–Gene Networks

Biomarker discovery in disease–gene networks aims to identify genes or gene modules that are strongly associated with specific diseases or disease progression. This often involves detecting network modules enriched for disease-associated genes or identifying genes that bridge multiple disease modules. Techniques like network-based gene prioritization and disease module detection are commonly used. These genetic biomarkers can provide insights into disease mechanisms, help in early disease detection, and guide personalized treatment strategies. They are particularly valuable in complex diseases with strong genetic components.

7.6.11 RNA-Related Networks

In RNA-related networks, biomarker discovery focuses on identifying RNA species or RNA–protein interactions that indicate specific cellular states or diseases. This might involve detecting changes in RNA expression patterns, identifying alterations in RNA splicing networks, or uncovering dysregulated RNA–protein interactions. Techniques like RNA sequencing and CLIP-seq are often used. These RNA biomarkers can provide sensitive indicators of cellular states and are particularly valuable in diseases where post-transcriptional regulation plays a crucial role, such as many neurological disorders and cancers (Farrel et al. 2023).

7.6.12 Transcription Factor Binding Networks

Biomarker discovery in transcription factor binding networks aims to identify specific binding patterns or regulatory interactions that are indicative of cellular states or diseases. This might involve detecting changes in transcription factor occupancy, identifying altered enhancer activities, or uncovering the rewiring of regulatory networks. Techniques like ChIP-seq and ATAC-seq are commonly used (Dirks, Stunnenberg, and Marks 2016). These regulatory biomarkers can provide insights into the mechanisms of gene regulation in different biological contexts and are particularly valuable in developmental biology and cancer research.

7.6.13 Cellular Compartment Networks

In cellular compartment networks, biomarker discovery focuses on identifying changes in protein localization or inter-compartment communication that indicate specific cellular states or diseases. This might involve detecting alterations in protein trafficking patterns, identifying changes in organelle morphology, or uncovering disruptions in inter-compartment signaling. Techniques like high-content imaging and spatial proteomics are often used. These subcellular biomarkers can provide detailed insights into cellular organization and are particularly valuable in diseases associated with protein mislocalization or organelle dysfunction, such as neurodegenerative disorders.

7.6.14 Pathway–Pathway Interaction Networks

Biomarker discovery in pathway–pathway interaction networks aims to identify higher-order network properties or pathway crosstalk patterns that indicate specific biological states or diseases. This might involve detecting changes in pathway coordination, identifying alterations in pathway crosstalk, or uncovering the rewiring of pathway interactions (Haider et al. 2018). Techniques like pathway enrichment analysis and network-based pathway analysis are commonly used. These systems-level biomarkers can provide holistic views of cellular states and are particularly valuable in complex diseases where the dysregulation of multiple pathways contributes to the pathology.

7.7 CONCLUSION

In conclusion, community detection in biological networks is a vital approach to unravel the complexities of biological systems. The identification of functional modules within these networks not only enhances our understanding of biological interactions but also has practical implications for therapeutic interventions and disease research. Future work in this field may focus on the following:

1. Algorithm Development: There is a need for the development of more efficient and scalable algorithms that can handle the increasing complexity and size of biological networks. Future research could explore hybrid approaches that combine existing algorithms or integrate machine learning techniques to improve accuracy and computational efficiency.
2. Integration of Multi-Omics Data: Future studies could aim to integrate multi-omics data (genomics, proteomics, metabolomics) into community detection frameworks. This integration would provide a more comprehensive view of biological systems and facilitate the identification of functional modules across different biological layers.
3. Dynamic Network Analysis: Biological networks are not static; they change over time due to various factors such as cellular processes and environmental influences. Future works could focus on developing methods for dynamic community detection that can track changes in network structure and function over time.
4. Application to Disease Mechanisms: There is significant potential for applying community detection techniques to understand disease mechanisms better. Future research could focus on specific diseases, using community detection to identify key biological pathways and potential therapeutic targets.
5. Validation and Benchmarking: Establishing standardized benchmarks and validation methods for community detection algorithms in biological contexts is crucial. Future works could focus on creating datasets and metrics that allow for the comparison of different algorithms and their effectiveness in real-world biological scenarios.
6. Visualization Tools: Developing advanced visualization tools to represent detected communities within biological networks could enhance interpretability and facilitate collaboration among biologists and computational scientists.
7. Interdisciplinary Collaboration: Encouraging interdisciplinary collaborations among computer scientists, biologists, and medical researchers could lead to innovative applications of community detection in understanding complex biological systems and improving healthcare outcomes.

By addressing these areas, future research can significantly advance the field of community detection in biological networks, ultimately contributing to a deeper understanding of biological processes and improved therapeutic strategies.

REFERENCES

Aittokallio, Tero, and Benno Schwikowski. 2006. "Graph-Based Methods for Analyzing Networks in Cell Biology." *Briefings in Bioinformatics*. https://doi.org/10.1093/bib/bbl022.

Al-Fatlawi, Ali, Eka Rusadze, Alexander Shmelkin, Negin Malekian, Cigdem Ozen, Christian Pilarsky, and Michael Schroeder. 2023. "Netrank: Network-Based Approach for Biomarker Discovery." *BMC Bioinformatics* 24 (1). https://doi.org/10.1186/s12859-023-05418-6.

Ata, Sezin Kircali, Min Wu, Yuan Fang, Le Ou-Yang, Chee Keong Kwoh, and Xiao Li Li. 2021. "Recent Advances in Network-Based Methods for Disease Gene Prediction." *Briefings in Bioinformatics*. https://doi.org/10.1093/bib/bbaa303.

Banf, Michael, and Seung Y. Rhee. 2017. "Computational Inference of Gene Regulatory Networks: Approaches, Limitations and Opportunities." *Biochimica et Biophysica Acta (BBA)-Gene Regulatory Mechanisms* 1860 (1): 41–52.

Chen, Chen, Jie Hou, Xiaowen Shi, Hua Yang, James A. Birchler, and Jianlin Cheng. 2021. "DeepGRN: Prediction of Transcription Factor Binding Site across Cell-Types Using Attention-Based Deep Neural Networks." *BMC Bioinformatics* 22 (1). https://doi.org/10.1186/s12859-020-03952-1.

Chen, Di, Huamin Zhang, Peng Lu, Xianli Liu, and Hongxin Cao. 2016. "Synergy Evaluation by a Pathway-Pathway Interaction Network: A New Way to Predict Drug Combination." *Molecular BioSystems* 12 (2). https://doi.org/10.1039/c5mb00599j.

Chen, Yan, Pei Zhao, Ping Li, Kai Zhang, and Jie Zhang. 2016. "Finding Communities by Their Centers." *Scientific Reports* 6. https://doi.org/10.1038/srep24017.

Dirks, René A.M., Hendrik G. Stunnenberg, and Hendrik Marks. 2016. "Genome-Wide Epigenomic Profiling for Biomarker Discovery." *Clinical Epigenetics*. https://doi.org/10.1186/s13148-016-0284-4.

Erten, Sinan, Xin Li, Gurkan Bebek, Jing Li, and Mehmet Koyutürk. 2009. "Phylogenetic Analysis of Modularity in Protein Interaction Networks." *BMC Bioinformatics* 10. https://doi.org/10.1186/1471-2105-10-333.

Farrel, Alvin, Peng Li, Sharon Veenbergen, Khushbu Patel, John M. Maris, and Warren J. Leonard. 2023. "ROGUE: An R Shiny App for RNA Sequencing Analysis and Biomarker Discovery." *BMC Bioinformatics* 24 (1). https://doi.org/10.1186/s12859-023-05420-y.

Faskowitz, Joshua, Richard F. Betzel, and Olaf Sporns. 2022. "Edges in Brain Networks: Contributions to Models of Structure and Function." *Network Neuroscience*. https://doi.org/10.1162/netn_a_00204.

Gligorijević, Vladimir, P. Douglas Renfrew, Tomasz Kosciolek, Julia Koehler Leman, Daniel Berenberg, Tommi Vatanen, Chris Chandler, et al. 2021. "Structure-Based Protein Function Prediction Using Graph Convolutional Networks." *Nature Communications* 12 (1). https://doi.org/10.1038/s41467-021-23303-9.

Gupta, Parul, and Sunil Kumar Singh. 2019. "Gene Regulatory Networks: Current Updates and Applications in Plant Biology." In *Energy, Environment, and Sustainability*. https://doi.org/10.1007/978-981-15-0690-1_18.

Haider, Syed, Cindy Q. Yao, Vicky S. Sabine, Michal Grzadkowski, Vincent Stimper, Maud H.W. Starmans, Jianxin Wang, et al. 2018. "Pathway-Based Subnetworks Enable Cross-Disease Biomarker Discovery." *Nature Communications* 9 (1). https://doi.org/10.1038/s41467-018-07021-3.

Hall, Peter A., Jorge S. Reis-Filho, Ian P.M. Tomlinson, and Richard Poulsom. 2010. "An Introduction to Genes, Genomes and Disease." *Journal of Pathology*. https://doi.org/10.1002/path.2652.

Hase, Takeshi, Kaito Kikuchi, Samik Ghosh, Hiroaki Kitano, and Hiroshi Tanaka. 2014. "Identification of Drug-Target Modules in the Human Protein–Protein Interaction Network." *Artificial Life and Robotics* 19 (4). https://doi.org/10.1007/s10015-014-0178-5.

Hashemi, Rastegar, and Hassan Darabi. 2022. "The Review of Ecological Network Indicators in Graph Theory Context: 2014–2021." *International Journal of Environmental Research*. https://doi.org/10.1007/s41742-022-00404-x.

Hellmuth, Marc, David Schaller, and Peter F. Stadler. 2023. "Clustering Systems of Phylogenetic Networks." *Theory in Biosciences* 142 (4). https://doi.org/10.1007/s12064-023-00398-w.

Holt, E A, and S W Miller. 2011. "Bioindicators: Using Organisms to Measure Environmental Impacts." *Nature Education Knowledge* 3 (10).

Hsu, Chia Lang, and Ueng Cheng Yang. 2012. "Discovering Pathway Cross-Talks Based on Functional Relations between Pathways." *BMC Genomics* 13 (Suppl 7). https://doi.org/10.1186/1471-2164-13-s7-s25.

Itzhak, Daniel N., Stefka Tyanova, Jürgen Cox, and Georg H.H. Borner. 2016. "Global, Quantitative and Dynamic Mapping of Protein Subcellular Localization." *ELife* 5 (JUN2016). https://doi.org/10.7554/eLife.16950.

Jiang, Peng, Alejandra C. Ventura, Eduardo D. Sontag, Sofia D. Merajver, Alexander J. Ninfa, and Domitilla Del Vecchio. 2011. "Load-Induced Modulation of Signal Transduction Networks." *Science Signaling* 4 (194). https://doi.org/10.1126/scisignal.2002152.

Judge, Ayesha, and Michael S. Dodd. 2020. "Metabolism." *Essays in Biochemistry* 64 (4): 607–647. https://doi.org/10.1042/EBC20190041.

Kanter, Itamar, Gur Yaari, and Tomer Kalisky. 2021. "Applications of Community Detection Algorithms to Large Biological Datasets." In *Methods in Molecular Biology* 2243. https://doi.org/10.1007/978-1-0716-1103-6_3.

Karczewski, Konrad J., Michael Snyder, Russ B. Altman, and Nicholas P. Tatonetti. 2014. "Coherent Functional Modules Improve Transcription Factor Target Identification, Cooperativity Prediction, and Disease Association." *PLoS Genetics* 10 (2). https://doi.org/10.1371/journal.pgen.1004122.

Klimm, Florian, Enrique M. Toledo, Thomas Monfeuga, Fang Zhang, Charlotte M. Deane, and Gesine Reinert. 2020. "Functional Module Detection through Integration of Single-Cell RNA Sequencing Data with Protein–Protein Interaction Networks." *BMC Genomics* 21 (1). https://doi.org/10.1186/s12864-020-07144-2.

Koch, Ina, and Jörg Ackermann. 2013. "On Functional Module Detection in Metabolic Networks." *Metabolites* 3 (3). https://doi.org/10.3390/metabo3030673.

Koch, Ina, and Bianca Büttner. 2023. "Computational Modeling of Signal Transduction Networks without Kinetic Parameters: Petri Net Approaches." *American Journal of Physiology. Cell Physiology*. https://doi.org/10.1152/ajpcell.00487.2022.

Lei, Xiujuan, Thosini Bamunu Mudiyanselage, Yuchen Zhang, Chen Bian, Wei Lan, Ning Yu, and Yi Pan. 2021. "A Comprehensive Survey on Computational Methods of Non-Coding RNA and Disease Association Prediction." *Briefings in Bioinformatics*. https://doi.org/10.1093/bib/bbaa350.

Li Song, Sarah M. Assmann, and Réka Albert. 2006. "Predicting Essential Components of Signal Transduction Networks: A Dynamic Model of Guard Cell Abscisic Acid Signaling." *PLoS Biology* 4 (10). https://doi.org/10.1371/journal.pbio.0040312.

Liang, Lifan, Vicky Chen, Kunju Zhu, Xiaonan Fan, Xinghua Lu, and Songjian Lu. 2019. "Integrating Data and Knowledge to Identify Functional Modules of Genes: A Multilayer Approach." *BMC Bioinformatics* 20 (1). https://doi.org/10.1186/s12859-019-2800-y.

Luo, Cuihua, Fali Li, Peiyang Li, Chanlin Yi, Chunbo Li, Qin Tao, Xiabing Zhang, et al. 2022. "A Survey of Brain Network Analysis by Electroencephalographic Signals." *Cognitive Neurodynamics* 16 (1). https://doi.org/10.1007/s11571-021-09689-8.

Luo, Feng, Yunfeng Yang, Jianxin Zhong, Haichun Gao, Latifur Khan, Dorothea K. Thompson, and Jizhong Zhou. 2007. "Constructing Gene Co-Expression Networks and Predicting Functions of Unknown Genes by Random Matrix Theory." *BMC Bioinformatics* 8. https://doi.org/10.1186/1471-2105-8-299.

Martz, Eric. 2012. "Introduction to Proteins—Structure, Function, and Motion." *Biochemistry and Molecular Biology Education* 40 (3). https://doi.org/10.1002/bmb.20603.

Mohyedinbonab, Elmira, Mo Jamshidi, and Yu Fang Jin. 2014. "A Review on Applications of Graph Theory in Network Analysis of Biological Processes." *International Journal of Intelligent Computing in Medical Sciences and Image Processing* 6 (1). https://doi.org/10.1080/1931308X.2014.938492.

Neudorf, Josh, Shaylyn Kress, and Ron Borowsky. 2022. "Structure Can Predict Function in the Human Brain: A Graph Neural Network Deep Learning Model of Functional Connectivity and Centrality Based on Structural Connectivity." *Brain Structure and Function* 227 (1). https://doi.org/10.1007/s00429-021-02403-8.

Omranian, Sara, Angela Angeleska, and Zoran Nikoloski. 2021. "Efficient and Accurate Identification of Protein Complexes from Protein-Protein Interaction Networks Based on the Clustering Coefficient." *Computational and Structural Biotechnology Journal* 19. https://doi.org/10.1016/j.csbj.2021.09.014.

Pang, Yin, Lin Bai, and Kaili Bu. 2015. "An Energy Model for Detecting Community in PPI Networks." In *Lecture Notes in Computer Science (Including Subseries Lecture Notes in Artificial Intelligence and Lecture Notes in Bioinformatics)* 9261. https://doi.org/10.1007/978-3-319-22849-5_9.

Pavlopoulos, Georgios A., Maria Secrier, Charalampos N. Moschopoulos, Theodoros G. Soldatos, Sophia Kossida, Jan Aerts, Reinhard Schneider, and Pantelis G. Bagos. 2011. "Using Graph Theory to Analyze Biological Networks." *BioData Mining*. https://doi.org/10.1186/1756-0381-4-10.

Picard, Martin, and Orian S. Shirihai. 2022. "Mitochondrial Signal Transduction." *Cell Metabolism*. https://doi.org/10.1016/j.cmet.2022.10.008.

Pita-Juárez, Yered, Gabriel Altschuler, Sokratis Kariotis, Wenbin Wei, Katjuša Koler, Claire Green, Rudolph E. Tanzi, and Winston Hide. 2018. "The Pathway Coexpression Network: Revealing Pathway Relationships." *PLoS Computational Biology* 14 (3). https://doi.org/10.1371/journal.pcbi.1006042.

Rahiminejad, Sara, Mano R. Maurya, and Shankar Subramaniam. 2019. "Topological and Functional Comparison of Community Detection Algorithms in Biological Networks." *BMC Bioinformatics* 20 (1): 1–25. https://doi.org/10.1186/S12859-019-2746-0/FIGURES/6.

Sato, Kengo, and Michiaki Hamada. 2023. "Recent Trends in RNA Informatics: A Review of Machine Learning and Deep Learning for RNA Secondary Structure Prediction and RNA Drug Discovery." In *Briefings in Bioinformatics* 24. https://doi.org/10.1093/bib/bbad186.

Schläpfer, Pascal, Peifen Zhang, Chuan Wang, Taehyong Kim, Michael Banf, Lee Chae, Kate Dreher, et al. 2017. "Genome-Wide Prediction of Metabolic Enzymes, Pathways, and Gene Clusters in Plants." *Plant Physiology* 173 (4). https://doi.org/10.1104/pp.16.01942.

Segal, Eran, Michael Shapira, Aviv Regev, Dana Pe'er, David Botstein, Daphne Koller, and Nir Friedman. 2003. "Module Networks: Identifying Regulatory Modules and Their Condition-Specific Regulators from Gene Expression Data." *Nature Genetics* 34 (2). https://doi.org/10.1038/ng1165.

Seifuddin, Fayaz, and Mehdi Pirooznia. 2021. "Bioinformatics Approaches for Functional Prediction of Long Noncoding RNAs." In *Methods in Molecular Biology* 2254. https://doi.org/10.1007/978-1-0716-1158-6_1.

Shi, Wen, Hong Yang, Linhai Xie, Xiao-Xia Yin, and Yanchun Zhang. 2024. "A Review of Machine Learning-Based Methods for Predicting Drug–Target Interactions." *Health Information Science and Systems* 12 (1): 1–16.

Su, Kenong, Ataur Katebi, Vivek Kohar, Benjamin Clauss, Danya Gordin, Zhaohui S. Qin, R. Krishna M. Karuturi, Sheng Li, and Mingyang Lu. 2022. "NetAct: A Computational Platform to Construct Core Transcription Factor Regulatory Networks Using Gene Activity." *Genome Biology* 23 (1). https://doi.org/10.1186/s13059-022-02835-3.

Sulaimany, Sadegh, Mohammad Khansari, and Ali Masoudi Nejad. 2018. "Link Prediction Potentials for Biological Networks." *International Journal of Data Mining and Bioinformatics* 20 (2): 161. https://doi.org/10.1504/IJDMB.2018.093684.

Tripathi, Beethika, Srinivasan Parthasarathy, Himanshu Sinha, Karthik Raman, and Balaraman Ravindran. 2019. "Adapting Community Detection Algorithms for Disease Module Identification in Heterogeneous Biological Networks." *Frontiers in Genetics* 10 (MAR). https://doi.org/10.3389/fgene.2019.00164.

Watson, Joanne, Michael Smith, Chiara Francavilla, and Jean Marc Schwartz. 2022. "SubcellulaRVis: A Web-Based Tool to Simplify and Visualise Subcellular Compartment Enrichment." *Nucleic Acids Research* 50 (W1). https://doi.org/10.1093/nar/gkac336.

Wen, Dingqiao, Yun Yu, Jiafan Zhu, and Luay Nakhleh. 2018. "Inferring Phylogenetic Networks Using PhyloNet." *Systematic Biology* 67 (4). https://doi.org/10.1093/sysbio/syy015.

Wu, Zengrui, Weihua Li, Guixia Liu, and Yun Tang. 2018. "Network-Based Methods for Prediction of Drug-Target Interactions." *Frontiers in Pharmacology*. https://doi.org/10.3389/fphar.2018.01134.

Yamada, Takuji, and Peer Bork. 2009. "Evolution of Biomolecular Networks Lessons from Metabolic and Protein Interactions." *Nature Reviews Molecular Cell Biology*. https://doi.org/10.1038/nrm2787.

Zahiri, Javad, Abbasali Emamjomeh, Samaneh Bagheri, Asma Ivazeh, Ghasem Mahdevar, Hessam Sepasi Tehrani, Mehdi Mirzaie, Barat Ali Fakheri, and Morteza Mohammad-Noori. 2020. "Protein Complex Prediction: A Survey." *Genomics*. https://doi.org/10.1016/j.ygeno.2019.01.011.

Zhang, Xiuwei, and Bernard M.E. Moret. 2010. "Refining Transcriptional Regulatory Networks Using Network Evolutionary Models and Gene Histories." *Algorithms for Molecular Biology* 5 (1). https://doi.org/10.1186/1748-7188-5-1.

Zhao, Wei, Peter Langfelder, Tova Fuller, Jun Dong, Ai Li, and Steve Hovarth. 2010. "Weighted Gene Coexpression Network Analysis: State of the Art." *Journal of Biopharmaceutical Statistics*. https://doi.org/10.1080/10543400903572753.

Zhou, Jizhong, Ye Deng, Feng Luo, Zhili He, Qichao Tu, and Xiaoyang Zhi. 2010. "Functional Molecular Ecological Networks." *MBio* 1 (4). https://doi.org/10.1128/mBio.00169-10.

Zhou, Yuanzhe, and Shi-Jie Chen. 2024. "Advances in Machine-Learning Approaches to RNA-Targeted Drug Design." *Artificial Intelligence Chemistry* 2 (1). https://doi.org/10.1016/j.aichem.2024.100053.

8 Influential Node Detection Based on Implicit Communities

Neda Binesh and Mehdi Ghatee

8.1 INTRODUCTION AND RELATED WORK

In today's digital age, the influence of social networks and virtual communication has become increasingly significant. Consequently, influence maximization (IM) has emerged as a critical issue within social networks (Li et al., 2020; Chen et al., 2009, 2012; Peng et al., 2018). This problem encompasses various approaches to identifying influential nodes within the network's graph (Li et al., 2020). However, it presents challenges due to networks' high dimensionality and continuous growth. The diffusion of information in social networks is influenced by numerous factors, particularly the methods used for disseminating news, which specific diffusion models determine. Two of the most important and widely recognized diffusion models are the independent cascade (IC) model and the Linear Threshold (LT) model. Building upon these foundational models, various other diffusion models have been developed (Shakarian et al., 2015; Kim et al., 2014). Numerous algorithms have been designed to identify optimal initial nodes for broadcasting information. These initial nodes play a crucial role in the diffusion simulation, activating other nodes in the network in successive steps. This activation process continues, gradually increasing the number of active nodes until no new nodes are activated. In the independent cascade (IC) model, active nodes independently trigger adjacent nodes. For example, if node u becomes active, it will independently activate its neighboring nodes, such as v and w, without being influenced by other active neighbors. In contrast, the activation of a target node, v, in the linear threshold (LT) model depends on the status of its neighboring nodes. Thus, the simultaneous activation of nodes u and w enhances the probability of v becoming active.

The characteristics of models like the linear threshold (LT) model help us identify influential nodes within clusters. In this diffusion model, selecting initial active nodes from the same cluster that share more common neighbors maximizes the effectiveness of these nodes. This highlights the importance of community discovery in networks. Properly clustering and identifying the right communities, as well as selecting influential initial nodes within them, can significantly accelerate the

DOI: 10.1201/9781003515890-11

speed of information propagation and increase the number of final active nodes. However, many existing algorithms do not consider the properties of different diffusion models. Greedy algorithms are widely used for influence maximization (Kempe et al., 2003; Leskovec et al., 2007; Goyal et al., 2011). Under the independent cascade (IC) and LT models, greedy algorithms often yield optimal results. However, they are unsuitable for large-scale networks due to their long execution times and high memory consumption. In contrast, metaheuristic methods, such as genetic algorithms, centrality-based methods, and random walk-based methods, focus on reducing execution time, though they do not guarantee optimal solutions. While these methods are faster than greedy algorithms, their accuracy and reliability depend on various factors (Sumith et al., 2018; Liu, 2017). The study of eigenvalues has gained considerable attention in various fields in recent years. Eigenvector centrality and its derived methods are commonly used to assess the importance of nodes (Ahajjam and Badir, 2018). These methods operate on the principle that a node's significance is directly proportional to the importance of its neighboring nodes, leading to the computation of eigenvectors. Certain techniques utilize community discovery to tackle different iterations of the influence maximization problem. For example, the GCC algorithm (Tripathi and Reza, 2019) employs eigenvalue analysis on the network's adjacency matrix and uses the k-means clustering algorithm for clustering. It then selects initial nodes from the center of these clusters. Additionally, singular value analysis can be used for clustering and identifying effective structures.

Some approaches focus on detecting communities based on existing techniques for community detection and subsequently identifying initial influencers. Hajdu et al. (2021) integrated community detection with influence maximization (Hajdu et al. 2018). They employ various overlapping community detection methods in conjunction with their algorithm, first computing the communities using a known algorithm and then utilizing a greedy approach to identify initial influencers within the communities.

Bozorgi et al. (2017) introduced a novel propagation model with node decision-making to tackle competitive influence maximization. Their approach involves extending the LT model and utilizing community structure to identify the minimum number of seed nodes for maximum advantage over competitors. Given the substantial size of social networks, identifying communities within them is a challenging and time-consuming task. To address this, the researchers propose constructing a smaller network based on social distances between candidate nodes. Subsequently, they introduce an algorithm called distance aware LT (DALT) supported by a strong mathematical foundation.

The chapter delves into an introduction to social networks, influence maximization, and diffusion models. It also discusses the construction of a smaller network containing candidate nodes, the computation of social similarity, and the definition of social distance between candidate nodes. Finally, the researchers present a mathematical model for influence maximization, define the Laplacian Plus matrix, and determine the eigenvectors corresponding to the largest eigenvalues. Additionally, they provide results for sample networks to validate the theoretical theorems and the DALT algorithm.

8.2 SOCIAL NETWORK SYMBOLS

Social networks can be modeled as a graph $G=(V,E)$, where V contains nodes representing real or virtual people and E contains edges indicating relationships between nodes. Their sizes are $|V|=n$ and $|E|=m$. These graphs can be weighted, directional, dynamic, multi-level, heterogeneous, multi-part, etc. Adj denotes the adjacency matrix of these graphs including zero and one elements, where 1 refers to the presence of an edge. In the case of weighted graphs, W is defined to save edges' weights. In directed networks, when exist an edge from node u to node v, it is said that node u follows node v, and two sets are defined for each node u corresponding to the nodes following u (followers), denoted with Fo_u, and the nodes that u follows them (friends), denoted with Fr_u . The input degree u is $D_{in}(u)$ and the output degree u is $D_{out}(u)$. Trivially $D_{in}(u)=|Fo_u|$ and $D_{out}(u)=|Fr_u|$. In undirected networks, for each node u, $\deg(u)$ denotes the degree of u.

8.2.1 Influence Maximization Problem (IM)

In the influence maximization problem, the goal is to select a set of initial nodes using network structural data that are expected to influence the largest number of network nodes. The diffusion method occurs based on a given model. In the general framework of all proposed models, each node is either passive or active. Information dissemination is done in separate time steps $t=0,1,2,\ldots,T$. At step $t=0$, the active nodes are given by A_0. A_t will be the set of active nodes in step t. In each step, active nodes can influence their neighbors to be activated, and so on. The termination meets when all nodes are activated. The details are as follows (Chen et al., 2013):

- **The random diffusion model** is a random process that occurs in a social network $G=(V,E)$ with discrete time steps. It involves generating the active set A_T for the initial influencers A_0.
- **The influence spread function** in the social network $G=(V,E)$ for an arbitrary set $S\subseteq V$ and the network parameters P, is denoted as $\sigma_{\{G,P\}}(S)$, representing the mathematical expectation of the number of users affected by the set S under the network parameters P. The parameters in the set P can include the type of release model, content information, and other necessary parameters depending on the problem. For simplicity, we use $\sigma(.)$ to denote $\sigma_{\{G,P\}}(S)$ when G and P are known. Expanding the influence of $\sigma(.)$ gives the number of active nodes after the publication process is complete.
- **The influence maximization problem** for the social network G and diffusion model M, with a positive number, aims to discover the set A_0 including k primary nodes such that the influence spread $\sigma_{G,M}(A_0)$ is maximized. In other words,

$$A_0 = argmax\, \sigma_{G,M}(S)\ s.t.\quad S \subset V \wedge |S| = k$$

- **The monotone influence function** is an influence function that meets $\sigma_{G,M}(S) \leq \sigma_{G,M}(S')$ for every $S \subseteq S' \subseteq V$.
- **The submodular influence function** is an influence function that satisfies

$$\sigma_{G,M}(S \cup \{v\}) - \sigma_{G,M}(S) \geq \sigma_{G,M}(S' \cup \{v\}) - \sigma_{G,M}(S')$$

for every $S \subseteq S' \subseteq V$ and $v \in V\, S'$.

To intuitively check this property, it is possible to empirically test whether or not adding a member to the set when the number of members of the set is small has a greater effect than when the number of members of the set is large. This point is used in the greedy algorithms presented for this problem.

8.2.2 Diffusion Models

Diffusion models can be divided into two general categories: progressive and non-progressive. In progressive models, an active node cannot be deactivated in subsequent steps. These models are usually used to show the acceptance of a new technology or product, such as watching a new movie or buying a smartphone.

However, in non-progressive models, activated nodes can revert to an inactive state. Non-progressive models are usually used to spread ideas and opinions about new events, etc., which may change their state and opinion based on new information.

Most Influence maximization algorithms use progressive models. Among the most important progressive models are the independent cascade diffusion (IC), the linear threshold diffusion (LT) (Kempe et al., 2003), and the mathematical modeling of infectious diseases such as susceptible, infectious, or recovered (SIR) (Jung et al., 2012). Common non-progressive models include Voter (Clifford and Sudbury, 1973) and multiple disease models SIS (Kimura et al., 2009). Contagion models are originally used to study the spread of disease in biological populations (Chen et al., 2013). In infection models, each person or node moves between several possible states, which generally include Susceptible, Exposed, infected, and removed (recovered) states.

8.2.3 Independent Cascade Diffusion Model

Goldenberg et al. (2001) explained the IC model, focusing on the propagation of information and emotions within a network (Wang et al., 2017). The IC model is sender-oriented, meaning that when a user v is activated, it attempts to independently activate each of its followers with a probability of influence $p(u,v)$ for the edge $e=(u,v)$. The relation $p(u,v)=1-(1-\alpha)^{W(u,v)}$ is used to determine the probability of propagation and the weighting of network edges. Here, α represents the importance of the news and models the activation speed of the nodes. In unweighted networks where W is equal to Adj, the influence probability is the same for all edges and is equal to α. During propagation, a random threshold $\theta(u,v)$ is assigned to each edge. If node u follows node v and node v is active in step t, then node u will be activated in step $t+1$ if the influence probability $p(u,v)$ is greater than or equal to the assigned threshold $\theta(u,v)$. The following rule outlies the results:

If $v \in \{Fr_u \cap A_{t-1}\}$ *and* $p(u,v) \geq \theta(u,v)$, **then** u **is added to** A_t **.**

Therefore, an active node in step t can activate each of its followers separately and independently in step $t+1$. This process continues until no more nodes are activated, and the number of final steps is denoted by T. In the case of an undirected network, the calculations outlined above are performed for the neighbors of node u. In the IC model, selecting primary active nodes from various areas of the network can lead to better spread throughout the network, and nodes with higher degrees have a greater probability of activating more nodes in the first round.

8.2.4 Linear Threshold Diffusion Model

In LT, an inactive user can become active if enough neighbors are active (Kempe et al., 2003, Granovetter, 1978). Thus, LT is receive-oriented and it is important to select the initial influencers with more neighbors.

Here, the influence of one node on another is represented by the weight (u,v), where this weight is determined from network information. The total weight of the output edges of each node should be less than or equal to 1. If the network is unweighted, then for each $v \in Fr_u$, this weight will be calculated as

$$\gamma(u,v) = \frac{1}{D_{out}(u)}.$$

where $D_{out}(u)$ represents the number of friends of u. If the network is weighted, this weight is calculated as

$$\gamma(u,v) = \frac{W(u,v)}{\sum_{j \in Fr_u} W(u,j)}.$$

In the LT model, there is a threshold $\eta(u)$ for any node u, which is a random number between 0 and 1 and changes randomly in each diffusion process. If the summation of the weight of the edges connected to its active neighbors is greater than $\eta(u)$, then the node u will be activated. Therefore, we can write if

$$\sum_{v \in \{Fr_u \cap A_{t-1}\}} \gamma(u,v) \geq \eta(u)$$

then u will be added to A_t. In the undirected network case, calculations are performed for the neighbors of node u, and $deg(u)$ is used instead of $D_{out}(u)$.

The propagation process continues until no new nodes are activated. In this model, the more friends of a node that are activated in step t, the more likely it is to be activated in step t+1. Therefore, it's important to distribute primary influencers in different communities, and within each community, select those that are closer to each other and have more common neighbors.

8.3 GENERAL FRAMEWORK OF THE PROPOSED ALGORITHMS

In the realm of influence maximization, the adjacency matrix serves as the primary data structure. The objective of the algorithms is to identify key influencers capable of disseminating information across diverse communities. To facilitate this, the initial data undergoes dimensional reduction, resulting in a more compact network of candidate nodes. The edges within this network are weighted according to the social distances present in the original network. The algorithms presented in this dissertation adhere to a generalized framework to tackle this challenge.

8.3.1 Candidate Node Selection

First, the approach for identifying candidate nodes using structural information in the influence maximization problem is outlined. In real-world social networks characterized by a large number of nodes, processing the entirety of network information can be computationally intensive. To mitigate this issue, candidate nodes are extracted, thereby reducing the dimensionality of the input data. These nodes are collected in the set V', and the total number of candidate nodes is represented by l. The value of l must be carefully selected to strike a balance between computation time and the accuracy of the method.

A subset of candidate nodes is selected to reduce the dimensionality of the input data and make subsequent computations more efficient. For undirected graphs, the Neighborhood Index (NI) measure is used to select candidate nodes based on their local influence as the following:

$$NI(u) = \frac{\deg(u)}{bn(u)+1} \tag{8.1}$$

in this relation, $bn(u) = \left|\{v | v\, is\, a\, neighbor\, of\, u\, and \deg(v) \geq \deg(u)\}\right|$. This local index aims to identify nodes that outperform their immediate neighbors within their local scope. A higher NI value for node u indicates that it not only has a high degree but also outperforms its neighbors.

Candidate nodes which have the highest NI values are stored in the set $V' \subset V$. Then, the NI values are normalized by dividing each component of the vector by the maximum value.

8.3.2 Number of Candidate Nodes

The number of candidate nodes denoted as $l = |V'|$ depends on processing power and is essential in generating different distance matrices affecting the spreaders. By changing the value of l for different networks, we selected different percentages of nodes. For each value of l, different distance matrices are generated that can affect the spreaders. The results show that the value of l does not significantly impact the output results because significant nodes are selected. Therefore, to save time and memory, a value like $l = 0.01 \times n$ can be applied in the algorithms.

After identifying candidate nodes, the computation of similarity features between these candidate nodes is described in the next section.

8.3.3 Similarity Graph Construction for Candidate Nodes

The concept of similarity can differ depending on the network being analyzed. Palla et al. (2005) proposed that similar nodes within a network often form communities. In a social network context, node similarity is defined by the number of direct and indirect communication pathways between them. To effectively capture these similarities as new features, we have developed algorithms based on random walks for their computation. This process entails calculating a similarity matrix using structural information, specifically the adjacency matrix of the network, to identify key nodes. The random walk process involves traversing a sequence of nodes over a defined number of steps, with each sequence representing a path to a randomly chosen destination node. These paths can be either direct or indirect. To quantify this movement, we utilize a probability matrix, π, which expresses the likelihood of transitioning from one node to another within the network. If the random walker begins at a specified node i at the start, the transition probabilities $\pi(j,i,st)$ are computed using the relationship:

$$\pi(:,i,st) = Q^T \pi(:,i,st-1),$$

where st is the step number of a random walker and $st = 1,\ldots,d$, and Q is a matrix obtained from the adjacency matrix and $Q(i,j) = Adj(i,j) / deg(i)$.

To determine the initial value for the vector $\pi(:,i,0) \in R^{n\times 1}$ in step zero, the ith component of this vector is set to 1 and the rest of the components are set to zero, which means that the random walker starts from the node i (Liu and Lü 2010, Wang et al. 2013). Now, in each step st, to determine the probabilities of the random walker moving between candidate i and j, we store the probabilities in the matrix $P(i,j,st) \in R^{l\times l\times d}$, taking into account the degrees of the nodes, as follows:

$$P(i,j,st) = P(j,i,st) = \frac{\deg(i)}{\Delta(G)} \times \pi(j,i,st) + \frac{\deg(j)}{\Delta(G)} \times \pi(i,j,st) \tag{8.2}$$

where Δ(G) is the maximum degree of all network nodes. For each pair of candidate nodes, the similarity is then stored in the symmetric matrix $Sim \in R^{l\times l}$ by summing the transition probabilities over all steps:

$$Sim(j,i) = \sum_{st=1}^{d} P(j,i,st)s \tag{8.3}$$

In the following sections, this similarity matrix is utilized to calculate the social distance in the proposed algorithms.

8.3.4 Social Distance (SD)

After selecting the feature vectors for candidate nodes, the next step is to determine the social distance between these nodes. The social distances should contain the necessary information to reach better answers. Social network data is initially represented by the adjacency matrix, which captures connections between nodes. Weighted networks use the weight matrix to encode the strength of these connections, enabling a more detailed measure of node similarity. In many scenarios, the distance between nodes is essential. Different algorithms, such as Dijkstra's algorithm, have been presented to calculate the distance between nodes. There are also methods to calculate the distance by inverting the similarity data or subtracting it from a constant in some references (Wang et al. 2013).

In the proposed social distance algorithm, it is assumed that the similarity matrix (Sim) containing the similarities between nodes is given. With the appropriate similarities calculated by the random walk process, in this algorithm, we first calculate the number of non-zero values for each node i from its similarity vector, $Sim(:,i)$, which contains the similarity between i and other nodes in the network, and show it by $f(i)$. Then, we sort the values of the vector $Sim(:,i)$ in descending order so that the values of the sorted data are stored in the vector C_i and their indices are stored in the vector Ind_i. Then, for each index $j \in \{1,...,l\}$, the distance between the node i and its jth neighbor in the list Ind_i, i.e., $Ind_i(j)$, is calculated using the following conditional structure:

$$SD(i, Ind\_i(j)) = \begin{cases} 0, & j = 1 \\ \dfrac{1}{f(i)}, & 2 \le j \le f(i) \; and \; C_i(j) < C_i(j-1) \\ SD(i, Ind\_i(j-1)) & C_i(j) = C_i(j-1) \\ 1 & otherwise \end{cases} \tag{8.4}$$

When $i \neq j$ and i and j are similar, the calculated value for $SD(i,j)$ should be small. For each node i, the index of the nearest node is in $Ind_i(1)$, and we set the smallest SD equal to $\frac{1}{f(i)}$. The index of others is saved in index $Ind_i(j)$, where $j = 2,..., f(i)$.

Here we have two cases:

1. If the similarity of this node to i is not equal to the similarity of the previous node in the list to i, i.e., $(C_i(j) < C_i(j-1))$, the distance will be equal to $\frac{j}{f(i)}$.
2. If the similarity of this node to i is equal to the similarity of the previous node in the list to i, i.e., $\left(C_i(j) = C_i(j-1)\right)$, then the distance of this node to i will not change and we have $Dis\left(i, Ind_i(j)\right) = Dis\left(i, Ind_i(j-1)\right)$.

Additionally, the node with the least similarity and nodes with zero similarity will also have a distance of 1 from the node i.

Figure 8.1 shows how the above algorithm works on a sample node. Since $SD(.,.)$ is not symmetric, we replace it as $SD = 0.5\left(SD + SD^T\right)$.

Binesh and Ghatee (2021) reported the effectiveness of the social distance metric SD compared to other distance metrics, where the social distance SD was more suitable for identifying communities and selecting spreaders, especially in large networks. For example, in the social network Zachary karate club in Figure 8.2, the neighbors of nodes 34, 8, and 7 are represented by squares, diamonds, and triangles, respectively. Based on the connections visible in this figure, it is evident that nodes 34 and 8 share more common neighbors and a shorter distance.

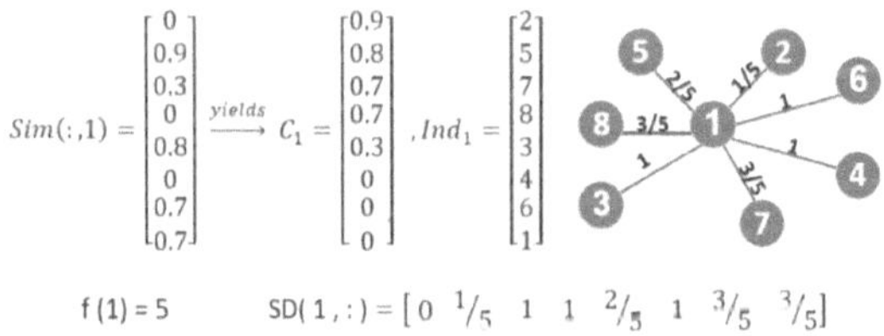

FIGURE 8.1 How to calculate the distance SD for node 1 from the similarity vector.

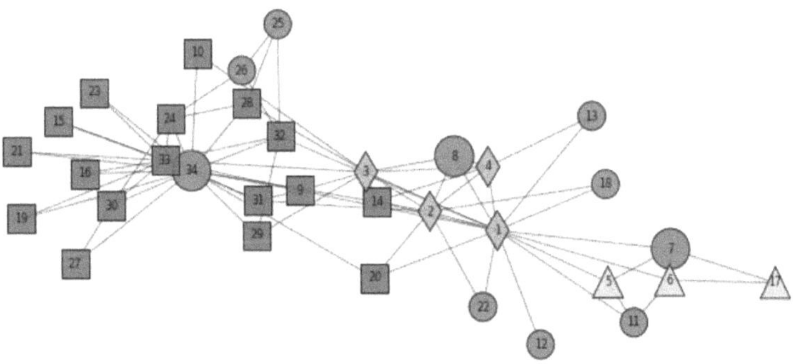

FIGURE 8.2 Zachary Karate Club network.

However, nodes 34 and 7 share fewer common neighbors (direct or indirect), and we expect the social distance between nodes 34 and 7 to be greater than the social distance between nodes 34 and 8. The SD results confirm these expectations so that $SD(34,8)=0.39$ while $SD(34,7)=0.6$. Similar results are observed for nodes 1 and 3 which have different closeness to 34, so that $SD(34,1)=0.22$ while $SD(34,3)=0.06$.

However, if we calculate the distance using basic shortest-path algorithms such as Dijkstra's algorithm, the distances between node 34 and nodes 7 and 8 are equal, as are the distances from node 34 to nodes 1 and 3 (Binesh and Ghatee, 2021). This is because these algorithms do not consider the various paths that exist between nodes. In social networks, however, these paths have a significant impact on information diffusion. These observations demonstrate that the SD method is more consistent in the selection of spreaders, thereby signifying its effectiveness.

8.4 MODEL FORMULATION FOR FINDING INFLUENCERS IN LINEAR THRESHOLD DIFFUSION

8.4.1 Model Objectives

In the linear threshold (LT) diffusion, a node will be active when a certain number of its neighbors are already active. Therefore, at the initial stage, selecting seed nodes from among those with the most common neighbors significantly increases the probability of activating their common neighbors.

Communities inherently foster a higher degree of interaction among their members compared to individuals outside the community. This localized interaction pattern has a decisive role in limiting the diffusion process within the boundaries of the community, preventing it from spilling over into other communities. Thus, we should identify implicit communities in a new candidate network and select some influencers from each community.

Consequently, in this model, influential nodes should be chosen from among the candidate nodes with the highest values, ensuring they are spread across different communities and have a higher number of common neighbors.

The proposed model should consider the following objective functions:

1. **Maximizing Global Coverage:** Seed nodes should be spread across different communities and have the maximum possible global distance from each other.
2. **Maximizing Local Overlap:** Seed nodes within a community should be close to each other to have the most common neighbors and the least local distance from each other.

8.4.2 Regularized Distance Measure

To achieve the mentioned objective functions, after calculating the social distance (SD), we regularize the distance between each pair of candidate nodes using their number of common neighbors (MN):

$$D_R^{'}(i,j) = \frac{SD(i,j)}{MN(v_i,v_j)+1} \tag{8.5}$$

where MN is calculated as follows:

$$MN = Adj * Adj$$

Here "*" denotes matrix multiplication. We also normalize these values to the range $[0,1]$ as follows:

$$MN = \frac{MN}{max(MN)}$$

As a result, $MN(i,j)$ represents the normalized number of neighbors between nodes i and j.

We then construct a graph consisting of the candidate nodes from set V' and consider $D_R^{'}(i,j)$ as the weight between candidate nodes i and j. If nodes i and j are close to each other and have many common neighbors, $D_R^{'}(i,j)$ will be small. On the other hand, for nodes inside various clusters that are far apart, this weight will be large.

8.4.3 Mathematical Representation of Objective Functions

If $D_R^{'}$ is the regularized distance matrix in the LT model, based on Equation (8.5), and we have two arbitrary sets of nodes A and B, we define the set distance $Set_{Dis}(A,B)$ as follows:

$$Set_{Dis}(A,B) = \sum_{a \in A}\sum_{b \in B} D_R^{'}(a,b)$$

We also denote the sum of NI weights, for the members of an arbitrary set A, by $\text{Set}_{\text{NI}}(\text{A})$:

$$\text{Set}_{\text{NI}}(\text{A}) = \sum_{a \in A} NI(a)$$

In a network containing c clusters, let c_i be the set of seed nodes in cluster i, so the union of these seed nodes form set A_0 is:

$$A_0 = U_{i=1}^{c}\, ci$$

It is important to pay attention to this point that we are currently in the candidate nodes space. When we talk about clusters, we're referring to groups created in this candidate node space. The weighted objective function below aims to maximize the distance between the seed nodes and the other candidate nodes in a cluster, while minimizing the distance between the seed nodes within a cluster. Additionally, the last part of this objective function encourages the selection of nodes with higher local weight within each cluster:

$$\max \sum_{i=1}^{c} \omega_1 \times Set_{Dis}\left(c_i, V'\right) - \omega_2 \times Set_{Dis}\left(c_i, c_i\right) + \omega_3 \times Set_{NI}\left(c_i\right) \tag{8.6}$$

We can assign various values to $\omega_1, \omega_2, \omega_3$ based on the importance of each object. For simplicity, let's set $\omega_1 = 1$, $\omega_2 = 1$, and $\omega_3 = l$, which is the size of the new network.

For each cluster $i = 1,...,c$, we define a binary vector $s_i \in R^{l\times 1}$ such that if node j is a seed node in cluster i, then $s_i(j) = 1$. This binary vector represents the cluster membership of the candidate nodes. Now, the set distance between node c_i and the rest of the candidate nodes, i.e., $Set_{Dis}\left(c_i, V'\right)$, can be written as $s_i^T \overline{D_R^{'}}\, s_i$, where $\overline{D_R^{'}}$ is a diagonal matrix which $\overline{D_R^{'}}(\mathrm{i},\mathrm{i})$ represents the sum of elements of the ith row in the regularized distance matrix $D_R^{'}$.

Similarly, the sum of distances between seed nodes within cluster i can be written as $s_i^T D_R^{'} s_i$. Additionally, $Set_{NI}\left(c_i\right)$ can be expressed as $s_i^T \widehat{NI}\, s_i$, where $\widehat{NI}$ is a diagonal matrix which $\widehat{NI}(i,i) = NI(i)$.

Substituting these expressions into Equation (8.6), we obtain the following reformulated objective function:

$$\max \sum_{i=1}^{c} \omega_1 \times \mathrm{s_i^T} \overline{\mathrm{D_R^{'}}}\, \mathrm{s_i} - \omega_2 \times \mathrm{s_i^T D_R^{'}\, s_i} + \omega_3 \times \mathrm{s_i^T}\, \widehat{NI}\, \mathrm{s_i} \tag{8.7}$$

8.4.4 Laplacian Plus Matrix

We define the Laplacian-Plus matrix L^+ as:

$$L^+ = \omega_1 \overline{D_R^{'}} - \omega_2 \mathrm{D_R^{'}} + \omega_3 \widehat{NI} \tag{8.8}$$

This matrix incorporates the regularized distance measure and the node importance values into a single representation based on our goals.

Using Equation (8.8), we can rewrite the objective function of Equation (8.7) as:

$$\max \sum_{i=1}^{c} \mathrm{s_i^T} L^+ \mathrm{s_i} \tag{8.9}$$

which is equivalent to the following optimization problem:

$$\max \sum_{i=1}^{c} \frac{\mathrm{s_i^T} L^+ \mathrm{s_i}}{\mathrm{s_i^T\, s_i}} \tag{8.10}$$

8.4.5 Definition of H Matrix

To solve this optimization problem, we introduce a normalized vector h_i for each cluster i as:

$$h_i = \frac{s_i}{\sqrt{s_i^T \; s_i}}$$

By substituting h_i into Equation (8.10), we obtain:

$$\max \sum_{i=1}^{c} \mathrm{h}_i^T L^+ \, \mathrm{h}_i$$

Let the normalized vector h_i represents the ith column of matrix H. Matrix H is an $l \times c$ matrix, where l is the number of candidate nodes and c is the number of clusters. The $H(j,i)$ is defined as:

$$H(j,i) = \begin{cases} \frac{1}{\sqrt{|c_i|}}, & \text{if } j \in c_i \\ 0, & \text{othewise} \end{cases} \tag{8.11}$$

In this equation, $|c_i|$ represents seed nodes number in cluster i.

The diagonal elements of the matrix $H^T L^+ \, H$ represent the normalized objective function for each cluster. Specifically, the $(i,i)^{\text{th}}$ element represents the "total distance between seed nodes within cluster i and the remaining candidate nodes" minus the "distance between pairs of seed nodes within cluster i."

Therefore, maximizing the diagonal elements of the matrix $H^T L^+ \, H$ aligns with the objectives defined in the LT model.

8.4.6 Simplified Optimization Problem

The columns of the matrix H are orthonormal, indicating that $H^T \, H = \mathrm{I}_c$, where I_c is the identity matrix of dimension $c \times c$. This property simplifies the optimization problem by removing the constraint on matrix H, and gives the following simplified optimization problem:

$$\begin{aligned} &max\, tr\left(H^T L^+ \, H\right) \\ &\text{s.t} \quad H^T \, H = I_c \end{aligned} \tag{8.12}$$

In this mathematical model, *tr* indicates trace of matrix as the summation of diagonal entities of matrix.

The matrix H is a crucial component of the eigenvector-based solution for the LT model.

8.4.7 Optimal Solution of the Model

The objective function in Equation (8.12) is maximized by the eigenvectors corresponding to the c largest eigenvalues of the Laplacian Plus matrix L^{+}, subject to the constraint $H^T H = I_c$. According to the Rayleigh-Ritz Theorem (Lutkepohl, 1997), which is a fundamental concept in linear algebra that applies to symmetric matrices, the optimal solution to the optimization problem defined in Equation (8.12) is the matrix H, where the columns are the mentioned eigenvectors.

Theorem: Let $A \in R^{n \times n}$ be a symmetric matrix with eigenvalues $\lambda_1 \leq \lambda_2 \leq \lambda_3 \leq \ldots \leq \lambda_n$ and orthonormal eigenvectors u_1 to u_n, respectively. For $k \in \{1, 2, \ldots, n\}$, the following relationship holds:

$$max\left\{tr\left(U^T AU\right) : U \in R^{n \times k}, U^T U = I_k\right\} = \lambda_{n-k+1} + \lambda_{n-k+2} + \ldots + \lambda_n$$

where U is the matrix that maximizes this objective function and can be stated as $U = \left[u_{n-k+1} + u_{n-k+2} + \ldots + u_n\right]$ whose columns are the k eigenvector of matrix A correspond to k largest eigenvalues.

Corollary

Based on the matrix H definition in Equation (8.11), we can calculate the highest absolute value in each row of H and construct the vector h_{max} as follows:

$$h_{max}(i) = \max_{j=1,\ldots,c} \# H(i, j) \#$$

$$h_{max} = \left(h_{max}(i)\right)$$

vector h_{max} represents the normalized maximum values for each cluster.

8.4.8 DALT Algorithm

The LT propagation model is used for understanding how information spreads in networks. Influential nodes are nodes that have a significant impact on the spread of information. The distance aware LT (DALT) algorithm explains how to select influential nodes in the LT diffusion model and is particularly useful for large networks. The DALT algorithm works in three phases:

- 1-Candidate Node Selection: Identify potentially influential candidate nodes.
- 2-Normalized Distance Matrix Calculation: Calculate a normalized distance matrix to show how similar candidate nodes are to each other.

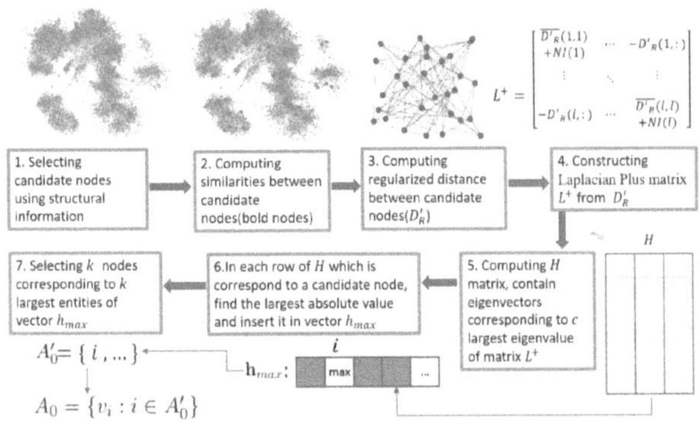

FIGURE 8.3 A schematic review of DALT algorithm.

- 3-Optimization Model Solving: Solve the optimization model to choose the most influential nodes from the candidate nodes.

In the DALT algorithm, the edge weight between two candidate nodes in the representation graph is determined based on the number of common neighbors between the two nodes. The algorithm calculates the Laplacian-plus matrix and determines the number "c" of eigenvectors corresponding to the largest eigenvalues of the Laplacian-plus matrix. These eigenvectors are stored in a matrix H. Finally, the largest element in absolute value in each row of the matrix H is selected and added to the vector. Then, the spreader nodes are greedily selected from the vector and added to the set $A_0^{'}$. The set contains the index of influencers in the candidate space, which is not equal to their main indices. In the next step, the corresponding indices from the set V are selected and stored in the set A_0. You can find a review of the DALT algorithm in Figure 8.3.

The pseudocode of this algorithm is as follows:

Algorithm: DALT

Input: Adj, k, l, d, c

Output: Initial influencer nodes (A_0)

1. **Selection of anchor nodes:**

Input: Adj, l.

Output: V', NI.

1.1. Calculation of $bn(i)$ and $deg(i)$ for all nodes.
1.2. Calculation of NI according to Equation (8.1).
1.3. Selection of l anchor nodes which have highest $NI(i)$ and store in V'.

2. Computation of regularized distance:

Input: Adj, V', d.

Output: $D_R^{'}$.

2.1. Running random walk d times, computing similarity values Sim for nodes in V' based on Equations (8.2)–(8.3).

2.2. For any $i \in V'$

2.2.1. Calculation of $(C_i, Ind_i) = sort(Sim(:,i))$ to finding the decreasing sorted values C_i and the corresponding indexes Ind_i

2.2.2. Computing $SD(i, Ind_i(j))$ based on Equation (8.4) For all $j \in \{1,...,l\}$.

2.2.3. Computing the regularized distance $D_R^{'}(i,j)$ according to Equation (8.5) For all $j \in \{1,...,l\}$.

3. Selection of spreaders based on the optimization model:

Input: V', $D_R^{'}$, NI, c and k .

Output: A_0.

3.1. Set $\omega_1 = \omega_2 = 1$, $\omega_3 = l$, and define $L^+ = \omega_1 \overline{D_R^{'}} - \omega_2 D_R^{'} + \omega_3 \widehat{NI}$.

3.2. Computation of the eigenvectors corresponding to c largest eigenvalues of L^+ and putting them to columns of H.

3.3. Calculation of $h_{max}(i) = \max_{j=1,...,c}\square|H(i,j)|$ and $\text{h}_{max} = (h_{max}(i))$, for all anchor nodes $i \in \{1,...,l\}$.

3.4. Extraction of the indices of the k greatest values of h_{max} and store them in the set $A_0^{'} \subset \{1,2,....,l\}$ in anchors space.

3.5. Find the corresponding indices from set V and construct spreader set $A_0 = \{v_i : i \in A_0^{'}\}$.

To see the performance of DALT on some benchmarks, one can refer to Binesh and Ghatee (2022).

8.5 DETERMINING THE NUMBER OF COMMUNITIES IN THE CANDIDATE NODE SPACE

In the previous section, the parameter c in the proposed mathematical model represents the number of hypothetical communities in the candidate node space, which may not directly correspond to the number of communities in the main network. In the DALT algorithm, c eigenvectors corresponding to the c largest eigenvalues of the Laplacian matrix should be considered based on this parameter. We can determine the number of required eigenvectors from the first gap among the largest eigenvalues of the Laplacian matrix. For this purpose, we need the following definitions:

- I_n is the identity matrix of size $n \times n$ and O_n is a matrix of size $n \times n$ where all entries are equal to 1. o_n is a vector of size $n \times 1$ where all entries are equal to 1.
- The eigenvalues of any symmetric matrix A of size $n \times n$ are denoted by $\lambda_1(A) \leq \lambda_2(A) \leq \ldots \leq \lambda_n(A)$, where $\lambda_1(A)$ is the smallest and $\lambda_n(A)$ is the largest eigenvalue of A.
- The set of eigenvalues of the matrix A is denoted by $\Lambda(A)$ and is given by:

$$\Lambda(A)=\{\lambda_i(A) \mid i \in \{1,2,\ldots,n\}\}$$

- If the eigenvalues of the matrix A are not distinct, this set contains repeated elements.
- If A is a symmetric matrix with size $n \times n$, then all its eigenvalues are real and it has n orthogonal eigenvectors (Lutkepohl, 1997).
- For any matrix A, the matrix $\Delta(A)$ is a diagonal matrix such as each diagonal element is equal to the sum of the corresponding row elements of A. This means that if A is the matrix of adjacency of a network with n nodes, and the degree of each node i is denoted by $deg(i)$, we have:

$$\Delta(A) = diag(deg(1), deg(2), \ldots, deg(n))$$

- For any symmetric matrix A, the Laplacian matrix of A is denoted by $L(A)$ and is calculated as follows:

$$L(A)= \Delta(A) - A$$

- Any Laplacian matrix of size $n \times n$ is a symmetric and positive semi-definite matrix, meaning all its eigenvalues are non-negative and it has at least one eigenvalue equal to zero, with the corresponding eigenvector being the vector o_n (Van Mieghem, 2010).
- If the graph G is an undirected graph with positive weights, the number of zero eigenvalues of its Laplacian matrix is equal to the number of connected components in the graph (Van Mieghem, 2010, Von Luxburg, 2007).
- If A is the network adjacency matrix with size $n \times n$, the distance matrix D is defined as follows:

$$D=O_n \quad I_n - A$$

Corollary 1: The Laplacian matrix is a symmetric matrix, and its eigenvectors are pairwise orthogonal. Furthermore, the vector $u_1 = o_n$ is the eigenvector corresponding to the smallest eigenvalue of the Laplacian matrix, and it is orthogonal to all other eigenvectors. This means that if $u_1, u_2, \ldots, u_n$ are the eigenvectors of the Laplacian matrix, we have:

$$\forall i \in \{2,3,\ldots,n\}, \qquad u_1^T u_i = 0.$$

As a result,

$$\forall i \in \{2,3,\ldots,n\}, \qquad o_n^T u_i = 0.$$

In other words, for the eigenvectors from the second to the last of the Laplacian matrix, the sum of their components is zero.

Theorem 1: If A is the network adjacency matrix and D is the corresponding distance matrix, the relationship between their corresponding Laplacian matrices is as follows:

$$L(D) = n \times I_n - O_n - L(A)$$

Proof

According to the Laplacian matrix definition:

$$L(D) = \Delta(D) - D \tag{8.13}$$

and in the matrix D, the sum of the elements of row i, for $i \in \{1,2,\ldots,n\}$, is equal to $n-1-deg(i)$, therefore, we have:

$$\Delta(D) = (n-1) \times I_n - \Delta(A)$$

Thus, Equation (8.13) can be rewritten as:

$$\begin{aligned} L(D) &= \Delta(D) - D \\ &= (n-1) \times I_n - \Delta(A) - (O_n - I_n - A) \\ &= n \times I_n - I_n - \Delta(A) - O_n + I_n + A \\ &= n \times I_n - O_n - (\Delta(A) - A) \\ &= n \times I_n - O_n - L(A) \end{aligned}$$

Theorem 2: If A is the networks adjacency matrix with size $n \times n$ and D is the corresponding distance matrix, the set of eigenvalues of their Laplacian matrices is identical, and we have

$$\Lambda(L(D)) = \Lambda(L(A))$$

and for $j \in \{2,\ldots,n\}$, if λ_j is an eigenvalue of the Laplacian matrix $L(A)$, $(n-\lambda_j)$ will be an eigenvalue of the Laplacian matrix $L(D)$.

Proof

If $u_1, u_2, \ldots, u_n$ are the eigenvectors of the Laplacian matrix $L(A)$, corresponding to the eigenvalues

$$\lambda_1(L(A)), \lambda_2(L(A)), \ldots, \lambda_n(L(A))$$

One can obtain: $\lambda_1(L(A)) = 0$ and $u_1 = o_n$. In the Laplacian matrix $L(D)$, the smallest eigenvalue is also 0, and the corresponding eigenvector is o_n.

For the other eigenvectors of the matrix $L(A)$, for $j \in \{2, \ldots, n\}$, according to Theorem 1, we have:

$$\begin{aligned} L(D) \cdot u_j &= (n \times I_n - O_n - L(A)) \cdot u_j \\ &= n \times I_n \cdot u_j - O_n \cdot u_j - L(A) \cdot u_j \end{aligned}$$

In the above expression, $n \times I_n \cdot u_j = n \times u_j$. Additionally, the value of $O_n \cdot u_j$ is zero, because based on Corollary 1, the sum of the elements in each of the eigenvectors of the Laplacian matrix, except for u_1, is zero. As a result, the above equation simplifies:

$$\begin{aligned} L(D) \cdot u_j &= n \times u_j - L(A) \cdot u_j \\ &= n \times u_j - \lambda_j(L(A)) \cdot u_j \\ &= (n - \lambda_j(L(A))) \cdot u_j \end{aligned}$$

As a result, u_j is an eigenvector of the Laplacian matrix $L(D)$, corresponding to the eigenvalue $(n - \lambda_j(L(A)))$.

Therefore, for $j \in \{2, \ldots, n\}$, if λ_j is an eigenvalue of the Laplacian matrix $L(A)$, $(n - \lambda_j)$ is an eigenvalue of the Laplacian matrix $L(D)$. The eigenvalue zero also exists in both Laplacian matrices, thus the proof is complete.

Theorem 3: If A is the network adjacency matrix, with size $n \times n$, and D is the corresponding distance matrix, and if the network contains c connected components, the number of $c-1$ eigenvalues in the Laplacian matrix $L(D)$ is equal to n, which are the largest eigenvalues of the Laplacian matrix $L(D)$.

Proof. If the network has c connected components, the number of eigenvalues of the Laplacian matrix $L(A)$ that equal to zero is c. Excluding the first smallest eigenvalue, according to Theorem 2, for $j \in \{2, \ldots, n\}$, if λ_j is an eigenvalue of $L(A)$, $(n - \lambda_j)$ will be an eigenvalue of $L(D)$. Therefore, for $j \in \{2, \ldots, c\}$,

$$n - \lambda_j = n - 0 = n$$

As a result, $c-1$ of the largest eigenvalues of the Laplacian matrix $L(D)$ is equal to n.

In real networks, the graph is typically connected and not composed of separate connected components. Consequently, the Laplacian matrix has only one eigenvalue equal to zero. The first gap in the eigenvalues of the Laplacian matrix can provide an estimate of the number of clusters, and the corresponding eigenvectors can serve as fundamental components.

The first eigenvector of the Laplacian matrix is a multiple of the vector o_n, in which all components are identical and provide no information. Hence, when using the eigenvectors of the Laplacian matrix, only around $c-1$ eigenvectors related to the second to the cth eigenvalues contain valuable information.

Referring to Theorem 3, in the distance Laplacian matrix, the approximate cluster number can be estimated from the first gap among the largest eigenvalues. In this context, if the first gap occurs after α large eigenvalues, we choose eigenvectors related to the α largest eigenvalues of the Laplacian of distance matrix as cluster indicator vectors.

To graphically observe the derived theorem, consider the network in Figure 8.4, composed of three connected components.

For this network, we computed the distance matrix D and the Laplacian of it as $L(D)$. Figure 8.5 presents their first 10 largest eigenvalues.

In this figure, it is observed that two of the largest eigenvalues are equal to 20, confirming Theorem 3. The eigenvectors corresponding to these two eigenvalues are shown in Figure 8.6, which can be used to identify the clusters in this network. The

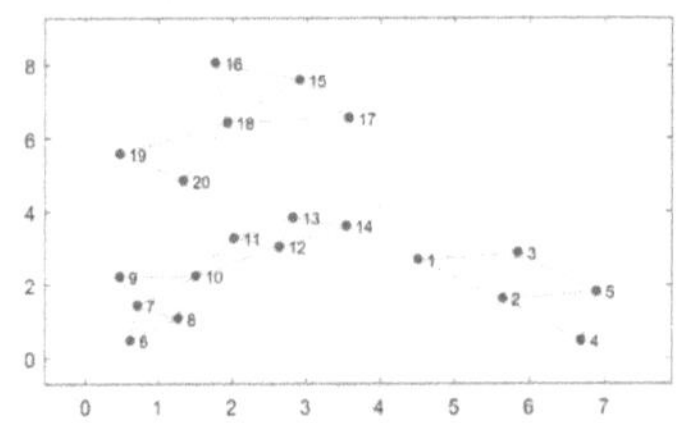

FIGURE 8.4 A sample network containing three connected components.

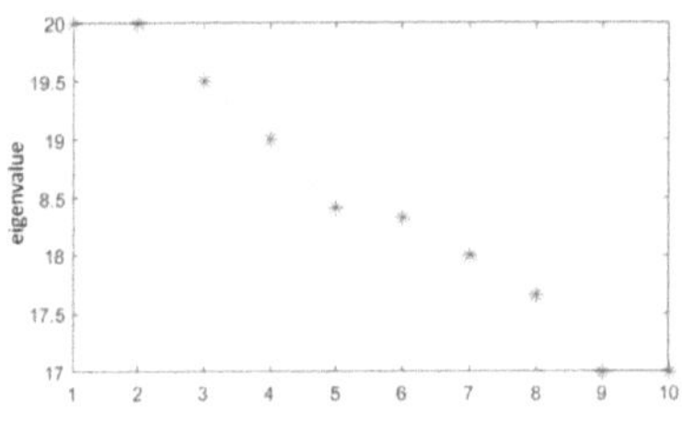

FIGURE 8.5 The 10 largest eigenvalues of Laplacian of the distance matrix, $L(D)$, for the network in Figure 8.4.

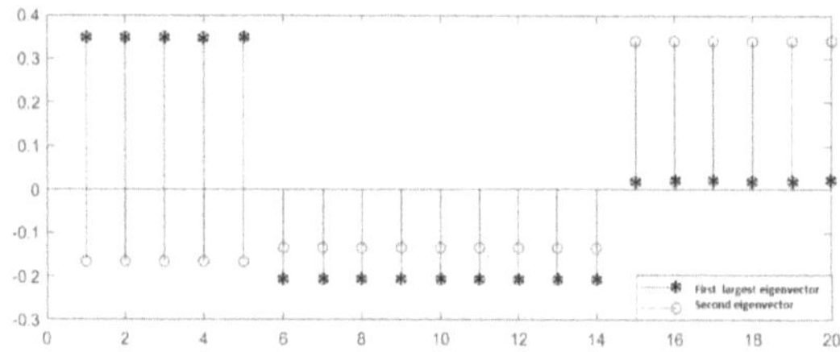

FIGURE 8.6 Two eigenvectors related to the first and second eigenvalues of Laplacian of the distance matrix, $L(D)$, for network in Figure 8.4.

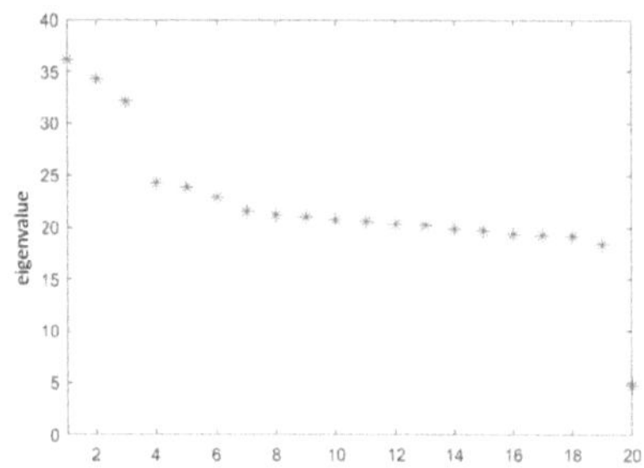

FIGURE 8.7 The eigenvalues of the Laplacian-plus matrix L^+ for the network in Figure 8.4.

eigenvectors are orthogonal to each other and all have a length of one, resulting in a mix of positive and negative values.

In this figure, the first cluster has positive values for the first eigenvector and negative values for the second eigenvector. The second cluster has negative values for both eigenvectors, while the third cluster has positive values for both eigenvectors.

To showcase the effectiveness of the DALT algorithm, we computed the Laplacian-plus matrix for this network and presented its eigenvalues in Figure 8.7.

In this figure, it is observed that the first largest gap occurs after the third eigenvalue. Consequently, the DALT algorithm selects three eigenvectors corresponding to these three eigenvalues as the columns of the matrix H.

Based on the algorithm, the maximum absolute value of each row of the matrix H is stored in the vector h_{max}. Based on the values obtained in this vector, the nodes 18, 2, 10, 12, and 15 are selected for $k = 5$.

8.6 SUMMARY

In this chapter, we delved into the intriguing concepts surrounding the influence maximization problem. We defined the problem and discussed various diffusion models, including the independent cascade (IC) and linear threshold (LT) models, while also introducing a novel perspective on the topic. The LT model is commonly utilized in real social networks to represent information diffusion. According to this model, when multiple friends share news, your likelihood of believing it increases.

Therefore, selecting influencers from various communities is essential in the LT model to maximize diffusion effectively. However, directly identifying communities within large social networks can be a time-consuming process. To address this challenge, we proposed a method to reduce the network size by strategically selecting candidate nodes. We then computed the similarities between these candidate nodes and all other nodes in the network. From there, we defined a social distance based on these similarities and introduced the DALT algorithm. DALT is a technique crafted to identify influencers aimed at maximizing diffusion across social networks. This approach encompasses the reduction of network size through the selection of key candidate nodes, followed by the calculation of social distances, ultimately leading to the application of a mathematical model to identify implicit communities within the reduced network. Solving the model requires computing the eigenvectors corresponding to the largest eigenvalues of the Laplacian matrix, constructed from the regularized social distances. After obtaining the eigenvectors, a new feature space is formed, from which influencers are extracted using a greedy approach.

REFERENCES

Ahajjam, Sara, and Badir, Hassan. Identification of influential spreaders in complex networks using hybrid rank algorithm. *Scientific Reports*, 8(1):1–10, 2018.

Binesh, N., and Ghatee, M. Distance-aware optimization model for influential nodes identification in social networks with independent cascade diffusion. *Information Sciences*, 581:88–105, 2021.

Binesh, N., ānd Ghatee, M. Using principal eigenvectors of Laplacian-Plus matrix to identify spreaders of social networks under linear threshold diffusion model. *AUT Journal of Mathematics and Computing*, 3(2):153–164, 2022.

Bozorgi, Arastoo, Saeed Samet, Johan Kwisthout, and Todd Wareham. "Community-based influence maximization in social networks under a competitive linear threshold model." *Knowledge-Based Systems*, 134:149–158, 2017.

Chen, Wei, Lakshmanan, Laks V.S., and Castillo, Carlos. Information and influence propagation in social networks. *Synthesis Lectures on Data Management*, 5(4):1–177, 2013.

Chen, Wei, Yajun Wang, and Siyu Yang. "Efficient influence maximization in social networks." In Proceedings of the 15th ACM SIGKDD international conference on Knowledge discovery and data mining, pp. 199–208, 2009.

Chen, Yi-Cheng, Wen-Chih Peng, and Suh-Yin Lee. "Efficient algorithms for influence maximization in social networks." *Knowledge and information systems*, 33:577–601, 2012.

Clifford, Peter and Sudbury, Aidan. "A model for spatial conflict." *Biometrika*, 60(3):581–588, 1973.

Goldenberg, Jacob, Libai, Barak, and Muller, Eitan. Talk of the network: A complex systems look at the underlying process of word-of-mouth. *Marketing Letters*, 12(3):211– 223, 2001.

Goyal, Amit, Lu, Wei, and Lakshmanan, Laks VS. Celf++ optimizing the greedy algorithm for influence maximization in social networks. In Proceedings of the 20th international conference companion on World wide web, 47–48, 2011.

Granovetter, Mark. "Threshold models of collective behavior." *American Journal of Sociology*, 83(6):1420–1443, 1978.

Hajdu, László, Miklós Krász, and András Bóta. "Community based influence maximization in the Independent Cascade Model." In 2018 Federated Conference on Computer Science and Information Systems (FedCSIS), pp. 237–243. IEEE, 2018.

Hajdu, László, Miklós Krész, and András Bóta. "Evaluating the role of community detection in improving influence maximization heuristics." *Social Network Analysis and Mining*, 11(1):91, 2021.

Jung, Kyomin, Heo, Wooram, and Chen, Wei. "Irie: Scalable and robust influence maximization in social networks." In 2012 IEEE 12th International Conference on Data Mining, pp. 918–923. IEEE, 2012.

Kempe, David, Kleinberg, Jon, and Tardos, Éva. "Maximizing the spread of influence through a social network." In Proceedings of the ninth ACM SIGKDD international conference on Knowledge discovery and data mining, pp. 137–146, 2003.

Kim, Jinha, Wonyeol Lee, and Hwanjo Yu. "CT-IC: Continuously activated and time-restricted independent cascade model for viral marketing." *Knowledge-Based Systems*, 62 (2014): 57–68.

Kimura, Masahiro, Saito, Kazumi, and Motoda, Hiroshi. "Efficient estimation of influence functions for sis model on social networks." In Twenty-First International Joint Conference on Artificial Intelligence, 2009.

Leskovec, Jure, Krause, Andreas, Guestrin, Carlos, Faloutsos, Christos, VanBriesen, Jeanne, and Glance, Natalie. "Cost-effective outbreak detection in networks." In Proceedings of the 13th ACM SIGKDD international conference on Knowledge discovery and data mining, pp. 420–429, 2007.

Li Jianxin, Taotao Cai, Ke Deng, Xinjue Wang, Timos Sellis, and Feng Xia. "Community-diversified influence maximization in social networks." *Information Systems* 92 (2020): 101522.

Liu, Dong, Jing, Yun, Zhao, Jing, Wang, Wenjun, and Song, Guojie. "A fast and efficient algorithm for mining top-k nodes in complex networks." *Scientific Reports*, 7:43330, 2017.

Liu, Weiping, and Lü, Linyuan. "Link prediction based on local random walk." *EPL (Europhysics Letters)*, 89(5):58007, 2010.

Lutkepohl, Helmut. "Handbook of matrices." *Computational Statistics and Data Analysis*, 2(25):243, 1997.

Palla, Gergely, Derényi, Imre, Farkas, Illés, and Vicsek, Tamás. "Uncovering the overlapping community structure of complex networks in nature and society." *Nature*, 435(7043):814–818, 2005.

Peng, Sancheng, Yongmei Zhou, Lihong Cao, Shui Yu, Jianwei Niu, and Weijia Jia. "Influence analysis in social networks: A survey." *Journal of Network and Computer Applications*, 106:17–32, 2018.

Shakarian, Paulo, Abhivav Bhatnagar, Ashkan Aleali, Elham Shaabani, Ruocheng Guo, Paulo Shakarian, Abhinav Bhatnagar, Ashkan Aleali, Elham Shaabani, and Ruocheng Guo. "The independent cascade and linear threshold models." *Diffusion in Social Networks*: 35–48, 2015.

Sumith, Nireshwalya, Basava Annappa, and Swapan Bhattacharya. "Influence maximization in large social networks: Heuristics, models and parameters." *Future Generation Computer Systems*, 89:777–790, 2018.

Tripathi, Richa, and Reza, Amit. "A subset selection based approach to structural reducibility of complex networks." *Physica A: Statistical Mechanics and Its Applications*, 540:123214, 2020.

Van Mieghem, Piet. *Graph spectra for complex networks*. Cambridge University Press, 2010.

Von Luxburg, Ulrike. "A tutorial on spectral clustering." *Statistics and Computing*, 17(4):395–416, 2007.

Wang, Qiyao, Jin, Yuehui, Yang, Tan, and Cheng, Shiduan. "An emotion-based independent cascade model for sentiment spreading." *Knowledge-Based Systems*, 116:86–93, 2017.

Wang, Wenjun, Liu, Dong, Liu, Xiao, and Pan, Lin. "Fuzzy overlapping community detection based on local random walk and multidimensional scaling." *Physica A: Statistical Mechanics and its Applications*, 392(24):6578–6586, 2013.

9 Connected Communities
The Role of Social Networks in Pandemic Preparedness and Mitigation

Shabir Ahmad Najar, Wakar Amin Zargar, Bilal Ahmad Khan, Mohammad Saleem Sofi, Shabnam Ahad, Fayaz Ahmad Bhat, and Mudasir Ahmad Nazar

9.1 INTRODUCTION

In people-centered communication, "connected communities" is understood as a group of people who can use such communication, a relationship that improves the way people exchange resources, information, or help. This is where contemporary technology and social media are helping relate people more closely to one another and with other institutions. Connected communities have high level of social capital, characterized by the creation and maintenance of trust and social networks among members for the purpose of collective benefit and efficacy [1]. To maintain ongoing relationships and facilitate communication and coordination in real time, these groups usually use some technology platform [2]. The use of these new ways of digital tools results in more efficacious and computerized forms of participation within civic engagement and community activities whereby many members actively join participatory initiatives including decision making [3]. This intrinsic connectivity helps overcome the barriers created by physical distances, making it easier for people to engage in productive relationships, regardless of their geographical location [4]. Oldenburg [5] also highlighted that connected communities particularly stress the importance of face-to-face meetings and the role of physical space in bringing people together and doing things. They do not function in a vacuum of only online activities. Connected communities foster benefits like ease of access to information, increase in collaboration opportunities and increased feelings of belongingness among the members [6]. Since these communities have developed social networks and structures, they are also more capable of addressing various issues and crises [1]. Furthermore, they promote inclusiveness by ensuring that each member belonging to the community is able to make their opinion known and heard, fostering a

DOI: 10.1201/9781003515890-12

background that is more of democracy and participation [3]. In general, acute communities alter how people interact and work with one another through the use of social networks and technology in building more integrated communities. These communities are kept active and adaptable to the conditions by giving more emphasis on virtual as well as conventional communication [4]. Social networks are relative structures composed of actors (tautologically called nodes) who are linked with each other in various relationships, such as close kin, common friends, common fields of interest, money relations, and/or information exchange. Such networks are of great importance in the social sciences as they explain the pattern of flow of resources, information and response patterns within and across units. Simply put, social networks are composed of actors who are contained in the nodes and social ties that connect them to each other. The type, direction, and magnitude of these relationships play crucial roles in the behavior of the network. The most common relationship is termed the "strong tie" between family or close friends, which is characterized by high emotional closeness and high contact, whereas the most common "weak tie" is the one that exists between acquaintances which opens up new opportunities and new information different from one's social circle [7]. Usually, the structure of a social network is presented in the form of graphs or matrices in which nodes illustrate people or other entities and edges indicate the links among these nodes. Density and centrality are two important parameters that help to break down these systems. Density is a measure of the connectivity of the system, in this context expressed as the fraction of existing connections relative to the possible connections in the network. Centrality identifies vital nodes in the network the importance of which is defined in terms of their position and their connection to other nodes [8]. Therefore there are professional social networks and career-based relationships, personal social networks and intra-member relationships, Internet-derived social networks, and organizational networks that are within and beyond organizational boundaries. Social Networks are very important in construction of the social behavior, culture, and identity, the provision of information or resources, influencing the actions of people, providing behavioral reward [9]. In situations such as pandemics or other public health crises, there is a strong emphasis and role that social networks play in information spread, promotion of health and emotional assistance [10]. Different models have been constructed in order to research social networks. The *Social Network Theory* has as its main premise the position occupied by the member in the context facilitates a member's possession of resources and information and that the structure of the system dictates how individuals act. The concept of *Social Capital* began with Bourdieu in [11] and underwent further development through Coleman [12] and Putnam [1] as its notable experts explain that social structures grant certain resources to individuals with respect to trust, aid, or collaboration. In the work by Burt [9], *the Structural Hole Theory*, it is pointed out that individuals having the capacity to link two or more different clusters within a network can obtain diverse information and relations, hence enabling them to compete effectively. The rising capabilities of computer technology have contributed to a transformation of social networks where social sites such as Facebook, LinkedIn, and X among others could be used for connecting large networks that are cross border. Furthermore, these tools help mobilize resources and disseminate information more effectively and quickly which has great implications in the social, political, and economic activities [13]. However, there are a number of drawbacks to the societal networks such as the hazards of spreading simulation of reality, reinforcing existing social inequalities, and "echo chamber" phenomena, whereby people only hear what they choose to believe and resist opposing views. The issue of data security and privacy, in social network analysis, for instance, is always a moral issue [14]. Contact with social networks is of great importance for public health because they improve health communication and promote health-related behaviors. Such integration, both offline and online, can help people in sharing information about various health risks, protective measures, and options of coping with health problems [15]. Popular social media platforms have helped people to know more about immunization campaigns and have encouraged them to participate or take part in the campaigns more actively [16]. Further, social channels provide other members of the society, friendship and kinship which are essential to the mental health of individuals. People try to obtain help whenever they have health problems through family members, friends, or the Internet [17]. It has been said that social support plays a constructive role by alleviating stress and enhancing recovery from illness [18]. However, social networks may have a better impact on health behaviors by creating norms and rules. If healthy food and regular exercise are the norms among their peers, they are likely to endorse healthy behavior [19]. The possibility of reaching different segments of the population because of social network outreach is beneficial also for health promotion activities. Social media outreach in particular can be effective in contacting specific demographic groups who are otherwise difficult to reach with other types of media [20]. Because these advertisements are able to be targeted toward specific communities around specific issues of their interest, the impact is even greater [21]. From other angles, social media can also be employed to identify and address health disparities among populations. Public health practitioners looking at social network data like that may be able to target individuals who are at a greater risk for certain illnesses and deliver disease prevention programs specifically to them [22]. By this means, the availability of such resources and interventions is ensured to be on the most appropriate populations [15]. Along with their capabilities to communicate information, provide social support, influence health behaviors, enhance health promotion programs, and eliminate health disparities, social networks play a critical role in the field of public health [10, 15, 20, 21]. Figure 9.1 highlights the information network flow in communities during pandemic.

Figure 9.1 reveals that by strengthening social ties, social networks are essential for pandemic preparedness and mitigation. They remove barriers to communication and foster timely and credible distribution of information which is important in enhancing the public's trust in health strategies and curtailing false assertions. This confidence decreases both the spread and effect by encouraging compliance with health behavior guidelines. Moreover, networks of social support also provide psychological and emotional assistance to individuals to help control stress levels and decrease feelings of disintegration as well as of integration within the community. This support is helpful in enhancing pandemic preparedness and response

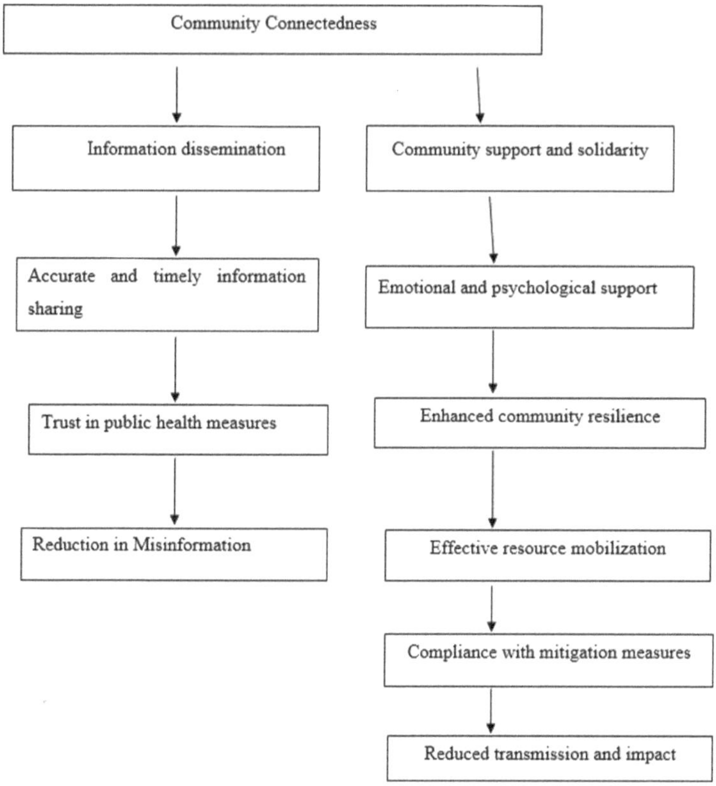

FIGURE 9.1 Information network flow process in communities during pandemic. Source: Framed by the authors on the basis of thorough analysis of the literature available on the topic.

by improving community's resilience. Additionally, effective acting to prospecting and deploying resources internally to an organization through a social network is assured. Looking at each of these factors it becomes clear why networks are so valuable in managing and reducing the effects of a pandemic and particularly in supporting central regions of heavily populated countries.

9.2 SIGNIFICANCE OF THE STUDY

The research topic "Connected Communities: The Role of Social Networks in Pandemic Preparedness and Mitigation" is importantly quite significant because it addresses the issue of how social networks may help in pandemic preparedness. They enable instantaneous transmission of information to millions through social media on critical health issues when several media channels could take too long to convey the message. They can be employed during a pandemic to instantly inform millions of people about important health information, measures, and schedules of vaccinations. Apart from educating the public, it may help alleviate panic and confusion.

Interpersonal interaction can also be facilitated by public health professionals to the communities to enhance interactions and answer any questions. Community leaders play an essential role in passing information to and from the health providers and the society, maximizing the effectiveness of the messages, as well as addressing the needs of the community. Apart from the family, they also help in fostering the probability of developing and cooperating in rivalry by following the health rules and consensus in the networks. Furthermore, there has to be the intervention of the government so as to be able to promote public health on social platforms, implement the policies, and provide accurate information. In order for the public to access appropriate information, governments may cooperate with social media companies to regulate and control free speech and refute fake news. Social media services have become a significant player in the battle against wrong propaganda, which is very common in times of public health crises and whose consequences can be serious. Understanding and leveraging the power of social networks will help policymakers and health agencies improve the efficacy features, inclusivity, and effectiveness of pandemic response measures. This chapter exposes how social networks bolster the participation and integration of families, government, and community leaders thus enabling effective planning of public health concerns to avert potential disasters and speed up recovery in the occurrence of epidemics, hence saving lives while reducing the adverse effects on societies.

9.3 OBJECTIVES

1. To investigate the role of social networks in promoting public health.
2. To assess how social networks help in mitigating the crisis of the pandemic.

9.4 METHODS

A secondary data analysis approach was employed in this study to explore the contribution of social networks to preparedness and response in the case of public health outbreaks. Relevant databases that were identified and chosen at the commencement of the study included PubMed, Web of Science, Google Scholar, and Scopus, owing to their vast evidence base and informative materials such as publications and reports. These databases were searched mostly with the terms "social networks," "pandemic preparedness," and "mitigation strategies." The scope of the search was also widened by adding additional terms such as "public health," "community resilience," "Covid-19," and "infectious disease management." A systematic review method was used to make certain the breadth and significance of the material found. Primary, an inclusive investigation was conducted crossways all databases by means of the chosen keywords. Further, Boolean operators (AND, OR) were used to further filter the searches, and results were filtered using language (English), publication date (last ten years), and document type (peer-reviewed papers, reviews, and policy documents) were used to further filter the results. Once nearly all of the pertinent sources were found, systematic abstracting and title searches were done to identify studies that exclusively addressed social networks in the context of health issues related to pandemic preparedness and mitigation. Following the recognition of pertinent publications, a full-text assessment was conducted to make certain that the research met the inclusion criteria, which included a focus on the role of social networks in public health emergencies, namely, pandemics. Some studies that did not fall within these parameters were excluded from the analysis, for instance, materials that were not published in English or materials that did not focus on social media or that were not on the preparedness for the pandemic were ignored. During data extraction, relevant information of every one of the chosen studies was recorded. Such aspects included the aims of the study, methodologies employed, authorship, year of publication, journal of publication, source of the study, social networks, and pandemic preparedness/mitigation aspects along with the findings and conclusions drawn from these aspects. The synthesized data was analyzed thematically. The communication, information dissemination, community engagement, and behavior change strategies in the social media cases were collated and analyzed to provide a better understanding of the role of social media in reinforcing communities and response strategies to pandemics. It also required synthesizing the results of different studies. A detailed summary of the results of the systematic search strategy and a flow chart (Figure 9.2) illustrating the article selection process are mentioned below.

A total of 1,500 articles were retrieved from four databases. After screening titles and abstracts, 400 articles were deemed relevant. A full-text review narrowed this down to 150 articles, which included 100 original research articles and 50 reviews/policy documents. These selected articles were then used for the thematic analysis to understand the role of social networks in pandemic preparedness and mitigation. This systematic and thorough approach ensures that the selected literature comprehensively covers the research topic, providing a solid foundation for understanding the impact of social networks on public health emergencies.

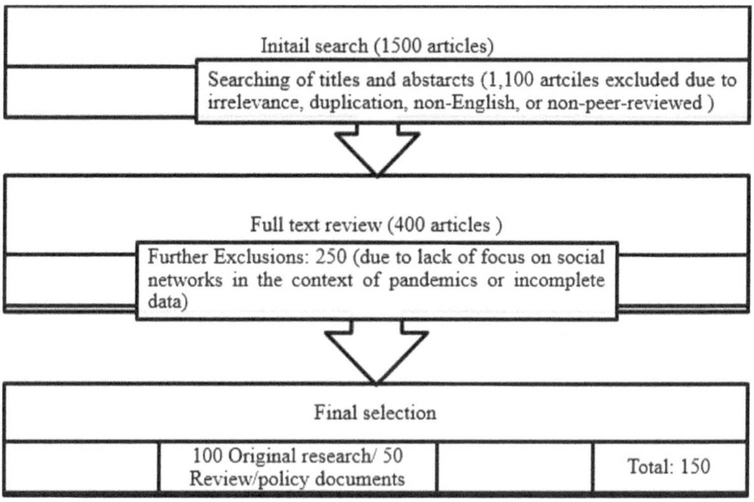

FIGURE 9.2 Selection of articles.

9.5 THEMATIC ANALYSIS

The role of social networks in the context of serving to prepare for and mitigate a pandemic remains a subject of great scholarly interest. The objective of this thematic analysis is to present the main conclusions from 150 research articles in order to analyze the impact of social networks on the response of the public to pandemics. The general themes available in the selected literature relevant to the research, for instance, Community Engagement through Use of Social, Dissemination of Misinformation, Communication for Public Health, Role of Influencers, and Policy Implication, have been utilized in this investigation. Themes that emerged from the selected research papers are discussed in a detailed manner below.

9.5.1 Theme: Community Engagement through Use of Social Networks

A common theme among the studies assessing the level of preparedness or mitigation strategies for the pandemic is Community Engagement through Use of Social Networks. During pandemics, social networks' power to communicate adequately and mobilize the whole community is vital for health interventions. The behavior of social networks in health emergencies has a functional ability to provide and consolidate great numbers of people within short notice [23]. As Garcia and Lee [23] argue, social networks in terms of reach and connectedness are critical in information distribution, especially during pandemics which is why they are so important for community mobilization. Public health organizations can provide regular or important updates, health warnings, or safety guidelines via social networks such as Facebook, X, and Instagram. It is especially useful in periods of pandemics when timely up-to-date information can assist in the conduct of the public's behavior to a better state of health. For example, various social media were used to provide information on vaccination: efforts, strategies and transmission of Covid-19. This real-time interaction played a major role in the pandemic response in terms of managing the public's understanding of and compliance with health norms [23]. Figure 9.3 as mentioned below highlights how various social institutions function during pandemic.

The picture provided outlines a community social structure in relation to epidemic prevention and management stressing the interrelated roles of certain key components. Central to this structure of social network is the Health authority whose responsibilities include formulation and distribution of relevant health messages. In between the two sides are community leaders who are essential in gaining confidence in the community and act as important communication links between the community and health authorities. One of the essential components of a health network is local hospitals since they are providers of critical healthcare services and information to the population. Social media marketing Figueroa is one of the efficient tools for communicating the message and raising interest among society since it utilizes the popularity of Facebook, Instagram, and other social networks. As the information's target group, the people need to adhere to the stated measures in order to mitigate the potential impacts of the pandemic. The news channels prevent the loss of a huge audience as they present facts and issues in a short period of time.

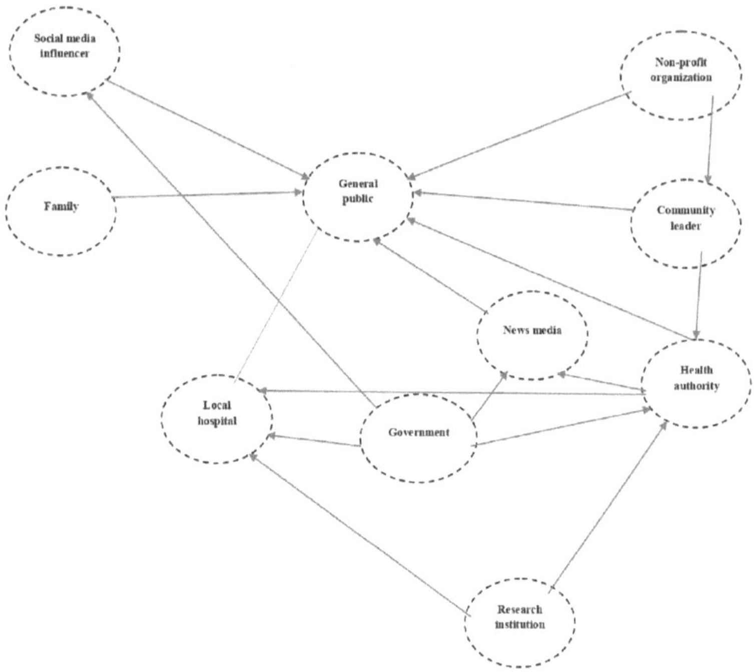

FIGURE 9.3 Connected social institutions during pandemic. Source: Framed by the authors on the basis of critical analysis of the literature available on social institutions and pandemic.

The wish of research institutions is to assist in changing the practice of healthcare by providing scientific information and research that is related to health. Such organizational structures operate at the grassroots level, provide support for designed public health initiatives, and ensure that local needs are addressed. Adherence to health guidelines is best enforced by families due to their capacity to spread within their network. Lastly, the government remains active in promoting health issues on social media as well as other platforms and implements the health rules, acting in this case, as the right source of information. This type of network also showcases how public health can be managed during a pandemic in terms of teamwork and every element's importance to maintaining the resilience and general health of the community. The focus of the research undertaken by Lopez and Miller [24] was to study the role of social networks in enhancing community resilience. A sense of belonging to a group and thereby creating support networks, as well as enabling activity sharing, contributes to the gaining and keeping of community resilience through these platforms [24]. Social networks facilitate information sharing across exactly these elements and therefore, can help the exchanged networks, encourage one another, and plan ways of responding to health challenges in their societies. Social media was especially efficient in uniting communities amid health crises such as the Ebola virus outbreak in West Africa. With these tools, health organizations were able to steadily inform populations of the symptoms, possible therapies, and prevention methods, thus inhibiting unnecessary virus transfer and empowering the population to stay healthy [24]. Good reasons exist for the use of social media for purposes of community mobilization and a few examples from the literature suffice in this regard. During the H1N1 pandemic, the public health community turned to social media for methodical announcements about the flu virus. The technique promoted active participation and continuous information flow that led to a reduction in panic and misinformation [23, 24]. Another case in this regard is that of the outbreak of Zika virus and how the internet, especially social networks, helped in educating the masses about mosquito control and its preventative measures. Public health campaigns utilized social media platforms to educate the public on healthy behaviors and how to prevent more people from contracting the virus.

9.5.2 Theme: Misinformation Dissemination

Another key area of focus within the literature on preparedness and response to the pandemic is the use of social media to share fake or distorted information. The public health efforts to promote health behavior change can be undermined by false information which creates problems such vaccine hesitance tendencies and adherence issues to health advice [25]. With the great audience and speed of social media, it becomes feasible for inaccurate information to reach large groups making it harder for public health measures. Many studies show that wrong information makes an adverse impact on the health of people in general. Zhao and Chen [25] also commented on the wave of false trends that surged on social networks regarding the unfounded safety and efficacy claims about vaccines during the Covid-19 pandemic which eventually influenced increased vaccine hesitancy. This disinformation finally contributed to a prolonged state of the pandemic due to significant delays in the realization of the wide-ranging vaccination campaign [25]. Lee and Park [26] similarly investigated the effects of misinformation on health guideline compliance. They found that widespread disregard of public health's instructions such as wearing a mask or keeping social distance was fueled by wrong beliefs about how the disease spreads and how it could be prevented [26]. This noncompliance complicated the public health emergency because it impeded the efforts to contain the disease [26]. Owing to their broad and speedy spread, these social networking sites have been acknowledged as important agents in the spread of disinformation. These sites support the fast and untrustworthy exchange of misleading or incorrect information by making it easy for users to share material in times of need usually on a high frequency without checks [25]. As per Lee and Park [26], the algorithms engaged by social media sites often give the material a superior priority than exactness based on engagement, which exacerbates the propagation of bogus information. During the Covid-19 plague and such, many false information about the virus what it entails, where it came from, and how it can be cured circulated over social media. In addition to this, Spanish flu's viral propagation has given rise to various other theories, for instance about the virus's applications as a bioweapon or even the fictitious information around clinical trials for drugs such as hydroxychloroquine, which also became prevalent on social networks [25]. These false narratives not only misled the citizens but also diverted attention from fact-based public health approaches. As Lee and Park [26] highlight, in order to stop the spread of misinformation, social media players and public health stakeholders need to work together. One possible outcome of this collaboration is to develop systems that prioritize likely truth and the use of fact-checking services for detection and rebuttal of false information [26].

9.5.3 Theme: Communication for Public Health

The referred articles explain the social networks use for health communication thoroughly. One major advantage of the use of social networks during pandemic situations is the speed and efficiency with which public health information disseminates to the people, thus affecting the overall public health. This ability for rapid dissemination however guarantees a wide coverage of health information, thus a quick response with the relevant health measures [27]. Johnson and Brown [27] focused on the role of social networks in delivering health communication especially in cases of pandemics. They pointed out that social networks such as Facebook, Instagram, and X are good sources of up-to-date information on how the virus is transmitted, preventive measures in place, and treatments available. For health policies to be adhered to, the public needs to be kept updated and so engaged and this takes a certain speed of reporting [27]. In addition, Harris and Johnson [28] also focused on the role of social networks in the implementation of health-enhancing behaviors. The researchers found that social networks could also help promote behaviors such as wearing masks, hand washing, and keeping distance by spreading interesting content along with health messages based on facts [27]. The role of such services is to consider offering some form of correction to any disinformation that might be availed on these products [27]. On the other hand, social networks provide a unique ability to reach various populations, including hard reaching populations. In the opinion of Johnson and Brown [27], social networks are especially effective in reaching teenagers and those in the young adult age group who are more users of these platforms for information. Health practitioners emphasize that this demographic reach ensures that important health promotion campaigns are effective and reach the intended target populations, hence bridging information gaps and health disparities. Harris and Johnson [28], on the other hand, delved into how "target" messaging is helpful in disseminating information to discrete groups such as the elderly or the lesser mass media accessible communities. Health authorities will assume that through targeting with the appropriate language and content, communication, the different aspects of society will be understood and reached [27]. Social networks also enhance community engagement by enabling communication between the public and the public health agencies in a more effective way. Interactive elements such as real-time Q&A sessions, survey options, and feedback choices give the public a forum to ask questions and get answers from government representatives in real time. This interaction encourages people to adhere to health-related behavior and develop faith, as suggested by Johnson and Brown [27].

Moreover, social networks can act as an avenue for public health as highlighted by Harris and Johnson [28]. Harris and Johnson [28] have revealed that user-associated content in the form of peer support and testimonials are valuable in promoting behavior and nurturing community in a pandemic situation. These community-based programs can educate the population regarding health issues and promote a culture that is more tolerant toward change in behavior [27].

9.5.4 Theme: Role of Influencers

Public health seeks to get audience participation by using different strategies and one of them revolves around whose voice is important that is, studying the role of influencers during the time of crises such as pandemics. The use of influencers especially social media influencers has been acknowledged to have a great effect on health outcomes during pandemics. Their duties include not only giving accurate information but also promoting healthy practices and combating incorrect information [29]. Activists who have a sufficiently large audience and are active on social networks tend to be good informants and information distributors. Influencers can act as a media outlet during pandemics and fast share health messages, information, and directives released by agencies like the World Health Organization (WHO) or the Centers for Disease Control and Prevention (CDC) as noted by Smith and Johnson [29]. Health campaigns are more successful in reaching followers as they tend to trust the information that is given by an influencer, thus extending the campaign's effectiveness. Further, influencers help in incorporating healthy practices. Influencers may set examples and encourage positive habits of hand hygiene, use of masks, and social distancing [30]. Such mundane acts help reconstruct the behavioral norms which taboo these activities as non-conventional, especially for young populations who are at risk of this effect due to their inclination toward social media stars [30]. Influencers can also be of great help in tackling the great challenge constraint of people spreading untrue information toward societies from time to time during the pandemics. Smith and Johnson [29] argue that influencers act as fact-checkers by correcting misleading information and sources often found on social media. Influencers are responsible for ensuring that people have the right information and supporting decision-making processes through engaging audiences with the right context [29]. Nguyen and Williams [30] highlight that influencers can effectively encourage their fans to receive vaccinations, if they share their vaccination experiences and correct misinformation surrounding vaccination. This is important in instilling vaccine confidence which is key to increasing vaccine uptake among populations [30]. Influencers have a unique ability to reach even the most marginalized populations, which regular public health interventions would have failed to address. In their work, Smith and Johnson [29] noted that these influencers have a good understanding of the preferences and problems of the audience that is why they are able to alter the nature of the messages sent out. This type of focused communication ensures that public health messages are appropriate, possible, and relevant to various sections of the population [29].

9.5.5 Theme: Policy Implications

Framing appropriate policy during the time of pandemic is very essential. Proper policies can alleviate the suffering of the people to a large extent. Figure 9.4 as mentioned below highlights how public health policy framed by the government works at the time of the pandemic.

Figure 9.4 reveals how the framed policy works on the ground during the time of the pandemic. Certain public health policies have wide-reaching effects, if social networks are used in health programs. This is especially true as far as readiness for and response to disasters such as pandemics is concerned. Social media can enhance the ability to engage communities, correct misperceptions and facilitate health communication. Lawmakers should consider this. Addressing those particular questions would increase the effectiveness of public health measures during the pandemics [22, 23]. One major policy implication is the institutionalization of social networks' involvement in public health communication planning processes and activities. Social networks enhance health communication, especially in providing fast and accurate information dissemination of health workers and their essential role in a health crisis that encompasses natural disasters. In order to ensure that the public receives information that is correct and to the point within the shortest time possible, the governing authorities should formulate policies guiding the use of social media sites [23]. In addition to that, public health institutions should also support capacity development programs aimed at enhancing the communication team's

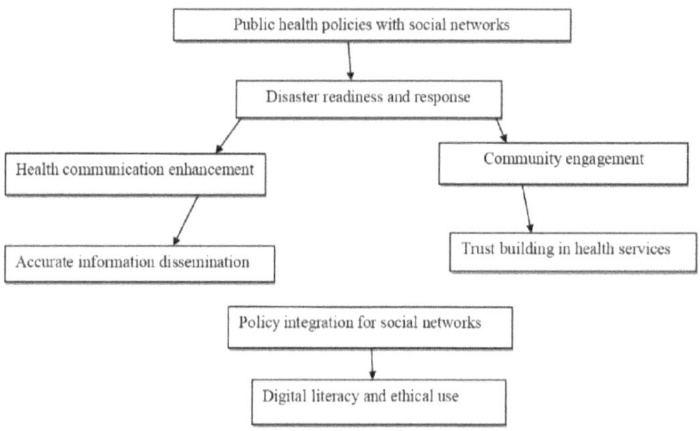

Figure: (04): Policy Implications Flow Chart

Source: *Framed by the authors of the basis of research results*

FIGURE 9.4 Policy implications flow chart. Source: Framed by the authors on the basis of research results.

digital skills. It is also believed that public health professionals would be able to actively and adequately communicate with members of the public on various social media sites with these programs [22]. Through bettering one's literacy, public health organizations are able to provide relevant information clearly to the intended target audience and all interested members [22]. Improving community participation with social networks should be another area for policy emphasis. There is synergy in social networks as public health organizations are able to relate with communities addressing their issues and creating goodwill [23]. As Garcia and Lee [23] state, the use of social media should be recommended by political agents as a way to organize people for social movements, particularly when such needs to be done with respect to the information on vaccination services and preventive measures. Lopez and Miller [24] argue that such policies should promote social networking for the purpose of supporting health programs that are community based. Community members as well as health officers can formulate a plan and organize activities to provide health messages to the community. Such collaborations can enhance the effectiveness and coverage of health promotion programs [22]. Unfortunately, the unregulated spread of fake news through social networks has been a significant drawback in the attempts to enforce public health policies. A number of strategies must be developed in order to reach the above goals so that the public does not receive information that is misleading [25]. For example, these approaches may involve partnerships with social media companies to identify and eliminate false information, or they may consist of campaigns to raise the public's understanding of the internet [25]. Regarding the importance of real-time systems that correct disinformation quickly, remarked on the need for improvement of these technologies. It should be noted that these great efforts must be made in the development and integration of these services into social media platforms by policy. It is also important for public health organizations to harness the influence and trust of community members and other reliable figures in the campaigns to counter myths and provide the people with the right information [29]. To ensure that all members of society are offered positive health information of high quality through networks, there is also a need for policies addressing the inequalities in digital technologies. Harris and Johnson [28] argue that some demographics in particular, the elderly and residents of low-income areas may not have such access to digital resources as others. Therefore, it is recommended that policy proponents make provision for resources targeting efforts to increase the ICT literacy and access levels of the vulnerable subgroups of the population [30]. Some measures to minimize the digital divide may include distributing electronic devices among people and establishing cheap internet services, as well as helping them learn how to use social media. Policymakers can promote health equity and improve public health by ensuring that all sections of society have access to and benefit from digital health communication [28]. Tempo is a very important aspect within the ethics of public health practice that relates to the timing of any social media strategies. Accountability is important, one way in which it is practiced is in campaigns involving influencers and social media. In order to maintain public trust, such policies should require the clear mention of all kinds of engagement or sponsorship [30]. There is also a need to formulate ethical policies pertaining to the participant's privacy and their health data in public health campaigns on social media. In such cases, it is essential to uphold the public credence that is associated with such projects by ensuring that all ethical measures regarding data collection and use are adhered to.

9.6 DISCUSSION

Despite the importance of each of these themes, the analysis of the literature selected for this study sheds light on the importance of social networks in preparedness and response to pandemics. First and foremost, one vital thing that sticks out is social network-based community mobilization. Due to social media platforms, people are able to have quick access to important health education. When essential and reliable information spreads at an exponential rate, it leads to improved health status of the population. Garcia and Lee [23] state that Facebook, Twitter, Instagram, and other social media platforms were actively used to communicate information regarding vaccinations, prevention, and the transmission of the virus during the Covid-19 pandemic. This information was very essential bearing a significant weight among public users leading to increased compliance toward health measures. In addition, social networks help to promote and encourage collective action by providing support networks and a sense of belonging to a community which increases community resilience. Lopez and Miller [24] demonstrated that health emergencies, the Ebola outbreak in particular, attracted and solicited social network resources, thus containing the spread of the virus and strengthening the communities in which it emerged. Further, evidence particularly from case studies of the Zika virus outbreak and H1N1 pandemic, supports how social media can be used as an effective tool for managing public awareness and mobilizing communities. On the other hand, it is worrisome to actively promote through social media is the problem of promoting misinformation. It is well documented that misinformation poses risks to health projects by creating vaccine hesitance and non-compliance to health treatment. Based on Zhao and Chen [25] and Lee and Park [26] vaccination safety and viral transmission embarrassment were a major challenge to the public health response during Covid-19 toward prevention and control. Add to this the fact that social networks themselves further compound the problem by rapidly spreading misinformation due to their prioritization of interaction rather than facts. Equally, these platforms have catered to the public health communication needs. Also, social media as a means of disseminating health information and promoting the good health practices of hand washing and wearing masks is equally effective according to Johnson and Brown [27] and Harris and Johnson [28]. The accumulative features of these platforms to capture the needs of a vast pool at least the young population in the context make it possible to disseminate essential health messages, address knowledge barriers, and promote health equity. Influencers play an important role even in pandemic communication using their large number of subscribers to disseminate relevant information, promote health behavior, and dispel misinformation. Finally, they help fasten the normalization of creating the bulwark and raising the chances of getting vaccinated among the youth who are easily influenced by social media idols [29, 30]. Last but not the least, there are important policy implications when social networks are incorporated into public health campaigns. Authorities have to adopt multicentric strategies to address disinformation, increase the level of the population's health professional's digital competence, and diversify the ways of communication with the audience. As an example, to ensure equal access to accurate health information for all populations, it is necessary to eliminate information inequality. Adhering to ethical aspects of health information issues such as openness and privacy of the information to the people concerned is paramount in restoring the civilians' faith in the digital health movement.

9.7 CONCLUSION

As noted above, social networks are considered with both opportunities and threats in the field of preparedness and response to any potential or actual pandemic. Recent pandemics have shown that their ability to disseminate information and mobilize communities in a short time frame is an asset in the health sector. However, there are many challenges in fighting these public health initiatives, since these channels allow for the mass spread of false information. Therefore, there is a need for social policy to protect the health of the public by also addressing the underlying factors of community organization and communication in social networks. That is why in order for social networks to be applied successfully and effectively in public health emergencies in the future, it will be necessary to adhere to ethical standard codes and ensure universal availability of digital means. When social networks are engaged for purposes of bringing together communities, they can significantly enhance preparation and response to pandemics which eventually is for the good of everyone.

REFERENCES

1. Putnam, Robert D. *Bowling Alone: The Collapse and Revival of American Community.* New York. Simon and Schuster, 2000.
2. Wellman, Barry. "Physical Place and Cyberplace: The Rise of Personalized Networking." *International Journal of Urban and Regional Research* 25, no. 2 (2001): 227–252.
3. Bimber, Bruce. *Information and American Democracy: Technology in the Evolution of Political Power.* Cambridge: Cambridge University Press, 2003.
4. Castells, Manuel. *Communication Power.* Oxford: Oxford University Press, 2009.
5. Oldenburg, Ray. *The Great Good Place: Cafés, Coffee Shops, Bookstores, Bars, Hair Salons, and Other Hangouts at the Heart of a Community.* Cambridge: Da Capo Press, 1999.
6. Hampton, Keith, and Barry Wellman. "Neighboring in Netville: How the Internet Supports Community and Social Capital in a Wired Suburb." *City & Community* 2, no. 4 (2003): 277–311.
7. Granovetter, Mark S. "The Strength of Weak Ties." *American Journal of Sociology* 78, no. 6 (1973): 1360–1380.
8. Freeman, Linton C. "Centrality in Social Networks: Conceptual Clarification." *Social Networks* 1, no. 3 (1978/79): 215–239.

9. Burt, Ronald S. *Structural Holes: The Social Structure of Competition.* Cambridge: Harvard University Press, 1992.
10. Christakis, Nicholas A., and James H. Fowler. "The Spread of Obesity in a Large Social Network Over 32 Years." *New England Journal of Medicine* 357, no. 4 (2007): 370–379.
11. Bourdieu, Pierre. "The Forms of Capital." In *Handbook of Theory and Research for the Sociology of Education*, edited by J. Richardson, 241–258. Westport: Greenwood, 1986.
12. Coleman, James S. "Social Capital in the Creation of Human Capital." *American Journal of Sociology* 94 (1988): S95–S120.
13. Boyd, Danah M., and Nicole B. Ellison. "Social Network Sites: Definition, History, and Scholarship." *Journal of Computer-Mediated Communication* 13, no. 1 (2007): 210–230.
14. Barabási, Albert-Lászl6. *Linked: The New Science of Networks.* Cambridge: Perseus Publishing, 2002.
15. Valente, Thomas W. *Social Networks and Health: Models, Methods, and Applications.* Oxford: Oxford University Press, 2010.
16. Thackeray, Rosemary, Brad L. Neiger, Ann K. Smith, and Sarah B. Van Wagenen. "Adoption and Use of Social Media Among Public Health Departments." *BMC Public Health* 12, no. 1 (2012): 1–6.
17. House, James S. *Work Stress and Social Support.* Reading: Addison-Wesley, 1981.
18. Cohen, Sheldon, and Thomas A. Wills. "Stress, Social Support, and the Buffering Hypothesis." *Psychological Bulletin* 98, no. 2 (1985): 310–357.
19. Christakis, Nicholas A., and James H. Fowler. *Connected: The Surprising Power of Our Social Networks and How They Shape Our Lives.* New York: Little, Brown and Company, 2009.
20. Hawn, Carleen. "Take Two Aspirin and Tweet Me in the Morning: How Twitter, Facebook, and Other Social Media Are Reshaping Health Care." *Health Affairs* 28, no. 2 (2009): 361–368.
21. Freeman, Becky, Suzanne Potente, Vanessa Rock, and Jan Mclver. "Social Media Campaigns That Make a Difference: What Can Public Health Learn from the Corporate Sector and Other Social Change Marketers?" *Public Health Research & Practice* 25, no. 2 (2015): e2521517.
22. Luke, Douglas A., and Jenine K. Harris. "Network Analysis in Public Health: History, Methods, and Applications." *Annual Review of Public Health* 28 (2007): 69–93.
23. Garcia, Miguel, and Henry Lee. "Community Mobilization During Pandemics: The Role of Social Networks." *Journal of Public Health* 15, no. 3 (2019): 200–210.
24. Lopez, Anna, and Bruce Miller. "Social Networks and Community Resilience in Public Health Emergencies." *Health Communication* 33, no. 4 (2018): 340–350.
25. Zhao, Yuhui, and Xiaojun Chen. "Influence of Social Media on Public Health Communication During Pandemics." *Journal of Health Communication* 25, no. 6 (2020): 500–510.
26. Lee, Susan, and Jinho Park. "The Impact of Misinformation on Public Health During Pandemics." *Public Health Journal* 34, no. 2 (2021): 210–220.
27. Johnson, Peter, and Thomas Brown. "Social Networks and Pandemic Preparedness: A Review of Literature." *Journal of Public Health Communication* 12, no. 4 (2021): 345–357.
28. Harris, Rachel, and Karen Johnson. "Analyzing the Effectiveness of Social Network Interventions in Pandemics." *Health Promotion Journal* 15, no. 2 (2020): 150–165.

29. Smith, Laura, and Peter Johnson. "The Influence of Social Media Personalities on Public Health During Pandemics." *Journal of Public Health Communication* 14, no. 3 (2021): 275–289.
30. Nguyen, Thuy, and Robert Williams. "Social Media Influencers and Public Health: A Crisis Communication Perspective." *Health Promotion Journal* 28, no. 2 (2020): 123–135.

10 Identifying Spread Blockers Using Overlapping Community Detection for Pandemic Management

Sajid Yousuf Bhat and Arjumand Akbar

10.1 INTRODUCTION

Pandemics have historically caused widespread disruption across the globe. In many instances, outbreaks progress in waves, with the disease spreading exponentially among populations primarily through social interactions. Governments often respond by implementing strict social distancing measures and lockdowns to curb the spread and aim to flatten the infection curve. While effective, complete lockdowns are challenging to sustain due to their profound negative impact on economies and the social and mental well-being of communities. An alternative approach involves minimizing the spread of contagion during its early stages, specifically before community transmission becomes widespread. This can be achieved by identifying and targeting the most influential spreaders, or spread blockers, within the social network of the population. These individuals can be subjected to interventions such as testing, quarantine, restricted socialization, or prioritized vaccination. By focusing efforts on these key nodes, the diffusion dynamics of the contagion can be significantly curtailed, reducing its overall spread. The number of spread blockers, i.e., k can range from a few to a small subset of the entire population depending upon the degree of precaution that a government wants to take before it is compelled to issue a complete lockdown advisory. The spread blockers thus identified can further be used to design and prioritize vaccination strategies in countries with high population and relatively less access to vaccines. This can be helpful in creating more effective vaccination drives in terms of minimizing the risks of consecutive infection waves that wreak havoc across communities. Identifying influential nodes from social networks has been a long-standing and challenging task with numerous methods based on different approaches being proposed in the literature.

 DOI: 10.1201/9781003515890-13

Most commonly, nodes are ranked based on some network node-centrality measure and the top-k ranked nodes based on the centrality measure are taken as most influential. However, calculating global centrality measures like the betweenness centrality is computationally exhaustive and requires the complete network to be in memory. This renders most of the existing influential-node detection methods based on centrality measures inapplicable to very large-scale social networks. One of the inherent characteristics of real-world social networks is the existence of communities in their underlying structure. Communities in a social network represent nodes that are connected more within the community in terms of similarity, interaction (physical or virtual), function, ideas, proximity, and so on than across the community. Community detection focuses on identifying densely connected groups within social networks, which are significant as they often represent functional units within a networked system. This area of research has garnered considerable attention in recent years and continues to evolve rapidly. A key challenge in community detection is addressing overlapping communities, where a single node in the network belongs to multiple communities simultaneously. Nodes at which communities overlap represent structural holes (Lou and Tang 2013) which indicate the scarcity of connections across communities at that point in the network. In information diffusion theory, nodes that occupy structural holes have higher influential power in the network (Katona, Zubcsek and Sarvary 2011). Traditional methods for overlapping community detection often face scalability challenges in large-scale social networks due to their reliance on global network metrics. Building on earlier work by Bhat and Abulaish (2013) which emphasized the importance of their overlapping community detection method (Bhat and Abulaish, 2012) for identifying influential nodes, the authors later introduced a distributed version of this algorithm in Muhammad, Majid, and Bhat (2020). This paper highlights the significance of the overlapping community detection approach proposed in Muhammad, Majid, and Bhat (2020) for identifying spread blockers in social networks. The performance of the proposed method is evaluated and compared against other state-of-the-art overlapping community detection methods in the literature. The significance of overlapping nodes, detected by various overlapping community detection methods, as spread blockers is verified by comparing their degree of overlap with their betweenness centrality score. Since the betweenness centrality score of nodes is often used to rank nodes in a network for influence, if the degree of overlap for a node positively correlates with betweenness centrality then an overlapping community detection method can simply be used to identify spread blockers in a social network. The chapter is organized as follows: Section 10.2 presents the related work on influential node detection and overlapping community detection. Section 10.3 involves hypothesis testing and insights wherein the degree of overlap of a node as identified by the method presented in (Muhammad, Majid and Bhat 2020) is compared with the nodes' betweenness centrality. Section 10.4 presents the significance of the proposed approach to identify spread blockers by measuring the network split (in terms of connected components) after removing the detected influential nodes. Finally, Section 10.5 concludes the chapter.

10.2 RELATED WORK

Traditionally, influential node detection and influence maximization problems have been studied mainly under two categories, namely centrality measure-based approaches (Zhang, et al. 2019) and greedy approaches (Khomami, et al. 2021). In the centrality-based approaches, tradeoffs have been followed to balance computational overheads, scalability, and accuracy by incorporating either local measures like the degree centrality or global measures like betweenness centrality. In the greedy approach, various diffusion models like the SIR, Threshold, and Independent Cascade models have been used to find and rank the best spreaders after each diffusion iteration through the network. However, these approaches are computationally exhaustive and have poor scalability. One of the important structural features of real-world social networks is the existence of communities in the underlying structure. In the context of influential node detection, many researchers have presented the significance of community structures for the task of influence maximization. Katona, Zubcsek, and Sarvary (2011) analyzed an OSN dataset and found that dense groups or communities promote higher rates of word-of-mouth influence, with influencers occupying structural holes in the network exhibiting, on average, greater influential power. Similarly, the empirical analysis by Lerman, Ghosh, and Surachawala (2012) on various online social networking platforms underscores the importance of community structures in viral marketing, noting that dense community structures in social networks lead to a lower epidemic threshold. Hinz et al. (2011) further demonstrated that seeding hubs (nodes with high degrees) for viral marketing generates a higher number of referrals, as hubs play a more active role in the diffusion process due to their extensive connectivity. The community analysis of influential nodes in a social network by Kimura et al. (2008) highlights that based on the correlation, a modularity-based graph partitioning algorithm is an alternative to the greedy method (Kempe, Kleinberg and Tardos 2003) for detection of influential nodes in a social network. The analysis of Galstyan, Musoyan, and Cohen (2009) based on finding the largest cascades using a threshold model suggested that the selection of influential nodes can be limited to a small community within the community structure of the underlying network. The work of Wang et al. (2010) is a bit different in the sense that after a community structure is identified, the kth influential node is selected from a community that yields the largest increase of influence degree among all communities. Here the influence degree is measured in terms of the diffusion process modeled using the independent cascade model. Bhat and Abulaish (2013) have also presented empirical evidence that the overlapping community detection algorithm proposed in Bhat and Abulaish (2012) generates overlapping nodes that are potential influential nodes for viral marketing. Building on these findings, numerous techniques for influential node detection and influence maximization based on community structures have been proposed in the literature. Zhang et al. (2013) argue that the influential nodes detected by traditional methods based on measures like degree centrality may all lie in the same underlying larger community and thus only influence nodes lying in that single community. They propose a k-medoid-based graph partitioning method to ensure that the k-influential nodes are taken from k different communities. Gupta,

Singh, and Cherifi (2016) argue that global information related to a network may be unavailable or impractical to use (e.g., in the case of very large-scale networks) and thus suggest that local centrality measures should be used for influential node detection. They propose a new local centrality measure for nodes based on the position (hubs and bridges) of a node in the underlying community structure of the network. However, we argue that global metrics are better indicators of influence across the network and should be preferable in cases where the dynamics of epidemics are studied. Moreover, alternative scalable metrics to that of global centrality measures should also be identified and evaluated. Zhao, Li, and Jin (2016) model the influential node detection as the identification of core nodes from within the underlying communities of the social network. The core node identification is based on a label propagation mechanism which is restricted within a community. Further, their work is based on the assumption of Xiangwei et al. (2009) that diffusion across communities is not possible which according to our understanding overlooks the significance of structural holes, bridges, and overlapping nodes in a network reported in the literature and is thus flawed. Pozveh, Zamanifar, and Nilchi (2017) use the underlying community structure of a social network to propose community-based closeness measures to rank the nodes. These closeness measures, categorized as active and blocked, are calculated using the neighborhoods of nodes and their community affiliations. Tulu, Hou, and Younas (2018) base their approach on the works of Zhao et al. (2014) and Zhao et al. (2015) which map the importance of a node in the network to the number of communities to which the node is linked to in the underlying community structure. Several community-based approaches for influential node detection have been proposed in the literature. Tulu, Hou, and Younas (2018) measure a node's influence based on the entropy of random walks from the node to various communities within the network. Zhang et al. (2019) introduce the Community k-Shell Influence (CKI), which ranks nodes according to the number of nodes with a degree greater than k to which they are connected within their community. Zhao et al. (2020) use the Blondel community detection method (Blondel, et al. 2008) to identify community structures and propose a community-based centrality measure for ranking nodes. This measure considers a node's influence based on the strength of its local community and the neighboring communities it connects to, with community influence determined by size and the closeness of inter-community nodes. Khomami et al. (2021) select k influential nodes, one from each of the k largest communities, by evaluating a node's centrality and degree within its community. Zhang, Li, and Gan (2021) inspired by the theory of the strength of weak ties, emphasize the role of structural holes—sparse connections between communities—in influence spread. They identify boundary nodes as structural holes, rank them based on their influence spread, and use these rankings to select influential nodes. Despite their diverse methodologies, these strategies face notable challenges in their application and effectiveness, as outlined below:

1. All these studies consider that the underlying community structure of the network is distinct, i.e., non-overlapping. However, it is a well-established theory that real-world social networks exhibit overlapping community

structures wherein a node may belong to multiple communities. Moreover, it is these overlapping nodes that better suit the role of structural holes and thus as spreaders. Ghalmane et al. (2019) present an approach that utilizes overlapping communities for influential node detection; however, it is faced with the following issues.

2. Most of these methods lack a clear justification for the choice of the community detection algorithm employed and often imply that any community detection method is suitable for the task. However, different community detection methods often use different definitions of communities and the results often vary. Moreover, most of the community detection methods do not take into consideration the weighted and directed nature of social networks that might provide more insights to the diffusion behavior.
3. Another major issue related to these studies is that they are applicable to small networks as many community detection methods proposed in the literature use some kind of a global metric like modularity and are thus not scalable to very large-scale networks, typically against large human proximity networks which are important for studying contagion based epidemics.

To address these challenges, this chapter proposes a novel study aimed at highlighting the significance of various state-of-the-art overlapping community detection methods for identifying influential nodes (spread blockers) from social networks.

10.3 TESTING OF THE HYPOTHESIS

The main objective of this chapter is to present an alternative for the global centrality measure namely betweenness centrality. Being a global measure, betweenness centrality is computationally exhaustive and thus not scalable to large-scale networks. We argue that from the overlapping community structure of a network, the community memberships of nodes can be used as a good indicator for selecting influential nodes. We hypothesize that the greater the number of communities a node belongs to, the more significant it is as a seed (influential node or spread blocker), as such nodes are likely to facilitate the diffusion of infections across multiple groups within a social network. To test this hypothesis, we examine the relationship between nodes' community memberships and their corresponding betweenness centralities. For our experiments, we utilize the distributed overlapping community detection method proposed by Muhammad, Majid, and Bhat (2020) alongside six other state-of-the-art overlapping community detection methods summarized in Table 10.1.

The overlapping community detection methods are applied to three social network datasets to extract overlapping community structures. The list of datasets is summarized in Table 10.2.

The community structure detected by each of the methods is then analyzed to reflect the relation of the community membership count of nodes for each of these methods with the betweenness centrality of these nodes. Since the overlapping community membership count of different community detection methods for the same set

TABLE 10.1
Overlapping Community Detection Methods Used

Method and Source	Approach Used	Scalability
HOCTracker (Muhammad, Majid and Bhat 2020)	Density-based clustering	Distributed implementation using MapReduce
CFinder (Palla, et al. 2005)	k-Clique percolation	Not scalable
AFOCS (Greene, Doyle, and Cunningham 2010)	Louvains local search heuristic	Not scalable
SLPA (Xie and Szymanski 2012)	Label propagation	Not scalable
COPRA (Gregory 2010)	Label propagation	Not scalable
NECTAR (Gregory 2010)	Louvains local search heuristic	Theoretically scalable
DEMON (Coscia, et al. 2012)	Label propagation	Theoretically scalable

TABLE 10.2
Datasets Used

Dataset Name and Source	Number of Nodes	Number of Edges
Facebook (Leskovec and Mcauley, 2012)	4039	88234
Enron (Klimt and Yang, 2004)	13750	175253
Deezer (Rozemberczki and Sarkar, 2020)	28281	92752

of nodes belonging to a network varies, we divide the overlapping membership count (assigned by a community detection method to nodes) into bins containing fractions of the highest membership assigned by a method to any node in the underlying network. The bin width is set to 0.1, i.e., 10% of the highest overlapping membership. To highlight the relationship between the overlapping membership of a node (assigned by a community detection method) and its betweenness centrality, we extract the top 1% and 2% nodes according to their decreasing betweenness centrality and plot the confidence of an overlapping node bin to appear in the top 1% and 2% fraction of influential nodes according to their betweenness centrality. The confidence of an overlapping bin to appear in the top fraction is calculated as shown in equation 1. In simple terms, the confidence score [between 0 and 1] of an overlapping bin for a community detection method is the fraction of nodes assigned to an overlapping bin that appears in the top 1% and 2% influential fraction in terms of betweenness centrality. Along these lines, the results highlighting the relationship of overlapping node memberships and betweenness centrality using different overlapping community detection methods and datasets are shown in Figures 10.1, 10.2, and 10.3. Figure 10.1 shows results for the Facebook dataset wherein Figure 10.1a uses the top 1% nodes and Figure 10.1b uses the top 2% nodes according to the betweenness centrality. The method CFinder did not generate any results for this dataset due to the high

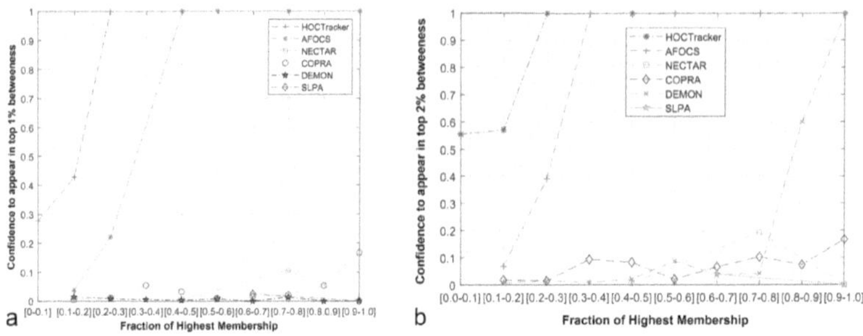

FIGURE 10.1 Confidence of overlapping node bins to appear in the top fraction of betweenness rank for Facebook Dataset. a) For top 1% of betweenness rank. b) For top 2% of betweenness rank.

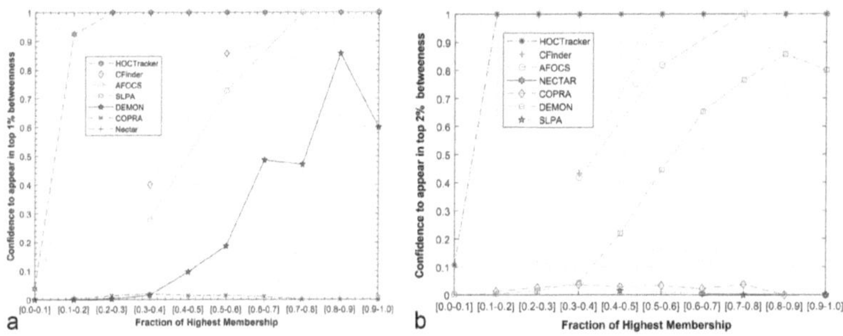

FIGURE 10.2 Confidence of overlapping node bins to appear in the top fraction of betweenness rank for Enron Dataset. a) For top 1% of betweenness rank. b) For top 2% of betweenness rank.

density of the input network and its memory requirements. It can be observed from Figure 10.1 that for the Facebook dataset the highly overlapping nodes bins identified by methods HOCTracker and AFOCS show positive relationship with betweenness centrality, i.e., the higher the overlapping membership of a node, the more likely (with confidence of 1) it belongs to the top 1% and 2% of nodes ranked based on the betweenness centrality. The same is not true for overlapping community detection methods including NECTAR, COPRA, DEMON, CFinder, and SLPA.

Figure 10.2 shows results for the Enron dataset wherein Figure 10.2(a) uses the top 1% nodes and Figure 10.2(b) uses the top 2% nodes according to the betweenness centrality. It can be observed from Figure 10.2 that for the Enron dataset, only the methods HOCTracker and AFOCS generate overlapping node bins that have a relatively high betweenness centrality. The results generated by other methods for Enron dataset are relatively insignificant.

Figure 10.3 shows results for the Deezer dataset wherein Figure 10.3(a) uses the top 1% nodes and Figure 10.3(b) uses the top 2% nodes according to the betweenness centrality. It can be observed from Figure 10.3 that for the Deezer dataset, methods HOCTracker, AFOCS, and CFinder show a consistent positive relationship pattern

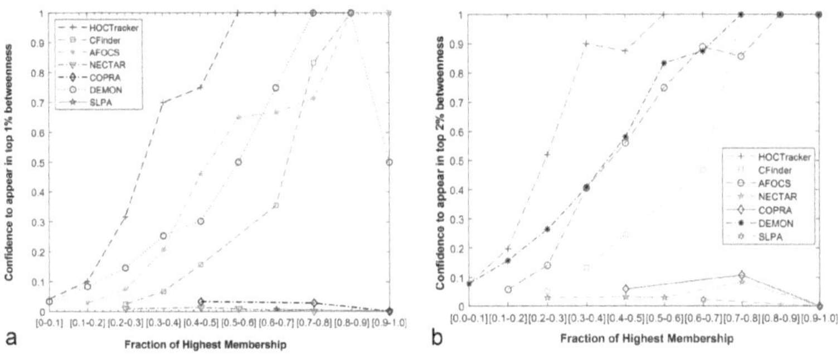

FIGURE 10.3 Confidence of overlapping node bins to appear in the top fraction of betweenness rank for Deezer Dataset. a) For top 1% of betweenness rank. b) For top 2% of betweenness rank.

between the overlapping node membership bins and betweenness centrality indicating high betweenness for highly overlapping node bins. On the other hand, the method DEMON shows an inconsistent relationship as it shows a relatively low confidence for the highest overlapping node bin [0.9 – 1.0] to appear in the top betweenness fraction. Other methods which include COPRA, NECTAR, and SLPA do not show any significant results for the Deezer dataset.

From the experimental results of Figures 10.1, 10.2, and 10.3, it can be argued that the overlapping community memberships assigned to nodes by overlapping community detection methods HOCTracker, AFOCS, and CFinder have a significant positive correlation with node influence measured in terms of node betweenness centrality. The method DEMON shows a relatively weaker relationship and the methods COPRA, NECTAR, and SLPA do not show any significant relationship. Since the different overlapping community detection methods used in question incorporate different definitions of communities and use different approaches, the variation in the results is expected. In the given context, methods HOCTracker, AFOCS, and CFinder show a relatively consistent positive relationship between the overlapping community membership of nodes and the influence of the nodes. In light of this observation, we can accept the hypothesis that nodes belonging to many communities qualify as influential nodes (spread blockers) for the underlying network as long as methods HOCTracker, AFOCS, and CFinder are used to detect the overlapping communities.

10.4 EVALUATION FOR SPREAD BLOCKING

Having accepted the hypothesis, for certain community detection methods, that nodes with high overlapping community memberships qualify as spread blockers, we now aim to present a practical picture of the usage of such spread blockers for reducing the spread of a pandemic. The methodology incorporates human mobility-based proximity data, in the form of a network, that is generated by many proximity detections-based smartphone apps as reported in ArogyaSetu[1] (accessed 15th July

TABLE 10.3
Information Format of the Check-In Dataset

user	check-in timestamp	latitude	longitude	location id

Source: Cho et al. (2011).

2021) and Roy et al. (2021). Although access to the human proximity data generated by such platforms is restricted, we use a similar human mobility dataset presented in Cho, Myers, and Leskovec (2011). The dataset comprises 6,442,890 check-ins, including time and location details, from the Gowalla location-based social networking platform, collected between February 2009 and October 2010, in the format illustrated in Table 10.3.

To construct the human proximity network from this dataset, a time window (TW) and an exposure threshold t are selected. For instance, with a time window of TW = [1, Jan 2010, 7, Jan 2010] and an exposure threshold of t = 5 minutes, the resulting contact network includes an edge between any pair of users whose check-in timestamps differ by no more than 5 minutes at the same location, provided the check-ins fall within the specified time window TW. The time window TW can be chosen based on the incubation period of the disease, i.e., the time it takes for an infected individual to exhibit symptoms. For example, COVID-19 symptoms typically appear 5 to 14 days post-infection, according to Azuma et al. (2020). The exposure threshold t is adjusted according to the dynamics of the epidemic, such as the time a virus remains active in an infected person's environment. For COVID-19, this ranges from minutes (in air) to hours (on surfaces), as reported by Setti et al. (2020), Domingos, Marques, and Rovira (2020), Nishiura et al. (2020), and Morawska and Milton (2020). For illustration, we use TW = [01, Feb 2010, 14, Feb 2010] and set t = m72 hours, resulting in a proximity network with 8,350 nodes and 31,359 edges.

Using this human proximity network, we apply the different overlapping community detection methods to extract the best spread blocker nodes for each method ranked according to their overlapping community membership counts. A top k-fraction of these ranked nodes (for each method) is then removed (along with their incident edges) from the network and the number of connected components resulting in the network is found. The idea is that the best set of spread blocker nodes for a proximity network is the one that when removed from the network (analogously given a work-from-home advisory and/or vaccinated) results in more number of connected components in the network, i.e., causes the network to split into more disconnected components so that the transmission of an infection is reduced. This indicates that for an overlapping community detection method if the removal of the top k-fraction of spread blocker nodes from the underlying network results in more number of connected components in the network, the better the method performs in selecting the best spread blockers from the network. To generate the results, we use two approaches for the removal of the top k-fraction of spread blocker nodes for each overlapping community detection method. In the first approach, each community detection method in question is applied once on the network to extract the overlapping nodes which are then ranked according to their overlapping community membership count. To extract the top k-fraction of spread blockers we simply vary the value of k from the top 1% to 15% of the ranked nodes and plot the resulting number of connected components after removal of each fraction from the network. The results of this experiment are shown in Figure 10.4. It can be observed from Figure 10.4 that the method AFOCS did not generate any results for this network typically due to the high density of the network. Furthermore, methods HOCTracker and CFinder show a relatively better split (more connected components) of the network upon the removal of their respective top fractions of candidate spread blockers. However, for higher fractions (greater than 9%) HOCTracker shows the best split. Other methods in question, although perform better than the random removal of nodes, do not perform significantly relative to HOCTracker and CFinder.

In the second approach, each community detection method in question is applied 15 times on the network. Each time, overlapping nodes are identified and then ranked according to their overlapping membership count. From this ranked list of nodes, the top 1% of nodes are selected and then removed from the network. The resulting number of connected components in the network after removal of this fraction is recorded and the community detection algorithm is run on the resulting network to

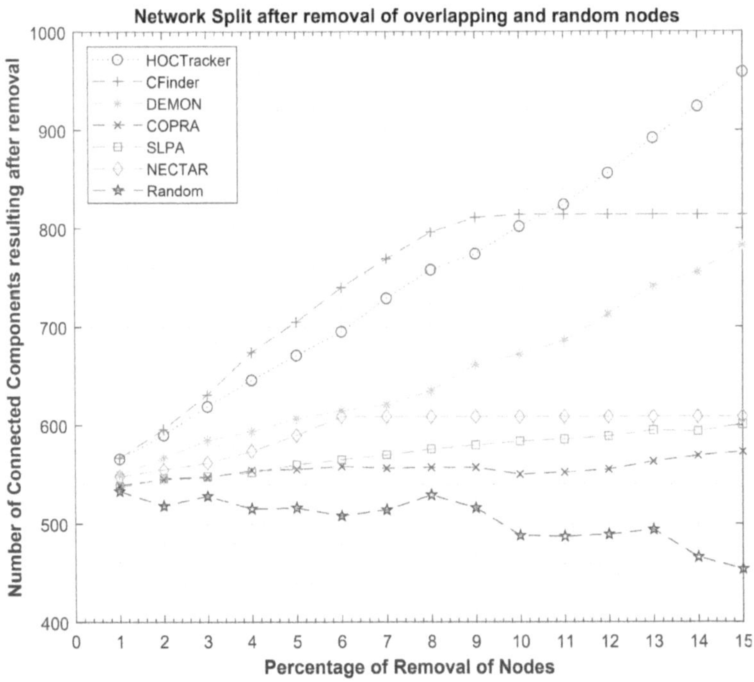

FIGURE 10.4 Confidence of overlapping node bins to appear in the top fraction of betweenness rank for Deezer Dataset. a) For top 1% of betweenness rank. b) For top 2% of betweenness rank.

select a new top 1% of spread blockers which is then eventually also removed from the network and the resulting number of connected components is recorded. This process is repeated 15 times and each time top 1% of overlapping nodes are removed from the network and the number of connected components is recorded. The results of this experiment for each community detection algorithm in question are shown in Figure 10.5.

It can be observed from Figure 10.5 that the method AFOCS did not generate any results for this network typically due to the high density of the network. Methods HOCTracker and CFinder show a relatively better split (more connected components) of the network upon the removal of their respective top fractions of candidate spread blockers. However, for higher fractions (greater than 10%) HOCTracker shows the best split. Comparing this iterative approach to the one used to generate results for Figure 10.4, it can be observed from Figure 10.5 that the iterative approach generates slightly more connected components, i.e., much better split of the network upon the removal of the top 1% spread blockers identified for each iteration. Other methods in question, although perform better than the random removal of nodes, do not perform significantly relative to HOCTracker and CFinder.

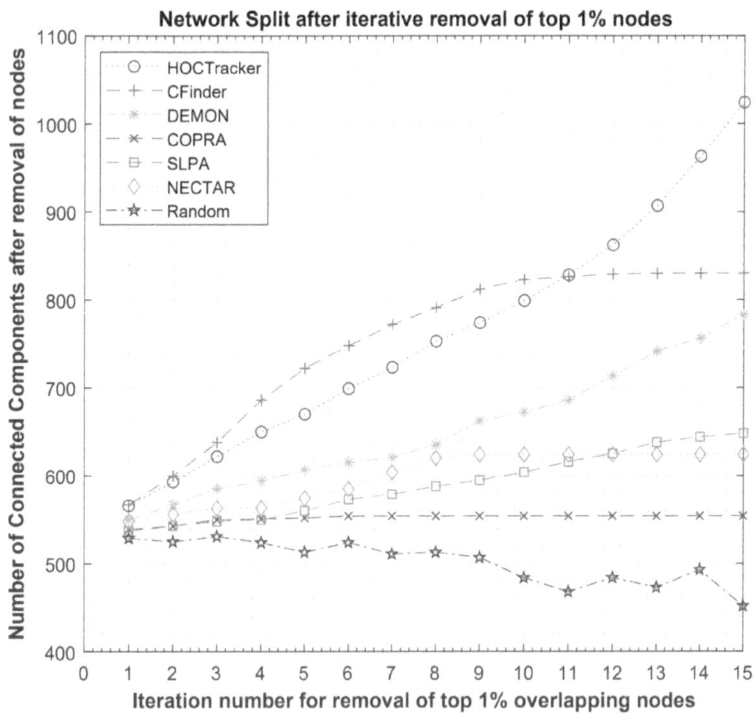

FIGURE 10.5 Confidence of overlapping node bins to appear in the top fraction of betweenness rank for Deezer Dataset. a) For top 1% of betweenness rank. b) For top 2% of betweenness rank.

10.5 CONCLUSION

This study provides a novel perspective on mitigating the spread of pandemics by leveraging overlapping community structures in social networks to identify influential nodes, termed as "spread blockers." The analysis demonstrates a significant correlation between overlapping community memberships and node influence measured through betweenness centrality. The HOCTracker and AFOCS methods consistently identify highly overlapping nodes as key influencers, supporting the hypothesis that nodes belonging to multiple communities are highly influential nodes and play a crucial role in identifying influential spreaders.

This study further evaluates overlapping community detection methods to identify optimal spread blocker nodes in a human mobility-based proximity data network by analyzing their effectiveness in splitting the network into disconnected components. Nodes were ranked based on their overlapping community memberships, and two approaches were used: a single application approach and an iterative approach. The single application showed that HOCTracker and CFinder achieved better network splits, with HOCTracker excelling at higher fractions of removed nodes, while AFOCS struggled with high-density networks. The iterative approach, which involved repeated node removal and re-application of the detection method, resulted in slightly better network splits, with HOCTracker consistently outperforming others.

In conclusion, this research underscores the importance of community memberships in identifying influential spreaders and offers a computationally efficient framework for targeted interventions during pandemics. Future work could explore the integration of real-time network data and evaluate the approach across diverse social network structures to enhance its applicability in real-world public health strategies.

NOTE

1. Aarogya setu mobile app. URL https://www. mygov.in/aarogya-Setu-app/.

REFERENCES

Azuma, Kenichi, U Yanagi, Naoki Kagi, Hoon Kim, Masayuki Ogata, and Motoya Hayashi. 2020. "Environmental factors involved in SARS-CoV-2 transmission: effect and role of indoor environmental quality in the strategy for COVID-19 infection control." *Environmental Health and Preventive Medicine 25* 1–16.

Bhat, Sajid Yousuf, and Muhammad Abulaish. 2012. "OCTracker: A density-based framework for tracking the evolution of overlapping communities in OSNs." *International Conference on Advances in Social Networks Analysis and Mining.* IEEE/ACM. 501–505.

Bhat, Sajid Yousuf, and Muhammad Abulaish. 2013. "Overlapping Social Network Communities and Viral Marketing." *International Symposium on Computational and Business Intelligence.* IEEE. 243–246.

Blondel, Vincent D , Jean-Loup Guillaume, Renaud Lambiotte, and Etienne Lefebvre. 2008. "Fast unfolding of communities in large networks." *Journal of Statistical Mechanics: Theory and Experiment 2008, no. 10.*

Cho, Eunjoon, Seth A. Myers, and Jure Leskovec. 2011. "Friendship and mobility: User movement in location-based social networks." *Proceedings of the 17th ACM SIGKDD international conference on Knowledge discovery and data mining.* ACM. 1082–1090.

Coscia, Michele, Giulio Rossetti, Fosca Giannotti, and Dino Pedreschi. 2012. "DEMON: A local-first discovery method for overlapping communities." *Proceedings of the 18th ACM SIGKDD international conference on Knowledge discovery and data mining.* ACM. 615–623.

Domingos, Jose L., Montse Marques, and Joaquim Rovira. 2020. "Influence of airborne transmission of SARS-CoV-2 on COVID-19 pandemic. A review." *Environmental Research 188.*

Galstyan , Aram, Vahe Musoyan, and Paul Cohen. 2009. "Maximizing influence propagation in networks with community structure." *Physical Review E—Statistical, Nonlinear, and Soft Matter Physics 79, no. 5.*

Ghalmane, Zakariya, Chantal Cherifi, Hocine Cherifi, and Mohammed El Hassouni. 2019. "Centrality in complex networks with overlapping community structure." *Scientific Reports 9, no. 1.*

Greene, Derek, Donal Doyle, and Padraig Cunningham. 2010. "Tracking the evolution of communities in dynamic social networks." *International conference on advances in social networks analysis and mining.* IEEE. 176–183.

Gregory, Steve. 2010. "Finding overlapping communities in networks by label propagation." *New Journal of Physics 12, no. 10.*

Gupta, Naveen, Anurag Singh, and Hocine Cherifi. 2016. "Centrality measures for networks with community structure." *Physica A: Statistical Mechanics and its Applications 452* 46–59.

Hinz, Oliver, Bernd Skiera, Christian Barrot, and Jan Becker. 2011. "Seeding Strategies for Viral Marketing: An Empirical Comparison." *Journal of marketing 75, no. 6* 55–71.

Katona, Zsolt, Peter Pal Zubcsek, and Miklos Sarvary. 2011. "Network effects and personal influences: The diffusion of an online social network." *Journal of marketing research 48, no. 3* 425–443.

Kempe, David, Jon Kleinberg, and Eva Tardos. 2003. "Maximizing the spread of influence through a social network." *In Proceedings of the ninth ACM SIGKDD international conference on Knowledge discovery and data mining.* ACM. 137–146.

Khomami, Mohammad Mehdi Daliri, Alireza Rezvanian, Mohammad Reza Meybodi, and Alireza Bagheri. 2021. "CFIN: A community-based algorithm for finding influential nodes in complex social networks." *The Journal of Supercomputing 77, no. 3* 2207–2236.

Kimura, Masahiro, Kazumasa Yamakawa, Kazumi Saito, and Hiroshi Motoda. 2008. "Community analysis of influential nodes for information diffusion on a social network." *IEEE International Joint Conference on Neural Networks (IEEE World Congress on Computational Intelligence).* IEEE. 1358–1363.

Klimt, Bryan, and Yiming Yang. 2004. "The enron corpus: A new dataset for email classification research." *European conference on machine learning.* Berlin, Heidelberg: Springer Berlin Heidelberg. 217–226.

Lerman, Kristina, Rumi Ghosh, and Tawan Surachawala. 2012. "Social contagion: An empirical study of information spread on Digg and Twitter follower graphs." *arXiv preprint* arXiv:1202.3162.

Leskovec, Jure, and Julian Mcauley. . 2012. "Learning to discover social circles in ego networks." *Advances in Neural Information Processing Systems 25.*

Lou, Tiancheng, and Jie Tang. 2013. "Mining structural hole spanners through information diffusion in social networks." *In Proceedings of the 22nd international conference on World Wide* 825–836.

Morawska, Lidia, and Donald K. Milton. 2020. "It is time to address airborne transmission of COVID-19." *Clinical Infectious Diseases: An Official Publication of the Infectious Diseases Society of America.*

Muhammad, Abulaish, Ishfaq Majid, and Sajid Yousuf Bhat. 2020. "Scaling density-based community detection to large-scale social networks via MapReduce framework." *Journal of Intelligent & Fuzzy Systems 38, no. 2* 1663–1674.

Nishiura,, Hiroshi, Hitoshi Oshitani, Tetsuro Kobayashi, Tomoya Saito, Tomimasa Sunagawa, Tamano Matsui, Takaji Wakita, MHLW COVID-19 Response Team, and Motoi Suzuki. 2020. "Closed environments facilitate secondary transmission of coronavirus disease 2019 (COVID-19)." *MedRxiv.*

Palla, Gergely, Imre Derenyi, Illes Farkas, and Tamas Vicsek. 2005. "Uncovering the overlapping community structure of complex networks in nature and society." *Nature 435, no. 7043* 814–818.

Pozveh, Maryam Hosseini, Kamran Zamanifar, and Ahmad Reza Naghsh Nilchi. 2017. "A community-based approach to identify the most influential nodes in social networks." *Journal of Information Science 43* 204–220.

Roy, Satyaki, Andrii Cherevko, Sayak Chakraborty, Nirnay Ghosh, and Preetam Ghosh. 2021. "Leveraging network science for social distancing to curb pandemic spread." *IEEE Access 9* 26196–26207.

Rozemberczki, Benedek, and Rik Sarkar. 2020. "Characteristic functions on graphs: Birds of a feather, from statistical descriptors to parametric models." *Proceedings of the 29th ACM international conference on information & knowledge management.* ACM. 1325–1334.

Setti, Leonardo, Fabrizio Passarini, Gianluigi De Gennaro, Pierluigi Barbieri, Maria Grazia Perrone, Massimo Borelli, Jolanda Palmisani, Alessia Di Gilio, Prisco Piscitelli, and Alessandro Miani. 2020. "Airborne transmission route of COVID-19: Why 2 meters/6 feet of inter-personal distance could not be enough." *International Journal of Environmental Research and Public Health 17, no. 8.*

Tulu, Muluneh Mekonnen, Ronghui Hou, and Talha Younas. 2018. "Identifying influential nodes based on community structure to speed up the dissemination of information in complex network." *IEEE Access 6* 7390–7401.

Wang, Yu, Gao Cong, Guojie Song, and Kunqing Xie. 2010. "Community-based greedy algorithm for mining top-K influential nodes in mobile social networks." In *Proceedings of the 16th ACM SIGKDD international conference on Knowledge discovery and data mining.* ACM. 1039–1048.

Xiangwei, Chu, Guan Jihong, Zhongzhi Zhang, and Zhou Shuigeng. 2009. "Epidemic spreading in weighted scale-free networks with community structure." *Journal of Statistical Mechanics: Theory and Experiment 2009* P07043.

Xie, Jierui, and Boleslaw K. Szymanski. 2012. "Towards linear time overlapping community detection in social networks." *Advances in Knowledge Discovery and Data Mining: 16th Pacific-Asia Conference, PAKDD 2012,Proceedings, Part II 16.* Kuala Lumpur, Malaysia: Springer Berlin Heidelberg. 25–36.

Zhang, Xiaohang, Ji Zhu, Qi Wang, and Han Zhao. 2013. "Identifying influential nodes in complex networks with community structure." *Knowledge-Based Systems 42* 74–84.

Zhang, Zufan, Xieliang Li, and Chenquan Gan. 2021. "Identifying influential nodes in social networks via community structure and influence distribution difference." *Digital Communications and Networks 7, no. 1* 131–139.

Zhang, Liangliang, Xiao Sun, Peng Wang, and Jinxin Hou. 2019. "Identifying influential nodes with a community structure measure." *In 2019 IEEE Fourth International Conference on Data Science in Cyberspace (DSC).* IEEE. 264–269.

Zhao, Yuxin, Shenghong Li, and Feng Jin. 2016. "Identification of influential nodes in social networks with community structure based on label propagation." *Neurocomputing 210* 34–44.

Zhao, ZY, H. Yu, Z.L. Zhu, and X.F. Wang. 2014. "Identifying influential spreaders based on network community structure." *Chinese Journal of Computers 37, no. 4* 753–766.

Zhao, Zhiying, Xiaofan Wang, Wei Zhang, and Zhiliang Zhu. 2015. "A community-based approach to identifying influential spreaders." *Entropy 17, no. 4* 2228–2252.

Zhao, Zi-Juan, Qiang Guo, Kai Yu, and Jianguo Liu. 2020. "Identifying influential nodes for the networks with community structure." *Physica A: Statistical Mechanics and Its Applications 551* 123893.

11 Spotting Plagiarism in Academic Social Networks by Community Network Identification

Tazeem Zainab, Irshad Ahmed Mir, and Zarka Malik

11.1 INTRODUCTION: PLAGIARISM, ITS DETECTION

The unethical representation or use includes copying of work or expression, stealing ideas, or paraphrasing without due credit which further violates the Intellectual Property Rights of an individual or damages the veracity of academic and inventive endeavors is Plagiarism. As per some dictionaries, the etymology of the word Plagiarism comes from the Latin word *plagiarius* which means hijacker, while Skandalakis and Mirilas argue that the word is derived from the Greek word *Plagios* which means obliquity. Plagiarism is considered to be a cardinal sin and a severest form of misconduct impacting negatively the academic aura and the publicity (Berlinck, 2011).

In higher education and academic publishing, plagiarism is an ongoing and rising concern. To combat plagiarism, thorough educational initiatives by Institutions, rigorous policies, and application of detection technologies particularly anti-plagiarism software have been instituted to endorse and maintain the standards of innovation and morality across scholarly and innovative fields. But the practice of Online Social Networks such as X, LinkedIn, Research Gate, Google Scholar, etc., in academia to publish research, get a following to increase citations, broadening of collaborations, etc., have undoubtedly increased the plagiarism of content due to increased visibility of research. The more accessibility a research article/chapter has, its vulnerability of being copied increases.

The awareness and education regarding plagiarism and avoiding it at all levels requires continuous efforts and comprehensible policies that elucidate the forms of plagiarism and its potential consequences when found. The identification of plagiarism requires complex judgments and cannot be dependent on using detection software only. Establishment of clear and vivid policies by journal managements

DOI: 10.1201/9781003515890-14

and social work programs for skirmishing plagiarism is crucial. Constant education, careful development of coursework, incident tracking within institutions, and establishment of clear policies might help trim down plagiarism and advance the quality of professional writing (Drisko, 2023). According to Foltýnek, Meuschke, and Gipp (2019) detection of plagiarism requires the identification of plagiarism type that has been done. Two main forms of plagiarism can be identified as (1) inappropriate use of someone else's words and (2) inappropriate use of someone else's ideas. Both forms involve lack of acknowledgment to the author or source. They further explain that Idea plagiarism is presentation of someone else's idea without proper citation of the source/author and year. In academic writing an idea or concept is written without proper in-text citation and linking it to the rest of the text and concluding it as your own is clearly plagiarism.

With the brisk advancement of information technology (IT), which offers expedient and immediate access to cosmic quantity of information, plagiarism has become much convenient. Information technology (IT) has considerably transformed the professional and academic milieu, mainly in relation to plagiarism. From one perspective, the explosion of digital content and effortlessness in information accessibility have made it trouble-free for researchers to copy and use someone's work without proper acknowledgment. The availability of massive online resources, including research articles, books, papers, and multimedia, simultaneously with the aid of sophisticated search engines, assists in quick and a lot unchecked misuse of content. In his study Park (2017) discusses how effortlessly digital resource accessibility amplifies plagiarism among students. The study proposes that the accessibility of papers and online essays entices students to use content directly in their assignments lacking proper citation. Selwyn (2008) supports this leaning in his research where he shows that more than 60% of students confessed to plagiarizing once at the minimum during their career, through Internet as their primary source of information.

The detection of plagiarism has been complicated by another major concern, i.e., the use of AI-generated text, which produces human-like manuscripts. A vast amount of research reflects that AI is being used in research and produces authentic scientific research papers, which has increased the deceitful academic and research output. In a research article published in Collonnaz (2024) it has been recorded that researchers establish that AI-generated abstracts may well deceive connoisseurs, stressing that robust plagiarism detection methods are required and also lucid guidelines on AI utilization in academic and research writing are required. Weber-Wulff et al. (2023) in their study reveal that existing AI-detection tools fail to detect rephrased or synonym-replaced or reworded AI content, which leads to an elevated rate of false negatives. This issue was further exacerbated during COVID-19 with increased shift to Online Learning and Assessments, where students were at ease to access, copy, and misuse the online resources. Plagiarism software used to check the originality during the period exposed a spike in educational dishonesty, compelled by the demands and challenges of distance learning (Eshet, 2024). On the whole, while IT has smoothed the development of new types of plagiarism, it has also prompted the design of sophisticated tools to spot and discourage such practices. Constant research and revision of policy are essential to maintain pace with these progressions and maintain scholarly integrity (Peytcheva-Forsyth et al. 2018). Information Technology has also empowered institutions to fight plagiarism extra efficiency. Academic organizations have implemented sophisticated plagiarism detection software such as Copyscape, Turnitin, or Grammarly which are based on some complex algorithms to evaluate submitted manuscripts against broad web databases be it academic or general content, spotting similarities and probable occurrences of plagiarism. In addition, IT enables enhanced opportunities and facilitates consciousness and education about plagiarism through seminars, workshops, online tutorials, and other channels that educate about attribution and citation practices and ethical research practices. The research study conducted by Ison (2015) exposed that the use of plagiarism software not only supports grabbing the hold of plagiarists but also acts as a restriction since students conscious of the software's potential are dubious to engage in fraudulent practices. Moreover, Heckler and Forde (2015) in their study draw attention to the efficacy of plagiarism detection software in recognizing copied content. The study verified that software like Turnitin have 95% efficiency in detecting the copied content, notably reducing the occurrence of plagiarism. Although IT has shaped novel avenues for plagiarism, it has also offered vigorous methodologies and tools to detect and avoid it, promoting a culture of honesty and originality in educational and professional bubble. In addition to this, educational institutions are facilitating IT to teach students about the significance of academic truthfulness. Sutherland-Smith (2008) in their study found that inclusive online plagiarism awareness tutorials and programs considerably reduce plagiarism occurrence. These programs educate students regarding appropriate citation methods and the fair use of information, endorsing a culture of integrity and reverence for intellectual property. Educational institutions are definitely at the forefront in the development and implementation of advanced plagiarism detection software/tools. In spite of their sophistication, this is also a fact that these tools struggle to accurately identify text generated by AI, mostly when it has been slightly changed.

11.2 PLAGIARISM DETECTION: TYPOLOGIES

A typology is an important aspect to understand and configure a research unit and also aids in the communiqué of a procedure. Numerous researchers have proposed diverse typologies to elaborate plagiarism in academics. Alfikri and Purwarianti (2012) distinguished academic plagiarism as the partial replication of smaller manuscript segments, presenting two types of paraphrasing that vary regarding whether the sentence formation modifies or whether translations occur.

Further Foltýnek, Meuschke, and Gipp (2019) presented the plagiarism topology as follows:

1. Characters-preserving plagiarism
2. Structural plagiarism
3. Synonym substitution
4. Technical disguise
5. Syntax-preserving plagiarism

6. Semantics-preserving plagiarism
7. Idea-preserving plagiarism

Mozgovoy, Kakkonen, and Cosma (2010) presented a typology that consolidates other classifications into five forms of academic plagiarism: (1) Verbatim copying, (2) Hiding plagiarism instances by paraphrasing, (3) Technical tricks exploiting weaknesses of current plagiarism detection systems, (4) Deliberate inaccurate use of references, (5) Tough plagiarism. John Walker (1998) presented a typology from a plagiarist's perspective, which is still accepted by current literature. Walker's typology characterizes between different types of plagiarism like Sham paraphrasing, Inadequate citation, Verbatim Copying, Recycling, ghostwriting, Purloining, etc. Velásquez and Taylor (2014) in their research categorized different forms of plagiarism. They placed plagiarism into two separate forms. One form contains technical disguise and verbatim copying, translation and paraphrasing, and categorized the conscious misuse of references as a separate form. Alzahrani, Salim, and Abraham (2012) distinguished plagiarism into two types:

1. Intelligent plagiarism and
2. Literal plagiarism which includes modified and near copies while intelligent plagiarism encompasses summary, paraphrases, idea plagiarism, and translation. This type of typology was followed by Eisa, Salim, and Alzahrani (2015) in their research. Further many researchers/authors (Chong, 2013; Chowdhury, et al.2018; Hourrane & Benlahmar, 2016) approved the classification of idea plagiarism as a separate type of plagiarism.

Based on the literature, some important factors like the nature, purpose, and severity of content copying, plagiarism can be grouped into various typologies.

1) **Incomplete Citation**

Definition: Incomplete citation refers to a fabricated citation that is misleading, incomplete, or incorrect. This makes it difficult to trace the original source of information (APA, 2020).

2) **Direct Plagiarism (Complete or Verbatim Plagiarism)**

Definition: In this type of plagiarism an author copies an entire research work and presents it as his/her own. This form of plagiarism is considered to be the severest misconduct in the research arena (Roig, 2015).

3) **Paraphrasing Plagiarism**

Definition: Rephrasing someone else's work in your own words without proper acknowledgment and credit. The structure and ideas of the manuscript remain the same; only the word formation differs (Walker, 1998).

4) **Self-Plagiarism**

Definition: If an author/researcher reuses his previous work including assignments. Research articles that have been published or submitted without acknowledgment it is considered to be self-plagiarism.

5) **Accidental Plagiarism**

Definition: Pecorari (2003) clarifies that if an author accidentally or unintentionally misses acknowledgment, citation, or paraphrasing of content it will be considered accidental plagiarism.

6) **Source-Based Plagiarism**

Definition: It includes fabrication and falsification. Fabrication as the name implies refers to creating fake data or research sources and citing them as original. Falsification includes altering existing data or sources to mislead readers (Steneck, 2003).

7) **Patch Writing or Mosaic Plagiarism**

Definition: Howard (1995) says that an unattributed copying or use of someone's work and mixing it with one's original content without interpretation and proper understanding is referred to as Mosaic Plagiarism.

8) **Secondary Source Plagiarism**

Definition: The failure of an author to cite an original source and referencing from another work (Stern, 2007).

9) **Misleading Attribution**

Definition: Misrepresenting an author's particular work by incorrectly attributing his/her work to any other author or your own will be considered misleading attribution (Gasparyan. et. al., 2017).

10) **Collusion**

Definition: This type of plagiarism happens in unauthorized research collaborations, particularly on individual assignments or allowing one's assignment to be copied by others (Park, 2017).

11.3 APPROACHES TO UNCOVERING PLAGIARISM

The augmentation of the digital content and the ease of access to huge quantity of information available online, the probability for plagiarism has amplified to a great extent. To spot, identify, and forestall this immoral practice, several plagiarism detection techniques and tools have been developed. Some of the techniques are discussed here.

11.3.1 Syntactical/Semantic Scrutiny

In research manuscripts, paraphrased content can be a source of plagiarism. Here, external matching tools or techniques particularly semantic analysis scrutinize the denotation of the wording rather than just the terminology. The methods of semantic or syntactic scrutiny include **natural language processing (NLP)** in which parts of speech, sentence structure, word dependencies, etc. are analyzed to identify the text context; **latent semantic analysis (LSA)** based on a mathematical technique called singular value decomposition to identify copying/paraphrasing and **Synonym Replacement Detection** which employs some sophisticated natural language detection tools to detect the synonyms underlying the replaced words. The use of NLP technologies can evaluate content at different levels, from full texts to just phrases, detecting faint plagiarism occurrences such as rephrasing/rewording or the AI application to rework the original documents. The detection of AI-generated content like ChatGPT lets precise identification of text created by analogous and parallel NLP models (Quidwai, Li, and Dube, 2023).

11.3.2 Text Matching Method

Being one of the most commonly used plagiarism detection techniques, it compares a specified document to an already existing document database to identify the similarity.

The chief procedures include fingerprinting, in which a fingerprint or hash is formed and then Winnowing Algorithm is used to spot the similarity.

1. **String Matching Algorithms** include Rabin-Karp Algorithm and Knuth-Morris-Pratt (KMP) Algorithm. These algorithms recognize precise or near-exact equivalents of word/phrase sequences.
2. **N-Gram Analysis**: This technique breaks down the text into smaller units called n-grams (e.g., sequences of two or three words) and compares these units across documents. It can detect similarities even when the text has been slightly modified.
3. **Program Dependency Graph (PDG) Analysis**, in which a graph created identifies the dependencies in a code which is a text document. The comparative similarities between these graphs can spot the copied content.
4. **Code Fingerprinting and Tokenization**: It resembles the fingerprinting method but here tokens are created and then compared.

11.3.3 Database and Web Crawling Integration

The integration of academic databases of books, research articles, research notes, thesis and dissertations, and other web content with the plagiarism detection software has to a greater extent helped to identify the unethical publishing of content. These tools have the ability to surf the databases on the internet and scan the latent sources of plagiarized content. The indexation and content in the databases of these tools are consistently updated and hence they ensure the new text/documents that are published are being monitored and remain in check.

11.3.4 Leveraging Artificial Intelligence and Machine Learning

With the huge advancement of artificial intelligence (AI) and machine learning (ML), the recognition accuracy of plagiarized content has definitely improved. But with the increase in AI-generated content, detection of such material has turned out to be gradually more imperative. Novel detection systems now center of attention on distinguishing between manually-written and AI-generated wording, by means of sophisticated metrics like sensitivity and specificity. Several tools/software/applications have been developed that classify text based on AI-generated probability like Copy Leaks, OpenAI tools, GPTZero, etc. (Elkhatat, Elsaid, & Almeer, 2023).

11.3.5 Hybrid Approaches

To improve the reporting and accuracy of plagiarism detection, countless contemporary plagiarism detection tools blend multiple methodologies. For instance, initially a plagiarism tool may apply text matching technique for primary detection for detection. Subsequently it may apply semantic analysis or linguistic fingerprinting for extensive scrutiny. These approaches can offer a more inclusive analysis and trim down the false positives. In artificial intelligence (AI), hybrid techniques that merge unsupervised preliminary training and supervised optimizing are excessively used to guide AI models that identify plagiarism. Because of their ability to polish or optimize to particular domains and content type, these models are flexible and predominantly successful OpenAI's GPT models are an example (Ibrahim, 2023).

11.3.6 Learning and Ethical Frameworks

To daunt and discourage the practice of plagiarism, special emphasis on moral education and creation of academic circles that depress the practice along with technological remedies is important. This includes promotion of sense of participation, community among students, offering varied assessments, and enhancing feedback systems. These practices facilitate to address the core problem of plagiarism, particularly in distant learning where occurrences of academic fraud have spiked.

11.4 ACADEMIC SOCIAL NETWORK

Academic social networks are digital spaces designed exclusively for academicians, researchers, and scholars to connect, work together, and share their research work. The aim of these networks is to ease research dissemination, promote academic teamwork, and enhance research visibility. These networks have become an important part of researchers' lives by connecting them across wide geographies and research areas. The key features of an academic social network are profile creation, sharing your own research, recommending the research work of others, networking and collaborating, and gauging your research impact. One of the popular ASNs is ResearchGate which is one of the largest networks of researchers where they connect, share their research, collaborate on research projects, and indulge in discussions. Some others are Mendeley, Zotero, Google Scholar, etc. The academic social networks benefit an academician or a researcher increasing his/her research visibility, providing a platform to enhance the collaborations. Through widely shared research, more accessibility options are available to an author and also these platforms provide a good opportunity for receiving feedback from peers. But there certainly have raised some grave considerations and concerns regarding its use. The peer-review or the quality check on these platforms is not considered meticulous which affects the research output quality. There are also some grave concerns regarding the privacy concerns of data and research and the bias of certain platforms toward the researchers. But Plagiarism and Intellectual Property Theft remains a concern. To curb the practice of Plagiarism, identification of users/researchers with similar activities/interests can be traced and hence will lead to identification, behavior, and interactions of Community Networks that exhibit similar behavior in a research environment.

11.5 SOCIAL NETWORK ANALYSIS

Social network analysis (SNA) is an integrated and methodological approach used to study social structures through the lens of network and graph theory. The main approach of using social network analysis is to focus on the relationships between individuals and groups, teams, and organizations (De Brún & McAuliffe, 2018). SNA allows exploration of the underlying structures of an organization or network pinpointing both informal and formal relationships that drive all the processes and outcomes (Wang, Yidong, et al. 2023). The social networks that are mostly visualized through SNA are social media platforms/networks, public health, marketing and business, community development, data science and technology, education, and research (Collonnaz et al., 2024; Sakamoto, 2021; Valdez et al., 2021). The sociogram, a graphical representation of the connections between these social units, is one of the essential components of an SNA. These sociograms provide a visual representation of the network's size, composition, and characteristics. They can also produce a number of quantitative metrics that can be tracked over time (Hoe et al., 2019; , Wasserman & Faust, 1994).

11.5.1 Key Characteristics of Social Network Analysis

Fundamentally SNA is characterized by:

1. **Nodes and Edges:** Nodes represent entities, individuals within a network such as organizations, members, and institutions. Edges signify the relationships and interactions between the communities, members, institutions, and organizations.

2. **Network Structure through Cohesion, Components, and Cliques:** Cohesion defines the interconnection of the network and is measured in density and distance. A component is a subset of the network where all nodes are connected, either directly or indirectly. A clique is a subset where each node is directly connected to every other node, signifying dense subgroups in the network (Mailman School of Public Health).
3. **Centrality Measures:** These are used to identify influential nodes within a network.
4. **Community Detection:** Identification of clusters of communities within a network. The community detection highlights networks where nodes are densely connected to each other rather than the rest of the network.
5. **Visualization:** Identification of patterns, relationships, and key players makes it significant for the representation of complex data.
6. **Multilevel Analysis:** SNA can be conducted at various levels, micro (individual), meso (group), and macro (entire network) levels. This multilevel approach is structured and allows for a comprehensive understanding of social structures, patterns, and dynamics across various contexts. Therefore, SNA offers a theoretical and methodological approach for identifying, analyzing, and visualizing network communities.

11.6 NETWORK COMMUNITIES

Social Network Analysis consists of an essential part of revealing veiled structures within complex networks termed as Community detection. It aids in knowing the patterns, roles, and relationships within various kinds of networks like social, technological, etc. by revealing groups of densely connected nodes. Network communities are essentially defined as groups, communities, or modules inside a network. These represent collections of individuals with common behaviors or traits, such as social network circles or collaborators in an academic research context, and are essential research facets in various fields, including the biological sciences, social sciences, physical sciences, and computer science. Groups of nodes (individuals, organizations, or other entities) that are more closely connected to one another than to the rest of the network make community networks. Identification of communities within networks provides insight into their functionality and organization. The network communities are characterized by high internal connectivity, low external connectivity, and diversity in structure. Network Communities are clusters that are the fundamental aspect of research in various fields, including sciences, social sciences, biology, and computer science.

In social network analysis, community detection is a fundamental technique that helps to identify members, groups, or individuals who interact and collaborate within a network, where nodes that signify individuals, entities, or documents are more compactly connected to each other than to the rest of the network. This process aids in the identification of communities, formation of new networks and patterns of relationships. Communities, in this context, characterize subgroups inside the wider network that show higher internal connectivity and have common patterns, characteristics, and connections. Similarly, in biology, community network analysis is used to identify the functional organization of complex biological systems.

In social networks, relations between nodes habitually form clusters, representing groups with common goals, interests, or roles and purposes. **Communities** may signify research groups, professional networks, friendship circles, or any other setting where entities are bound significantly to one another than to outsiders. The identification of these communities helps in the following:

- **Comprehension of Group Dynamics**: The detection of communities within a larger group helps to reveal the network structure unveiling the subgroups and their possible impact within a broader system.
- **Detection of Anomalies**: Community detection is very helpful for identification of abnormal behaviors, or spotting irregular behavior, such as detecting duplicitous activities in networks or doubtful forms or in plagiarism detection.
- **Identification of Influencers**: The identification of personal or professional communities in social media helps in locating the influencers or prominent entities who have a strong hold in a group and can influence opinions or behaviors.
- **Resource Allocation Optimization**: The identification of community networks helps in service delivery and resource distribution like in marketing where using these methods tailored interventions based on internal network structure can be offered.

For handling complex and large-scale data community detection algorithms are studied and developed in computer science. The exploration of community structures dates back to early sociological research (Hunt et al., 2012). The notable contributions include the famous works of Stuart Rice in the 1920s whose analysis of political blocs was later studied by Robert Weiss and Eugene Jacobson in the 1950s. These studies led to the development and evolution of modern approaches to network analysis particularly detection of communities (Porter, 2015). Also, notable works of Girvan and Newman included development of modularity for the identification of community structures. Some characteristics of network communities are explained by Mynatt et al. (1998):

- **Network Communities Are Technologically Mediated:** Network Communities rely on technology for bridging spatial distances in contrast to historical forms of communication mediums among communities. This mediation of technology ensures social cohesion among communities, despite the vast geographical dispersion, fostering engagement and intersections.
- **Network Communities Are Persistence:** Network communities are resilient and endure over time, across users and contexts. The persistence ensures continuous interactions among communities. Persistence ensures mobilization of communication channels over time.

- **Multiple Interaction Styles:** Network communities are defined by their capacity to provide various interaction styles. These communities function in such a style that enables both formal and informal discussions. This flexibility allows members to communicate in different ways through direct or peripheral interactions.
- **Real-Time Interaction:** Network communities are characterized by their capability for real-time interaction, which is vital for enhancing a dynamic social environment. This immediacy allows users to engage in interactions and activities that mimic face-to-face interactions, enhancing the overall experience of community engagement.
- **Multiple User Interaction:** Network Communities allow multi-user participation. This flexibility allows private interactions and social engagements, creating an expandable and functional space for community interactions.

Therefore network communities can help understand and examine the dynamics and structure of these communities can help us understand the interactions (Motschnig et al., 2021) which is important to understand the identification of similar patterns of behavior such as plagiarism or fraudulent activities, identifying influential nodes (like main miscreants) and also spotting abnormalities. Whether using sophisticated deep learning techniques or more conventional clustering algorithms, community identification methodologies aim to accurately locate these groups and examine their connections and stimuli within the larger network.)As an example, researchers use community detection techniques to determine how social media partnerships arise both with and without organizations, how social media support groups function, or how information/misinformation is displayed on online social media platforms.

11.6.1 Key Characteristics of Communities

Network communities are defined primarily by **density of connections**:

- **Internal Connectivity**: The nodes within a community are extremely interconnected, which means that the edges of a community have significantly higher connections between nodes in a same size random graph.
- **External Sparsity**: The nodes in this scenario have reduced connections, signifying that members of different communities interact less frequently.

11.6.2 Community Detection Methods

In a diversity of network structures, numerous algorithms have been established to spot communities. These algorithms often aim to maximize **modularity**, a measure that quantifies the strength of division of a network into communities (Mauro et al., 2014). Community detection algorithm can be used to identify the contextual meaning of the text. If the text is modeled as a complex network and community detection algorithms are applied, then the plagiarized content can be identified and flagged along with the source if the member has even changed the wording of the content (Rathin Raj & Ramya, 2023).

They further discuss the methods as given below:

1. **Louvain Method**: The most extensively used algorithms for community detection is the Louvain method. It intends to enhance **modularity**, a metric that is used to measure the concentration of links inside communities compared to links between communities. This method is particularly efficient for large networks and can handle networks with millions of nodes. It works in two phases:
   - **Modularity Maximization**: The modularity score at each step is aimed to be maximized in this phase by grouping nodes into communities.
   - **Hierarchical Clustering**: Once the community structure is established, the algorithm builds a hierarchical representation of the network, further refining community boundaries.
   - The community structure is established in the first phase, which acts a base for the algorithm to shape a hierarchical representation of the network, further filtering community boundaries.

2. **Label Propagation Algorithm (LPA)**: LPA is a quick and simple algorithm for community detection. Every node in the network is allotted a label, which is circulated to its fellow nodes. Slowly, nodes accept the most recurrent label between their neighbors, following groups of nodes sharing the similar label. While computationally competent, LPA does not continuously yield the best community detection outcomes, and the product may be contingent on the preliminary labeling.
3. **Girvan–Newman Algorithm**: The Girvan–Newman algorithm considers high betweenness centrality to spot the communities by gradually removing edges. Betweenness centrality is a graph theory measure that specifies how significant a node is in a network by gauging how often it appears on the shortest paths between other nodes. It measures the number of unswerving paths that pass over a given edge. By eliminating edges that join different communities, the link progressively splits into discrete clusters. This method is computationally affluent and is more appropriate for minor to medium-sized networks (Barthelemy, 2004).
4. **Clique Percolation Method (CPM)**: CPM focuses on finding **k-cliques**, or complete subgraphs of k nodes, that share edges. Communities are detected by identifying overlapping cliques in the network, where nodes are part of multiple cliques. This method is especially useful in networks where community structures overlap, such as in social and biological networks (Chang, Gamage, & Yu, 2024).
5. **Spectral Clustering**: The eigenvectors derived from the Laplacian matrix of a network are used here to detect the communities. The Laplacian matrix distinguishes the graph structure, and its eigenvectors are applied to divide the network into groups. This approach is effective in detection of well-bound communities and is frequently employed in networks where communities are not linearly divisible.

11.7 CITATION NETWORK

The analysis of citation networks can also reveal plagiarism among citing documents. A document citing the same documents can potentially reveal a pattern that the content is plagiarized. If the different patterns of citation networks are leveraged by different modeling techniques, they can possibly identify plagiarism in academic networks through research papers.

- **Feature-Based Detection by Neural Networks:** The features that neural network classifiers extract from the text are trainable for detection of plagiarism (Engel et al. 2017).. With the identification and detention of similarity features that capture syntactic, lexical, semantic aspects, and neural networks can learn to contrast between original and plagiarized text (Butakov & Scherbinin, 2009; El-Rashidy et al., 2022). Each of the approaches can be used individually for assessing and measuring plagiarism (Engel et al., 2017).

In general, community network research is essential to expanding our knowledge of the complex relationships and inter-dependencies across many systems, allowing scholars to make significant discoveries and provide creative solutions spanning several academic fields.

11.8 APPLICATIONS OF COMMUNITY DETECTION

The most common applications of community detection in social networks are discussed here:

1. **Telecommunication and Infrastructure Networks**: Community detection is pragmatically used in communication networks between users like emails, chats, or telephone calls. The identification of clusters of frequently interacting users aids telecom companies to augment their networks, detect different patterns of communication, offer tailored services, or spot the occurrence of fraud or system mishandling.
2. **Social media and Online Platforms**: Social Network Platforms like X, Instagram, Facebook, and LinkedIn use community detection to cluster users based on their communications, interests, and activities. Community detection helps corporations comprehend social constructions, identify vital influencers, and provide specific types of content to target user groups.
3. **Plagiarism Detection**: As discussed earlier, in plagiarism detection, community detection aids in identifying sets of documents that are extremely similar, signifying probable cases of replication or shared content. By bunching documents into communities, plagiarism can be detected across various sources.
4. **Fraud Detection**: Community detection is applied to recognize groups of entities like individuals and businesses that interact recurrently. This can support in catching scam rings, sensing insider transactions, or identifying illegal financial dealings.

11.9 CHALLENGES IN COMMUNITY DETECTION

- **Dynamic Networks:** The offline social networks and online social networks both are dynamic in nature and tend to evolve drastically over-time. The network changes quite frequently with the formation, merging, or dissolving of communities. This poses a great challenge to apply practical community detection methods.
- **Overlapping Communities**: In numerous real-world networks, nodes (individual, researcher, or group) may represent to multiple communities. For example, an individual may belong to a research group and also a friend group. Most of the algorithms for community detection cannot gauge this intersection except a few like CPM algorithm which can handle this overlap.
- **Large-Scale Networks**: The massive base of Social Media Platforms consisting of billions of nodes and edges poses a great challenge for Scaling community detection algorithms. Here compromising computational efficiency and accuracy remains a crucial challenge.

11.10 COMMUNITY NETWORK APPROACHES TO PLAGIARISM DETECTION

The integration of social network information, web data, and advanced semantic visualization improves plagiarism detection (Zrnec & Lavbič, 2018). The analysis of social media connections and networks between authors and documents and the patterns of plagiarism are detectable. The combination of web data, social media information, and semantic visualization increases the efficiency of plagiarism detection (Alsallal et al., 2013; Zrnecn & Lavbič, 2018). The identification of sharing pattern, reputation of the member, and content similarity analysis are also fundamental in this context. The application of community network identification for plagiarism detection within social networks comprises harnessing the data regarding the behavioral patterns of users, their communications, and their structural relationships. This can be achieved by:

11.10.1 Exploring Community Detection in Social Networks

Plagiarism detection in research collaborations can be detected profoundly by Community Network Analysis. The identification of clusters having the same content, tracking the flow of information, identifying the anomalies, and lastly recognition of the collaborative works a versatile approach may be developed through community networks to trace and detect plagiarism efforts. With amalgamation of traditional detection tools of plagiarism these methodologies can provide a robust mechanism to precise identification of the content that has been misused or mis-presented leading to plagiarism. By identifying clusters that interact and work together frequently the patterns of content sharing among them can be detected and the occurrence of plagiarism might be spotted. Torkaman et al. (2023) and Hamed, Rebhi, and Saoud (2024) in their study draw attention to various community detection techniques that can help in identification of plagiarized content. An intricate cognition into community structures for spotting plagiarism can be done by involving deep learning approaches that represent multifaceted relations between the researchers or authors. Further Hamed, Rebhi, and Saoud (2024) suggest the use of sophisticated multilayer networks that involve multiple types of interactions among consumers like collaborations, sharing content or friendships. As per them this method helps in plagiarism detection by presenting holistic view of such community networks and enhances the accuracy for detecting such network structures. Some studies suggest the application of spectral clustering or modularity optimization to identify communities with huge datasets. For instance, the assignments submitted by students in a class form an interconnected community owing to the high similarity in their text, which can point out the copying or illicit replicating from a common source (Motsching, et al., 2021; Vieira, Xavier & Evsukoff, 2020). Brzozowski, Siudem, and Gagolewski (2023) investigate the use of graph representation and measures of node similarity to detect the network communities which help to enumerate the node similarity predicated on the interactions and communications contributing another platform for spotting potential plagiarism through community structures. In nutshell, utilizing and employing different community detection techniques in academic social networks endows with a robust frame to recognize and address plagiarism.

11.10.2 Methodology for Plagiarism Detection

1. **Collection of Data and Pre-processing**: The researchers must in the first step collect the data which needs to be checked for plagiarism from the Social Networks. This data can be in the form of interaction (comments, likes, or shares), textual (shared posts and updates, research interests, participation in discussion, collaborations, citations), or metadata. The collected data then must be processed to remove noise and standardize it for study. This could involve consistent formatting, removing stop words and ensuring text normalization.
2. **Data Representation**: After processing the data, each dataset like a researcher or paper must be represented by a node. The between nodes edge formation must be established based on factors like similarity between texts and interactions between the researchers. Establish edges based on interactions studies suggest that techniques like Jaccard Index, Cosine similarity, Jaccard index, or TF-IDF can be utilized for this purpose.
3. **Application of Community Detection Algorithms**: Numerous methods have been developed in due course of time by scientists and researchers for community detection. Three main methods are discussed here:
   - **Deep Learning Approach**: This involves the application of advanced and sophisticated neural network architecture to gauge the purposeful node representation and their relations in a graph. Deep learning approaches mostly comprise graph neural networks (GNNs), deep graph convolutional networks (DGCNs), graph autoencoders (GAEs), and graph attention networks (GATs). By the application of these

techniques, researchers can efficiently identify and evaluate communities within complex networks. In particular, graph convolutional networks (GCNs) model is capable of learning complex network relationships and structures to spot communities more effectively.

- **Modularity Optimization**: The most basic representation of modular optimization in plagiarism detection is given below:

<table>
<tr><td>| Text Preprocessing |</td><td>⟶</td><td>| - Tokenization |</td><td>| - Stemming |</td><td>| - Stop Words |</td></tr>
<tr><td>| Similarity Detection|</td><td>⟶</td><td>| - String Matching |</td><td>| - Cosine Similarity|</td><td>| - Jaccard Similarity|</td></tr>
<tr><td>|Semantic Analysis|</td><td>⟶</td><td>|-Word Embeddings |</td><td>| -Contextual Embeddings|</td><td>| -Paraphrase Detection |</td></tr>
<tr><td>| Citation Analysis |</td><td>⟶</td><td>| - Citation Matching|</td><td>| - Reference Network Analysis |</td><td></td></tr>
<tr><td>| Machine Learning |</td><td>⟶</td><td>| - Supervised Learning |</td><td>| - Deep Learning |</td><td></td></tr>
<tr><td>| Post-Processing |</td><td>⟶</td><td>| - Result Aggregation |</td><td>| - Visualization |</td><td></td></tr>
</table>

This method allows for all the components to be designed and optimized separately, enhancing the total efficiency of the plagiarism detection structure.

Spectral Clustering: Spectral clustering is a dominant technique applied in various areas of research, including plagiarism detection, to recognize communities or clusters in spectrum data given by eigenvalues of a similarity matrix. The basic representation is:

- **Text Representation**
  - **TF-IDF**
  - **Word Embeddings**
- **Similarity Matrix**
  - **Cosine Similarity**
  - **Jaccard Similarity**
- **Laplacian Matrix**
- **Eigen Value Decomposition**
- **Clustering Algorithm**
  - **-k-means**
- **Clusters (Potentially Plagiarized Documents)**

11.10.3 Case Study and Applications

1. **Analysis of Academic Social Networks**: The analysis of academic social platforms can aid in spotting potential plagiarism by revealing the patterns

of apprehensive collaboration or abnormal similarities in research productivity. For instance, the identification of clusters that frequently corroborate and cross-cite can be a focal point to map the community network and detect potential plagiarism. Clusters that display characteristics for instance excessively high collaborations and co-authorship, particularly across an extensive sort of themes, may necessitate further inquiry. This may in the future reveal high rate of content recycling or collusion of research output. Honorary authorships and ghost authorships can also be uncovered. Overlapping of publications can also be detected. Identification of central authors who connect multiple groups, potentially coordinating plagiarism efforts is another breakthrough. Plagiarism detection software like iThenticate, Turnitin, etc. can be used to detect the similarity index of the research publications across and in-between the research groups or we may call them clusters. The citation behavior of such clusters can also to a greater extent reveal the potential case of plagiarism. Further, "Papermill operation" can be detected in clusters if the authors have rapid successive publications. Whistle-blowing and complaints/news from editors, ethical boards, and journals can also provide additional evidence. By analysis of the network data of such clusters, advanced Machine Learning Standards can qualify the occurrence of plagiarism like phrase frequency in text, collaborations, and citing patterns. For illustration, Eshet (2024) and Zrnec and Dejan (2017) in their study reveal that data from content analysis and social networks can be integrated into the system called social plagiarism detection framework (SPDF) to envisage the associations between suspected plagiarists. This method can discover communities where the chances of plagiarism are high by assessing both direct and indirect relationships, like common co-authors or frequent communications on academic social platforms. Such frameworks have been revealed to considerably improve the precision and effectiveness of plagiarism exposure, reducing the probability of false positives or negatives.

2. **Social Media Platforms**: Uncovering communities in networks like Social Media Platforms (X, Instagram, Facebook) have the ability to identify the clusters of users who recurrently share alike content or posts, signifying probable content stealing or coordinated copying campaigns. The careful monitoring of posts that are widespread can help in identifying the original creators and control the further publishing or reposting on these platforms hence containing plagiarized content.

11.11 CONCLUSION

Community network identification endows us with a resilient framework for identifying plagiarism within social networks by leveraging the behavioral and structural approach of user communications, relations, and similarities in content. The identification and mitigation of plagiarism can be efficiently done by utilizing prompt content analysis and community detection algorithms, hence preserving the reliability of research and academic output. The identification of plagiarism within academic social networks through community network analysis is a vigorous approach that surpasses traditional plagiarism detection methods, presenting an extra nuanced and inclusive interpretation of how immoral practices can reproduce within academia. By focusing on the interaction and relations between the clusters and communities that have a common research milieu investigators besides revealing individual plagiarism incidents can also highlight the widespread trends that signify institutional issues. The potency of this framework lies in its capability to contextualize apprehensive actions within the bigger network of academic collaborations. The reimbursement of using community network identification in plagiarism discovery is lucid and clear, but these methods also bring forth some grave concerns regarding the practical and ethical considerations. The trust in network data means that the privacy of users/people/entities under study must be cautiously protected. The unjust allegations due to wrong interpretations of network blueprints must be refrained from. Moreover, since the network data varies geographically and disciplinary, the efficacy is reliant on the accuracy and quality of the network data. To summarize, Community Network Analysis can offer a comprehensive development in plagiarism detection in academic social networks to fight academic fraud and misconduct. With the evolution in academia and overhaul of digital availability and exploitation of online content, the credence of such cutting-edge and advanced techniques will continue to evolve. It is the responsibility of the research centers and institutions to refine such technologies, complementary appropriate and vigorous detection models with the ethical concerns that are raised with scrutinizing complex social networks (Eshet, 2024; Zrnec and Dejan, 2017).

11.12 FUTURE RESEARCH DIRECTIONS

The future research may include:

- Focus to enhance and develop social network analysis with machine learning and artificial intelligence (AI) techniques which are capable of analyzing bigger multifaceted datasets like academic databases, social media, and citation networks.
- Ethical implications to be researched while using data derived from social media.
- Cross-disciplinary research applications of such techniques like non-academic sectors, law, business, etc.
- Additional studies to improve the accuracy of these approaches, dipping false positives and enhancing the trustworthiness of community detection for identification of collaborative efforts of plagiarism in academic circles.

REFERENCES

Alfikri, Zakiy Firdaus, and Ayu Purwarianti. "The construction of Indonesian-English cross language plagiarism detection system using fingerprinting technique." *Jurnal Ilmu Komputer dan Informasi* 5, no. 1 (2012): 16–23.

Alsallal, Muna, Rahat Iqbal, Saad Amin, and Anne James. "Intrinsic plagiarism detection using latent semantic indexing and stylometry." In *2013 sixth international conference on developments in esystems engineering*, pp. 145–150. IEEE, 2013.

Alzahrani, Salha M., Naomie Salim, and Ajith Abraham. "Understanding plagiarism linguistic patterns, textual features, and detection methods." *IEEE Transactions on Systems, Man, and Cybernetics, Part C (Applications and Reviews)* 42, no. 2 (2011): 133–149.

American Psychological Association. "Publication Manual of the American Psychological Association, (2020)." *American Psychological Association* 428 (2019).

Barthelemy, Marc. "Betweenness centrality in large complex networks." *The European physical journal B* 38, no. 2 (2004): 163–168.

Berlinck, Roberto GS. "The academic plagiarism and its punishments-a review." *Revista Brasileira de Farmacognosia* 21 (2011): 365–372.

Brzozowski, Łukasz, Grzegorz Siudem, and Marek Gagolewski. "Community detection in complex networks via node similarity, graph representation learning, and hierarchical clustering." *arXiv preprint arXiv:2303.12212* (2023).

Butakov, Sergey, and Vladislav Scherbinin. "The toolbox for local and global plagiarism detection." *Computers & Education* 52,no. 4 (2009): 781–788.

Chang, Lijun, Rashmika Gamage, and Jeffrey Xu Yu. "Efficient k-Clique count estimation with accuracy guarantee." *Proceedings of the VLDB Endowment* 17, no. 11 (2024): 3707–3719.

Chong, Man Yan Miranda. "A study on plagiarism detection and plagiarism direction identification using natural language processing techniques." (2013).

Chowdhury, Hussain A., and Dhruba K. Bhattacharyya. "Plagiarism: Taxonomy, tools and detection techniques." *arXiv preprint arXiv:1801.06323* (2018).

Collonnaz, Magali, Laetitia Minary, Teodora Riglea, Jodi Kalubi, Jennifer O'Loughlin, Yan Kestens, and Nelly Agrinier. "Lack of consistency in measurement methods and semantics used for network measures in adolescent health behaviour studies using social network analysis: a systematic review." *J Epidemiol Community Health* 78, no. 5 (2024): 303–310.

De Brún, Aoife, and Eilish McAuliffe. "Social network analysis as a methodological approach to explore health systems: a case study exploring support among senior managers/executives in a hospital network." *International journal of environmental research and public health* 15,no. 3 (2018): 511.

Drisko, James W. "What is plagiarism, how to identify it, and how to educate to avoid it." *Journal of Social Work Education* 59, no. 3 (2023): 744–755.

Eisa, Taiseer Abdalla Elfadil, Naomie Salim, and Salha Alzahrani. "Existing plagiarism detection techniques: A systematic mapping of the scholarly literature." *Online Information Review* 39, no. 3 (2015): 383–400.

Elkhatat, Ahmed M., Khaled Elsaid, and Saeed Almeer. "Evaluating the efficacy of AI content detection tools in differentiating between human and AI-generated text." *International Journal for Educational Integrity* 19, no. 1 (2023): 17.

El-Rashidy, Mohamed A., et al. "Reliable plagiarism detection system based on deep learning approaches." *Neural Computing and Applications* 34,no. 21 (2022): 18837–18858.

Engel, Jesse, Matthew Hoffman, and Adam Roberts. "Latent constraints: Learning to generate conditionally from unconditional generative models." *arXiv preprint arXiv:1711.05772* (2017).

Eshet, Yovav. "The plagiarism pandemic: inspection of academic dishonesty during the COVID-19 outbreak using originality software." *Education and Information Technologies* 29, no. 3 (2024): 3279–3299.

Foltýnek, Tomáš, Norman Meuschke, and Bela Gipp. "Academic plagiarism detection: a systematic literature review." *ACM Computing Surveys (CSUR)* 52, no. 6 (2019): 1–42.

Gasparyan, Armen Yuri, Bekaidar Nurmashev, Bakhytzhan Seksenbayev, Vladimir I. Trukhachev, Elena I. Kostyukova, and George D. Kitas. "Plagiarism in the context of education and evolving detection strategies." *Journal of Korean medical science* 32, no. 8 (2017): 1220–1227.

Hamed, Imen, Wala Rebhi, and Narjes Bellamine Ben Saoud. "A comprehensive view of community detection approaches in multilayer social networks." *Social Network Analysis and Mining* 14, no. 1 (2024): 103.

Heckler, Nina C., and David R. Forde. "The role of cultural values in plagiarism in higher education." *Journal of Academic Ethics* 13 (2015): 61–75.

Hoe, Connie, et al. "Using social network analysis to plan, promote and monitor intersectoral collaboration for health in rural India." *PLoS One* 14,no. 7 (2019): e0219786.

Hourrane, Oumaima, and El Habib Benlahmar. "Survey of plagiarism detection approaches and big data techniques related to plagiarism candidate retrieval." In *Proceedings of the 2nd international Conference on Big Data, Cloud and Applications*, pp. 1–6. 2016.

Howard, Rebecca Moore. "Plagiarisms, authorships, and the academic death penalty." *College English* 57, no. 7 (1995): 788–806.

Hunt, Andrea N., Christine A. Mair, and Maxine P. Atkinson. "Teaching community networks: A case study of informal social support and information sharing among sociology graduate students." *Teaching Sociology* 40,no. 3 (2012): 198–214.

Ibrahim, Karim. "Using AI-based detectors to control AI-assisted plagiarism in ESL writing: 'The terminator versus the machines.'" *Language Testing in Asia* 13, no. 1 (2023): 46.

Ison, David C. "The influence of the Internet on plagiarism among doctoral dissertations: An empirical study." *Journal of Academic Ethics* 13 (2015): 151–166.

Motschnig, Niko, Alexander Ramharter, Oliver Schweiger, Philipp Zabka, and Klaus-Tycho Foerster. "On comparing and enhancing common approaches to network community detection." *arXiv preprint arXiv:2108.13482* (2021).

Mozgovoy, Maxim, Tuomo Kakkonen, and Georgina Cosma. "Automatic student plagiarism detection: Future perspectives." *Journal of Educational Computing Research* 43, no. 4 (2010): 511–531.

Mynatt, Elizabeth D., et al. "Network communities: something old, something new, something borrowed..." *Computer Supported Cooperative Work (CSCW)* 7 (1998): 123–156.

Park, Chris. "In other (people's) words: Plagiarism by university students—literature and lessons." *Academic Ethics* (2017): 525–542.

Pecorari, Diane. "Good and original: Plagiarism and patchwriting in academic second-language writing." *Journal of Second Language Writing* 12, no. 4 (2003): 317–345.

Peytcheva-Forsyth, Roumiana, Lyubka Aleksieva, and Blagovesna Yovkova. "The impact of technology on cheating and plagiarism in the assessment–The teachers' and students' perspectives." In *AIP conference proceedings*, vol. 2048, no. 1. AIP Publishing, 2018.

Porter, Constance Elise. "Virtual communities and social networks." *Communication and technology* 1 (2015): 161–180.

Quidwai, Mujahid Ali, Chunhui Li, and Parijat Dube. "Beyond black box ai-generated plagiarism detection: From sentence to document level." *arXiv preprint arXiv:2306.08122* (2023).

Rathin Raj, R. S., and G. R. Ramya. "Detection of Plagiarism in Contextual Meaning Using Transformer Model and Community Detection Algorithm." *International Conference on Smart Trends for Information Technology and Computer Communications*. Singapore: Springer Nature Singapore, 2023.

Roig, Miguel. *Avoiding plagiarism, self-plagiarism, and other questionable writing practices: A guide to ethical writing*. United States Department of Health & Human Services. Office of Research Integrity, 2015.

Sakamoto, Maiko. “The role of social capital in community development: Insights from behavioral game theory and social network analysis.” *Sustainable Development* (2024).

Selwyn, Neil. “‘Not necessarily a bad thing…’: A study of online plagiarism amongst undergraduate students.” *Assessment & Evaluation in Higher Education* 33, no. 5 (2008): 465–479.

Steneck, Nicholas Hans. *ORI introduction to the responsible conduct of research.* Department of Health and Human Services, Office of the Secretary, Office of Public Health and Science, Office of Research Integrity, 2003.

Stern, Linda. “What every student should know about avoiding plagiarism.” *(No Title)* (2007).

Sutherland-Smith, Wendy. *Plagiarism, the Internet, and student learning: Improving academic integrity.* Routledge, 2008.

Torkaman, Atefeh, Kambiz Badie, Afshin Salajegheh, Mohammad Hadi Bokaei, and Seyed Farshad Fatemi Ardestani. “A four-stage algorithm for community detection based on label propagation and game theory in social networks.” *AI* 4, no. 1 (2023): 255–269.

Valdez, Anna. “New Year, New Updates: What to Expect From JEN in 2024.” *Journal of Emergency Nursing* 50, no. 1 (2024): 1–2.

Velásquez, Juan D., and Edison Marrese Taylor. “Tools for external plagiarism detection in DOCODE.” In *2014 IEEE/WIC/ACM International Joint Conferences on Web Intelligence (WI) and Intelligent Agent Technologies (IAT)*, vol. 2, pp. 296–303. IEEE, 2014.

Vieira, Vinícius da Fonseca, Carolina Ribeiro Xavier, and Alexandre Gonçalves Evsukoff. “A comparative study of overlapping community detection methods from the perspective of the structural properties.” *Applied Network Science* 5 (2020): 1–42.

Walker, John. “Student plagiarism in universities: What are we doing about it?.” *Higher Education Research & Development* 17, no. 1 (1998): 89–106.

Wang, Yidong, et al. "Pandalm: An automatic evaluation benchmark for llm instruction tuning optimization." *arXiv preprint arXiv:2306.05087* (2023).

Wasserman, Stanley, and Katherine Faust. "Social network analysis: Methods and applications." (1994).

Weber-Wulff, Debora, Alla Anohina-Naumeca, Sonja Bjelobaba, Tomáš Foltýnek, Jean Guerrero-Dib, Olumide Popoola, Petr Šigut, and Lorna Waddington. “Testing of detection tools for AI-generated text.” *International Journal for Educational Integrity* 19, no. 1 (2023): 26.

Zrnec, Aljaž, and Dejan Lavbič. “Social network aided plagiarism detection.” *British Journal of Educational Technology* 48, no. 1 (2018): 113–128.

Index

FSC
www.fsc.org
MIX
Papier | Fördert gute Waldnutzung
FSC® C083411

Kolibri 360 GmbH
Ferdinand-Jühlke-Straße 7
99095 Erfurt, Deutschland
produktsicherheit@kolibri360.de